GENERATING FORGIVENESS AND
CONSTRUCTING PEACE THROUGH
TRUTHFUL DIALOGUE:
ABRAHAMIC PERSPECTIVES

GENERATING FORGIVENESS AND CONSTRUCTING PEACE THROUGH TRUTHFUL DIALOGUE: ABRAHAMIC PERSPECTIVES

Hilarie Roseman

A thesis submitted in total fulfillment of the requirements for the degree of Doctor of Philosophy

Department of Media, Music, Communication & Cultural Studies
Faculty of Arts, Macquarie University AUSTRALIA

Easter 2013

Dignity Press
World Dignity University Press

Copyright © 2014 Hilarie Roseman
This work is licensed under the Creative Commons Attribution-Share-Alike 4.0 Unported License.
Please note: This license allows free use of the material with the restrictions that authors and editors have to be mentioned as the originators and that works making use of it have to stay open under the same license.
    For details see: https://creativecommons.org/licenses/by-sa/4.0/.

Published by:
World Dignity University Press,
an imprint of Dignity Press
16 Northview Court
Lake Oswego, OR 97035, USA
www.dignitypress.org/forgiveness

Front and back cover images by Hilarie Roseman

Printed on paper from environmentally managed forestry:
http://www.lightningsource.com/chainofcustody

ISBN 978-1-937570-48-4

Contents

Abstract	x
Declaration	xii
Acknowledgements	xii
Personal Statement	xiii

Chapter One
Introduction

Introduction	1
Foundational Flows of Information	2
Abrahamic Religions in Australia	5
Prior Research in Australia	6
The Problem	7
Background to the Abrahamic Religions	8
Interfaith Organizations	17
Social Science and Religion	18
Research Objectives	25
Structure of the Thesis	26
Summary	28

Chapter Two
Intercultural Communication and Conflict

Introduction	29
The Nature of the Human Being in the World	30
International Level	37
Cooperation at the International Level	43
Cooperation at an Organizational Level	52
Theories of Forgiveness	62
Signs of Reconciliation	67
Summary	69

Chapter Three
Peace, Forgiveness and Ethical Communication

Introduction	71
Social Science Review	73
Humanities Review	80
Religious Discourse Review	97
Non-Government Organization Discourse Review	102
Frames of Reference	107
Summary	117

Chapter Four
Communication and Conflict Resolution

Introduction	119
The Case of Blacks and Whites in South Africa	121
The Case of Northern Ireland and the Republic of Ireland	130
The Case of Israel and Palestine	141
The Role of Religion	149
The Process of Reconciliation	156
Summary	158

Chapter Five
Research Methodology

Introduction	161
Methodological Reflections	161
Social Change	166
Focus Group Interviews	176
Research Process	184
Summary	191

Chapter Six
Activity Report: Focus Groups

Introduction	193
The Participants	193
Introduction to Coding of Questions	201
Enemy Images in Responses to Set Questions	203
Focus Groups and the Journey from Fear to Friendship	214
The Construction of Peace	220
Summary	222

Chapter Seven
Behaviour and Attitudes of Participants in the Focus Groups

Introduction	225
Open Coding Analysis	226
Social Change: Values and Interests	229
Values and Leadership	236
Communication and Sustainability of Social Change	238
Soft Power or Propaganda	247
Key Ideas in the Focus Groups	252
Discussion of Findings in Terms of Theory	253
Sequence of Frameworks for Communication in the Focus Groups	259
Summary	265

Chapter Eight
Conclusion

Introduction	267
Social Change	268
Has the Research Question Been Answered and How?	269
Critical Self-Reflection	273
Future Prospects	274
Universal Themes	275
Future Research	280
Conclusion	282

Appendices

Appendix 1: Findings	283
Appendix 2: Interview Themes	354
Appendix 3: Gaining Access to Respondents	356
Appendix 4: Explanatory Statement	358
Appendix 5: Information for Focus Group Participants	360
Appendix 6: Consent Form	363
Appendix 7: Codification of Themes	365
Appendix 8: Final Ethics Approval	379
Bibliography	381
Table 5.1	190
Fig. 7.1	260

The Mercy Prayer

Eternal Father, we offer you the Body and Blood, Soul and Divinity of your Dearly Beloved Son, Our Lord Jesus Christ, in atonement of our sins, and the sins of the whole world.

There are 10 responses to this: for the sake of His sorrowful passion have mercy on us and the whole world. It is said on rosary beads. This prayer mirrors the kind of forgiveness that Derrida talks about, forgiving the unforgiveable.

I dedicate this thesis to the Patroness of Australia Mary, Help of Christians.

Abstract

In interfaith encounter groups, the people of the Abrahamic religions are drawing together in dialogue rather than conflict. The core research question in this thesis is "How are people of Abrahamic faiths, faiths that are implicated in a geopolitical confrontation, able to cooperate within religious organizations?" The analysis is comparative. On the analectic continuum, it stems from a deductive set of questions, but takes into account some inductive emerging issues. 15 participants, perceived as role models for the language of peace, were interviewed at great depth. Social, scientific, and religious knowledge from a questionnaire was discussed by four focus groups consisting of Jews, Christians and Muslims. Commitment to religion, enemy images of each other, ethical dialogue, forgiveness, and the construction of peace made up the discussions. Peace was constructed by remediation of negative attitudes and behavior that often involved hospitality and always involved deep listening. Differences and identities in Jewish, Christian and Muslim religions were clearly stated, but also their commonalities: human needs such as respect and safety, and the religious text to love God and neighbour. They defined this God as forgiving and compassionate, and neighbour as "everyone". There was a change in their interests, which expanded to all three Abrahamic religions and their language of peace included discussing difficult issues such as the re-examination of their texts, and the paramount need to be open, generous and brave. Their dialogue rose above differences to enable them to lay a reasonable, achievable foundation for a peace, based on human needs and common texts. All participants were reasonably well-informed and well-educated believers committed to their own faith tradition and able to communicate its inner values and spirit. A model was extracted from this research that shows the pathway from externally mediated images of geopolitical conflict to practical expressions of cooperation and peace within interfaith groups. This is an historical social change.

Declaration

This work contains no material which has been accepted for the award of any other degree or diploma in any university or other tertiary institution and, to the best of my knowledge and belief, contains no material previously published or written by another person, except where due reference has been made in the text.

I give consent to this copy of my thesis, when deposited in the University Library, being available for loan and photocopying.

Acknowledgements

I acknowledge and give thanks to Macquarie University, Sydney, NSW, and Monash University, Gippsland Campus, Churchill, Gippsland, Victoria. I also thank Dr. Amy Forbes (Communication), and Associate Professor Harry Ballis (Sociology), who were Auxiliary supervisors from Monash University. In particular, I want to deeply thank Professor Naren Chitty of Macquarie University for his loyalty as a friend in difficult situations and his remediating supervision which enabled me to produce this thesis.

Finally, it is also with gratitude that I acknowledge and thank the Interfaith Groups in Sydney. The Jewish Interfaith Executive, Uniting Church Executive Interfaith, and Affinity Interfaith Foundation (Muslim) sent voluntary members to help me research truth, reconciliation, forgiveness and peace. Men and women, young and old, shared their lives, their commitment to God and their thoughts and beliefs on the construction of peace with the help of the common text, to Love God and neighbour. I thank them from the bottom of my heart.

Personal Statement

A Personal Odyssey

It is not uncommon for researchers to acknowledge that their research merges from and reflects their autobiographies. Atkinson & Shakespeare (1993:8) note that "personal histories are germane to the conduct of research and construction of knowledge". A Catholic heritage and a Jewish name define my personal journey. That journey has become an odyssey to create a new memory of history, a memory that responds to the sadness of the past with friendship for the future. As a Roman Catholic with close family affiliations to the Judaic tradition, and as a social scientist, I am interested in the ways people of the Abrahamic religions are engaging in dialogue rather than conflict. The purpose of this research, therefore, explores how members of Jewish, Christian, and Islamic organizations address intra-organizationally the extra-organizationally unresolved questions of reconciliation and forgiveness in local and worldwide settings. The philosopher Derrida identified the need for an "urgency of memory". For Derrida, this memory is a Judaic/Christian legal and religious legacy. For this reason reconciliation necessitates a turning back towards the past. This process is an act of memory, of self indictment, of repentance and of justice beyond the level of the country and the nation-state (Derrida 2004). As a Catholic with a Jewish name, I view myself as being a type of link in the chain of memory of both religions.

This study considers ways to repair the broken links in that chain of memory through interfaith encounter groups. Such groups are flourishing under the authority of Pope Benedict XVI and 138 Muslim scholars (www.acommonword.com). Mending links means forgetting and disposing of old hurtful memories, looking carefully at human needs, and with the love and forgiveness that religions teach, working together to construct peace. To link religion and peace is to link religion and philosophy, one of the social sciences. It is my personal and intellectual odyssey to find that link within the traditional concepts of international communication and conflict resolution. The study examines the thoughts and experiences of many scholars and peoples of religions other than the Abrahamic religions but who are working on theories of international communication, or who have experienced and resolved deep seated conflicts.

This research coincides with the growth of diasporas under globalisation, the gathering together of different cultures, for many reasons in many nations. The notion of us and them has become a notion of cultural togetherness. This forces new ways of thinking and acting and new ways of being together. Electronic communication is the primary vehicle by which this process is extended beyond national borders. Used for war propaganda in the history of international communication, communication technologies can now be used to promote conflict resolution and peace. This information, taken into our own minds and memories and with our own insight to be turned into knowledge, provides an opportunity for peace. Conflict resolution helps us to construct friendships with those whom we may have thought of in negative terms.

There is revealed knowledge, which has been cut off from traditional scholarship since the Enlightenment, and there is, of course, the knowledge that comes from the five senses. This thesis began at the "time" of the Festival of Pentecost. In my "mind space" (my centre of personal energy) I thought about the coming of the Holy Spirit for the Christians, Shavuot, the receiving of the Torah, for the Jews, and the birthday of Muhammad, for the Muslims. The Spirit brings gifts, different, but all from the same Spirit, to build community. In Isaiah 11:2-3 the Spirit is described as "A spirit wise and discerning, a spirit prudent and strong, a spirit of knowledge and piety and fear of the Lord" (Knox 1966). These gifts are precursors of truth, reconciliation, and forgiveness, the necessary attributes for leadership. Or as Goleman, speaking of social intelligence, says "the social responsiveness of the brain demands that we be wise, that we realize how not just our own moods but our very biology is being driven and moulded by the other people in our lives" (Goleman 2006, p. 12).

Chapter One
Introduction

Introduction

The polities of nations that belong to Abrahamic faiths have for centuries been involved in intercivilizational wars and conflicts. Polities associated with Christianity, Islam and Judaism continue to have discomfiting geopolitical relationships. Despite this, individuals and communities belonging to these faiths live together in cultures of peace in several parts of the world, even if others are at war. This is an intercultural, international communication thesis which presents the living construction of a language and culture of peace. With great cooperation and wisdom, a peace language is put into practice by authorized Jewish and Muslim leaders, and self-chosen Christians. In four focus groups, 15 participants, both old and young, men and women, dialogued together over two days, resulting in 80,000 words of interfaith understanding from three interfaith Abrahamic religious organizations. They dialogued truthfully about enemies, remediation[1], forgiveness, reconciliation and a common religious text. Intercultural communication for peace is very important to the world today, and this thesis truly charts a way

---

1 Remediation: "the action of remedying something" (oxford-dictionaries.com), the word "remedy" "means of countering or removing something undesirable" (Cowie 1994 p. 1065) which in this case, is the historical conflict within Abrahamic communities.

to the possibility of peace in troubled times. With regard to remediation, the remedy for the prejudice that has been handed down to families for generations is documented. It is available to us all. The remedy is truthful information and hospitality, both of which exist at the heart of moving from prejudice to friendship. There are two foundational flows of information in this thesis.

Foundational Flows of Information[2]

1. Literature of Conflict and Cooperation Covering Both International and Intra-Group Levels

Foundational knowledge of the attributes of human beings, their language, culture, communication and cooperation, as well as the practice of conflict resolution runs right throughout the whole thesis. Embracing, as well, theorists from the social sciences and humanities, the thesis also presents the lived life of global and local Abrahamic communities. It can be seen that forgiveness has a political context.

---

[2] Operational definitions are often used in this thesis because they show the process of information coming from different sources which define identity, cultural and religious foundations of thought. The operational definitions that are quoted have a common-sense, rather than theoretical quality. This makes them to be more proximate to the language of the ordinary religious people who are the participants of my research. The definitions also have resonance with the deeper theoretical underpinnings that inform my framework.

Forgiveness "is an act that joins moral truth, forbearance, empathy, and commitment to repair a fractured human relation" (Shriver, 1995, p. 9). Reconciliation is a "word best reserved, perhaps, for the end of a process that forgiveness begins." (ibid., p. 8)

2. What It Is To Be a Jew, Christian and Muslim: The Research Process

Participants from the Jewish, Christian and Muslim interfaith groups dialogue truthfully about prejudice and peace in Sydney, NSW, Australia, beginning with their family histories. It needs to be stated clearly, that both the Jewish and Muslim interfaith movements gave their authority to the Jewish and Muslim participants to present their attitudes on enemies, values, forgiveness and the construction of peace. The Christians were self-chosen, but they were the risk takers, the leaders of the Uniting Church. All participants were reasonably well-informed and well-educated believers committed to their own faith tradition and able to communicate its inner values and spirit. In a small way, this thesis begins to construct a "conceptual framework for the systematic study of differential commitment to religion" (Glock & Stark 1965, p. 19).

Attentive, concentrated "listening" to a person telling their story brings forth empathy and understanding. As modeled in this thesis, the process of positive thoughts and words leading into good actions and cooperation can be called the peace process. Friendship is an outcome. Only limited research has been done on cross group friendship (Pettigrew & Tropp 2011).

Foundational Flows of Information Brought Together

Peace is not only the absence of conflict, individually it can mean to make one's peace with somebody and end a quarrel, especially by apologizing" ... or in groups, "to make peace (of two people, countries), agree to end a war or a quarrel" (Cowie: 1994: p. 910).

A coherent picture is presented from interdisciplinary theorists of how the human person has the capacity to think, to form thoughts into words, and words into language. The relationship between reality, thought and language is a correspondence "between thought and reality" (Grice 1989, p. 284), what Grice calls psychophysical correspondence.

Evidence is given that this human being has the capacity to use what is called a "will" – a "mental power by which a person can direct his thoughts or actions" (Cowie 1994, p. 1461), that is, an intention to think, speak and act in a certain way. Also, there is evidence of individual and group change of mind. This is strikingly shown by the Catholic Vatican Council II. Pressure to change attitude (Neal 1965, p. 71) was cited in the focus groups as the terrorist attack of 9/11 on the Twin Towers. Leaders called on Jews, Christians and Muslims to pray together.

The authentic identity of each person, pictured within their free commitment to their religion, is very important. "Modern freedom and autonomy centers us on ourselves, and the ideal of authenticity requires that we discover and articulate our own identity" (Taylor 1991, p. 81). The participants did this. Using dialogue they proposed models of society. "To come together on mutual recognition of difference – that is, of the equal value of different identities – requires that we share more than a belief in this principle; we have to share also some standards of value on which the identities concerned check out as equal" (ibid., p. 52).

Respect and knowledge of self and others were cited by all in the focus groups. With hospitality they grew into positive communication, from which came friendship and even love. Love can be defined as "a warm liking or affection, affectionate, devotion" (Cowie, p. 741). The traditional idea of friendship had three essential contents. "Friends must enjoy one another's company, they must be useful to one another, and they must share a common commitment to the good" (Bellah et al. 1985, p. 115). A friend, the groups say, will tell you the truth. And "Let us designate the first social cognition of friendship as communication ... communication is noted by mutual understanding, 'a mutual, deep knowledge, an acceptance' of your friend" (Gurdin 1996, p. 32). As this is a communication thesis it also needs to be said, that within extended family groups, and the Abrahamic communities fall into this category as they are the descendants of Abraham, "communication emerges as the key to family satisfaction and to the full human development of family members" (Eastman 1989, p. 63).

Abrahamic Religions in Australia

The first Jews in Australia arrived in the First Fleet in 1788. There were at least 10 Jews among the convicts (Porush 1977, p. 1). Christians also arrived in Australia in the same boat. From 1850 Muslim fisherman had communicated with Aboriginals in Australia's north and in the 1860's 3,000 camel drivers, with camels, arrived from Afghanistan and the Indian sub-continent. Significant Muslim migration occurred in the 1960's, and also in the 1990's, (Australian Broadcasting Commission, religion, Islam).

The percentage of religions in the 2006 census was 64% Christians, 1.7% Islam, and 0.4% Jews (Australian Bureau of Statistics 2006 Census).

Prior Research in Australia

Cahill's research, of 2004, mapped the interrelationship between religion and cultural diversity in the context of Australia's social cohesion and internal security, especially in the aftermath of the terrorist attacks of September 11th, 2001 in the U.S.A.. The report, itself, was written in the shadow of the Muslim terrorist bombing in Bali on 12th October, 2002 (88 Australians killed) (Cahill et al. 2004, p. 6). An overwhelming majority of those consulted, "(78%), agreed (43%) or strongly agreed (35%) that 'religious extremism has the potential to destroy the fabric of Australia's civil, pluralist and democratic society'" (Cahill et al. 2004 p. 83). This research showed the wide spate of abuse, physical assaults on persons and property and hate mail in Australia after these events. There was a significant increase in vandal attacks on Islamic mosques and schools (ibid., p. 84). However, stress was placed by the consultees on: (1) The importance of change in inter-faith relationships at the local level where issues are best dealt with. (2) The importance of long term contact and friendship between religious leaders at all levels of society. (3) The achievement of inter-religious co-operation. (4) The need for cross-cultural and inter-faith education for all religious personnel. (5) The need for government to take the lead in times of crisis through the development of quick response strategies. (6) The need for the faiths to work together for religious education to be offered by government schools (ibid., p. 83).

Seven years later, research by Bouma et al., taken in 2011, shows the outcome from the implementation of Cahill's recommendations. Regarding freedom of religion in Australia, it shows that while there are concerns about how society in general, and government in particular, are managing religious affairs, "many participants in the research felt – and felt strongly – that the situation is quite satisfactory in Australia, the nation has a good and working model of freedom of religion and belief that does not need to be changed" (Bouma et al. 2011, p. 22). The message of those consulted "was to 'retain the status quo' because Australia is a peaceful country without serious interreligious tensions" (ibid., p. 22). Further on in the research, Bouma reports that, "while there was some concern about the impact of security legislation and security technology, little mention was made of these" (ibid., p. 74). He concludes that "the consultations and submissions have made it clear that this is an area much affected by local, national and transnational factors, and one with which many Australians are ready to engage in the spirit of dialogue and with the clear presentation of views characteristic of a healthy, genuinely democratic society" (ibid., p. 90).

The Problem

Sociologist C.W. Mills had a deep understanding of the historical phases and the historical reasons for varying directions of development and lack of development (Mills 1959). The emerging issue of our time is the urgent need to come to terms with the fact that religions, especially fundamental arms of some religions, have caused violence and pain in the world. To counteract this, today, role models in the Abrahamic religions are gathering in interfaith to make the world a better place.

How the authorised and self-chosen leaders gather up the yearnings of their communities to pursue peace shows how deep problems can be solved with intercultural communication: "The ability to understand other cultures may represent the cornerstone of international understanding and world peace" (Mowlana 1997, p. 157). "Sheer ignorance, as well as malice, accounts for much of the harm that strangers inflict on each other" (Shriver 1995, p. 233). To live together peacefully, we have to understand that it is through sending and receiving messages that "human beings assure their psychological survival and define their personal identity" (Willet 1989).

This thesis records behaviour and beliefs broadly in relation to intercultural communication, conflict, and cooperation. It also records cooperative relationships between academic, religious and Non-Government Organisation discourses on peace, and conflict resolution in interfaith contexts. It then goes on to introduce the social scientific matrix within which the studies method and analysis will be embedded before proving outlines of the objectives and structure of the thesis. It answers the question "How are people of the three Abrahamic faiths that are implicated in a geopolitical confrontation able to cooperate within interfaith organizations at the local level?"

Background to the Abrahamic Religions

While religious and cultural issues underpin the clashes between particular communities adhering to Abrahamic religions, Rouhana (1998, p. 762) sees a political economic dimension to the contemporary conflict. He notes that "Zionism and Palestinian nationalism clashed over the ownership of the land, the right for self-determination, and statehood". Wallensteen (2002, p. 15) views the conflict in terms of a severe disagreement between at least two sides, where their demands cannot be met by the same resources at the same time. The conflict model Rouhana and Wallensteen describe could apply also to Christian/Muslim conflict identified in nations where the practice of Christian rites is prohibited. Jamieson (2006, p. 208), however, views the contemporary Christian/Muslim as a clash between materialism and religion, stating that "The new conflict between the post-Christian West and Islam is more a clash between secular materialism and a revived religion". In the end, conflicts are carried forward by states and states-in-waiting, and are often about the control of land and resources – including people. A state is more than just land and government: "a state is not, like the ground which it occupies, a piece of property (patrimonium). It is a society of men whom no one else has any right to command or to dispose except the state itself. It is a trunk with its own roots" (Kant 1795), and often the leaves, or the people, are sustained by religious ideologies which give their communities shape.

To understand the present clash of discourses and emergent dialogue and potential for dialogue, it is necessary to outline the three Abrahamic religions definitionally. The following description does so by identifying key differences between each of the three religions that recognize that God is One, and also note key beliefs that they have in common.

Judaism

Judaism is "the religion of the Jews, a monotheistic faith having a basis in Mosaic and rabbinical teachings. Judaism was founded, according to the Bible, on the covenant made between God and Abraham, which ordained the Jewish people's special relationship with God" (Moore 1999, p. 715). "The people of Israel believed that their response to the divine presence in history was central not only for themselves but for all humankind. Furthermore, God – as person – had revealed in a particular encounter the pattern and structure of communal and individual life to this people. Claiming sovereignty over the people because of his continuing action in history on their behalf, he had established a covenant (berit) with them and required from them obedience to his teaching, or law (Torah)" (Encyclopaedia Britannica: Judaism). Fundamental to Judaism is the belief that the Jews are a chosen people of God, and must serve as a light for other nations. Their One God is omnipotent (all powerful), omniscient (all knowing), omnipresent (in all places at all times) and just and merciful (Judaism: Answers).

The Torah includes the Five Books of Moses that have also been incorporated into the Bible: These are Genesis, Exodus, Leviticus, Numbers and Deuteronomy. It became an important vehicle of sanctuary after Judaism became a religion of exile in the year A.D. 70. Replacing the temple and temple rites were synagogues. The Torah, as sanctuary, contained a belief in the return to the Promised Land, Zion; a rebuilding of the temple in Jerusalem and the promise of Messianic redemption (Judaism 101: Torah). The Synagogue governance is seen as "a sacred trust to represent the whole congregation in building a sustainable future. Through leadership, the Board sets the tone for congregational life (Judaism: Effective Board Membership). Religious judges or rabbis expert in the Torah have special authority. Communal control over non-halakhic public affairs devolved upon the "elders" whose authority derived from their age, wealth, family lineage, gender, and personal qualities.

Christianity

Christianity is the religion of those who believe in and follow Jesus Christ (Crim et al. 1981, p. 169). The largest religion in the world today, it consists of some 38,000 denominations with approximately 2 billion adherents. "Christianity developed when a group of Jews two thousand years ago gathered around the Rabbi Jesus of Nazareth" (Crim et.al. 1981, p. 69). They saw him executed and proclaimed he had risen from the dead and that his death was an act of sacrifice and love for them. The resurrection held the promise for them of victory over death and the enemies of their soul. The Jews who believed in Jesus Christ continued to hold on to the Jewish religious texts now called the Old Testament (or old agreement with God) by Christians. They added their own stories of Jesus Christ into a New Testament (new agreement).

Many of the key Christian beliefs were formalized some three hundred years following the death and resurrection of Christ, at an assembly of bishops convened in Nicaea. The Church Fathers concentrated on the issue of Jesus' Divine son-ship, and agreed that the doctrine of the Trinity was central to the uniqueness of Christianity. This teaching holds that God exists as three 'persons', Father, Son and Holy Spirit, and each 'person' is fully God, and there is one God.

Jesus gave Christians a new commandment, to love one another as I have loved you (John 13.34). Christians also are called upon to love their enemies (Matthew 5.44). The key Christian attitudes are embodied in the prayer Jesus instructed his followers to pray:

Our Father in heaven, hallowed be your name. Your kingdom come, Your will be done, on earth as it is in heaven. Give us this day our daily bread, and forgive us our debts, as we also have forgiven our debtors. And do not bring us to the time of trial, but rescue us from the evil one. For if you forgive others their trespasses your heavenly Father will also forgive you, but if you do not forgive others, neither will your Father forgive your trespasses. (Matthew 6:9)

Jesus also taught that his followers are to "love the Lord your God with all your heart, and with all your soul, and with all your mind ... [and to] love your neighbor as yourself; On these two commandments hang all the law and the prophets" (Matthew 22.36-8). The commands to love others, including one's enemies are pivotal to Christianity regardless of denomination. The governance is of Episcopal polity, a form of Church governance that is hierarchical in structure, with the chief authority over a local Christian Church resting in a Bishop. In Catholic and Eastern Orthodox systems, Bishops may be subject to higher ranking Bishops, Metropolitans and/or Patriarchies or Popes (http:en.wikipedia.org/wiki/Episcopal_polity). Governance in Protestant denominations includes priests/ministers and laity working together. The governance goes from local church, to regional synods, presbyteries, to national general assemblies. In the case of the Anglican Church there is an international sharing of the gospel, and they also kept the Episcopal system.

Islam

Islam is a "major world religion promulgated by the Prophet Muhammad in Arabia in the 7th century CE. The Arabic term islām, literally "surrender," illuminates the fundamental religious idea of Islam—that the believer (called a Muslim, from the active particle of islām) accepts surrender to the will of Allah (in Arabic, Allāh: God). Allah is viewed as the sole God—creator, sustainer, and restorer of the world" (Encyclopaedia Britannica: Islam). Muslims believe that the prophet Muhammad received Divine revelations from the Angel Gabriel "which became the doctrine and legislative basis of Islam" (Moore 1999 p. 887). The Quran, the religious text that arose from these revelations, does corroborate, update and expand the Old and some of the New Testament. A key teaching of the Quran concerns the umma, or community. "Muslims represent many races and socioeconomic settings. There have been however significant divisions of opinion within the umma (commonwealth of Islam or Islamic Community). Despite these differences, Islam brings unity by incorporating divergent interpretations of basic beliefs" (Dolphin).

Islam has two denominations, the Sunni and the Shi'a; the larger of these is the Sunni. There are principal duties for all Muslims. It is obligatory for every Muslim to pray five times a day at prescribed times facing the Holy City of Mecca. The five Pillars of faith in Islam are as follows:

(1) The profession of faith in a prescribed form
(2) Observance of ritual prayer (the obligatory prayer sequences each day as well as non-obligatory prayers)
(3) Giving alms to the poor
(4) Fasting during the month of Ramadan

(5) Performing the pilgrimage (Hajj) to Mecca (Moore 1999, p. 695).

A communal prayer to Allah on Eid Day, the end of the fasting of Ramadan is reproduced below:

„O" *the High and the Great [God]! „O" the Forgiving and the Merciful [God]! You are the Great Lord like whom there is nothing. He is the All-Hearing, the All-Seeing. This is the month that You have exalted, honoured, glorified, and preferred over the other months; it is the month whose fasting You have made obligatory on me; it is the month of Ramadan in which You revealed the Qur'an as a guidance for people, as clear signs of guidance and as a means of separating the right from the wrong. And You placed in it the Night of Destiny which You have made better than a thousand months. So „O" the Lord who favours others and none can oblige Him, favour me by releasing my soul from the hell-fire... and admit me in the Heaven by Your mercy. „O" the Most Merciful of the Mercifuls. (Eid al Fitr Prayer/Supplication)*

With a membership estimated at 1.5 billion Muslim followers, Islam is the second-largest religion in the world, and fast growing (Islam: Major Religions of the World ranked by number of adherents). Islam is the predominant religion in the Middle East, North Africa and a large part of Asia. Islamic law (Sharia) touches on virtually every aspect of life and society.

The major principles of Islamic governance revolve around the belief that Allah Subhanahu wa ta'ala is sovereign. The head of the state and all those in positions of power must practice shura or Common Consultation. Sharia law provides a broad framework within which the people under the umbrella of Divine Guidance participate in developing a civil society (Siraj Islam Mufti: Muslim Access).

What is of relevance in the present study – exploring as it does the role of dialogue and reconciliation in bringing adherents of the Abrahamic faiths together – is that notwithstanding their individual origins and differences in their teachings, the three religions have in common the belief to serve the One God, who is forgiving, merciful and compassionate, and the commandment to love God and ones neighbour. The 138 Muslim scholars[3] declare:

> Love of God in Islam is thus part of complete and total devotion to God". And "Love of the neighbour is an essential and integral part of faith in God and love of God because in Islam without love of the neighbour there is no true faith in God and no righteousness. The Prophet Muhammad said: "None of you has faith until you love for your neighbour what you love for yourself. (Sahih Muslim, Kitab al-Iman, 67-1, Hadith no.45)

The Shema in the Book of Deuteronomy (6:4-5), a centerpiece of the Old Testament and of Jewish liturgy states:

> Hear, O Israel: The Lord our God, the Lord is one! You shall love the Lord your God with all your heart, and with all your soul, and with all your strength." "You shall not hate your brother in your heart. You shall surely rebuke your neighbor, and not bear sin because of him. You shall not take vengeance, nor bear any grudge against the children of your people, but you shall love your neighbor as yourself; I am the Lord. (Leviticus 19:17-18)

Likewise, Christians accept that when in the New Testament Jesus Christ the Messiah is asked about the greatest commandment, he answers thus:

> But when the Pharisees heard that he had silenced the Sadducees, they gathered together. Then one of them, a lawyer, asked Him a question, testing Him, and saying 'Teacher, which is the great commandment in the law?' Jesus said to him 'You

---

3 The 138 Muslim scholars were responding to a public address by Pope Benedict XVI delivered in Regensburg which was negative to the Muslim tradition. Pope Benedict XVI was quoting an ancient text.

shall love the Lord your God with all your heart, with all your soul and with all your mind. This is the first and greatest commandment. And the second is like it: 'You shall love your neighbour as yourself.' On these two commandments hang all the Law and the Prophets.' (Matthew 22:34-40)

In addition to exploring whether these common beliefs about loving God and one's neighbour can provide a basis for genuine dialogue and reconciliation, this study seeks to better understand how the practitioners interpret current religious conflicts, in the light of their religious texts, promoting love to God and neighbour.

Religious Schism

The roots of religious division run deep. A theme of this research, traditions of conflict resolution from within different religious and ethnic cultures, gives us an historical view of separation. First there was the division between the Catholic and Orthodox churches. Later, during the Reformation, various Protestant denominations arose in distinction from the Roman Catholic Church. The roots of division with the Church of England are here provided from a Catholic viewpoint: At the time of "[t]he breach with Rome under Henry VIII ... [t]he bishops were made to sue out their faculties from the King, and, that the meaning of this humiliation should be unmistakable, the very form of the licence granted them affirmed the plain Erastian principle that the Crown was the source of their jurisdiction" (Catholic Encyclopaedia). On the road to reconciliation, at its Vatican Council II in 1965, the Catholic Church stated when large communities became separated from full communion with the Catholic Church "developments for which, at times, men of both sides were to blame ... men who believe in Christ and have been properly baptized are brought into a certain, though imperfect, communion with the Catholic Church ... all those justified by faith through baptism are incorporated into Christ" (Abbott (b) 1966, p. 345).

The contemporary Protestant wing of the Church is also divided. For instance, the Church of England, members of which are now called "Anglicans", is a long way from being united with the Continuing Presbyterian Church. In 1977 the Methodist Church and majority of the Presbyterian Church of Australia and the Church of the Congregational Union of Australia formed the Uniting Church of Australia (www.abc.net.au/religion/stories/).

The roots of the Presbyterian Church may be traced back to John Calvin. Calvin trained for the Catholic priesthood, but later led the Reformation in Geneva, Switzerland in 1541 (Fairchild). Calvin taught that we are predestined to go to heaven or hell at birth – and if we were members of the Elect of God we were obliged to fill our lives with good works. The Calvinist outlook, found among Afrikaners, travelled with the Dutch to South Africa. Afrikaners thought they were the Elect and the Nationalist Government made sure that "Afrikaner interest would take precedence over everything else" (Rebirth Africa Life). The Afrikaners' apartheid with its racism and segregation was drawn from Calvinist thought even if Calvin himself did not prescribe apartheid. "The South African Government of the 1970's had in many ways and at many times declared that its policies rested on Western civilization and Christian principles ... (but) when we looked at the policies it was impossible to conclude that these policies characterised love of God and neighbour" (Boraine 2000, pp. 19-20).

While the conflict around apartheid has now been resolved, that between Muslims, Christians and Jews across the world has not abated. Violent tensions continue between groups of Muslims, Christians and Jews in various countries. At the same time there are various ways in which these communities try to get together in various countries, not the least of which are the Interfaith Encounter Groups, the micro-dynamics of which are examined in this thesis in a Sydney context.

Interfaith Organizations

The Vatican Council II opened up the 21st century's windows to interfaith relationships.

Although ... many quarrels and hostilities have arisen between Christians and Muslims, this most sacred Synod urges all to forget the past ... (and) ... make common cause of safeguarding and fostering social justice, moral values, peace, and freedom... (also) ... The Church decries hatred, persecutions, displays of anti-Semitism ... (and) ... awaits the day, known to God alone, on which all peoples will address the Lord in a single voice and serve him shoulder to shoulder. (Soph. 3-9 (12) (Abbott 1966a, pp. 663-5)

The new thinking from the Vatican Council II, was very specific with regard to the historical basis of conflict with the Jews. "With regard to the trial and death of Jesus, the Council recalled that 'what happened in his passion cannot be blamed on all the Jews then living, without distinction, nor upon the Jews of today ... upon the Muslims, too, the Church looks with esteem, they adore one God, living and enduring, merciful and all powerful'" (Abbott 1966b, pp. 65-6).

There are now many 'secular' interfaith organizations in operation. For instance, the Jewish-Palestinian Living Room Dialogue Group in the USA initiated a public peace process in July 1992 that drew American Palestinians and Jews into a long term dialogue. This was done to discover common ground and improve the environment for reconciliation and change in America (Traubman). Others, such as Encounter Faith Association in Israel and the JCMA of Melbourne, Australia, are less secular in that they incorporate religious values as well, even if they do not belong to a synagogue, mosque or church.

Social Science and Religion

The present study draws comparatively on religious concepts but within a framework of social science. It explores the notion of remediation, the dialogue of understanding, with "dialogue being a discussion with people of different opinions" (Cowie 1989, p. 331). This dialogue leads to peace between local and international groups belonging to Abrahamic religions, the religions that are in a contemporary clash of civilisations. Huntington (1993) argues that the challenge for the West is "to accommodate non-Western modern civilizations whose power approaches that of the West, but whose values and interests differ". Social science scholars have been accused of sidelining religion and this has led to a misunderstanding of developments in the relations between civilizations.

The present study is based on the premise that an understanding and acceptance of the importance to people of religious values are foundational to achieving dialogue between religious organizations and faith communities. Only dialogue will abate current conflicts. Hamid Mowlana (2003, p. 19) endeavours to bridge the gap between approaches that sideline, and those that affirm, religion by noting that the "border between philosophy and religion must be rethought". Naren Chitty (2004, p. 54) asks, "can we assume that the path of academic secularisation is forever correct? Certainly we should from time to time re-examine our core beliefs". While the borders of philosophy and religion, social science and science, may be porous, the language and methods we use to examine religion within social science cannot belong to any domain other than social science.

As a social scientist looking at religion, Hervieu-Leger (2000) argues that knowing about religious leadership is important for understanding religion. Religion exists when the authority of tradition supports the act of believing. There is a chain of belief that depends on authority. Bellah argues that "the capacity for religion to provide ideals and models for new lines of social development increases with the growing symbolic, individual, and social differentiation" (Bellah 1970, p. 17).

In a phenomenological sense this project takes a reflective, evidential and descriptive approach to both encounterings and objects as encountered" (Centre for Advanced Research in Phenomenology). In other words, religious activities and objects cannot be considered in isolation from relationships. The phenomenological approach focuses "particularly on emotions seeking to explain their ongoing commitment to their faith in One God" (Smith 2007, p. 165).

International Communication

The present study is located in the field of international communication. International communication as a field of study was founded on propaganda studies and modernization studies (Chitty 2005). It was after World War II that key guidelines were established for the study of international communication. The social conditions, attitudes and institutions that influenced the production and reception of images among people were the main subject of post war research. So were elite leadership, communication and mediation, or opinion leadership. The design at the American University in 1968 for International Communication was based on "the belief that mass communications, information technology and intercultural communication should not be arbitrarily separated, but should be united, as they are all inextricably linked" (Mowlana 2004, p. 11). A changing world has brought different emphases to international communication. "In the area of international and intercultural communication, the culture and human components of international and societal relations have been overshadowed by technical, political and economic aspects" (Mowlana 1988, p. 1).

According to Chitty, "[i]nternational communication arose from the coalescing of specialised fragments arising out of political philosophy ... the fragmentation occurred along with a distancing from theology" (Chitty 2004, p. 54). While the West has accepted the values of the European Enlightenment, many Islamic communities have not subscribed to them. "The Enlightenment was a volatile mixture of classics, impiety, and science; the philosophers in a phrase, were modern pagans" (Gay 1997, p. 8). Gay understands that "When Lucretius spoke of dispelling night, lifting shadows, or clarifying ideas, he meant the conquest of religion by science" (Gay 1997, p. 103).

International communication thus not only defines the broad contours of this study, but also signals that it is cognizant and respectful of the different cultures that are examined, seeks to employ a language that values the commonalities between participants, and does not pass judgment on the views of others. At the same time, the perspective of international communication upholds human rights and strives to capitalize on the common acceptance of rights between groups and for developing a vision for the future.

Cross-Cultural and Trans-Generational Experiences

Like most, if not all, international communication research, the present work is an exercise in cross-cultural study in that it examines the views and interactions of members of three groups across borders of faith and faith related cultural histories and cultural practices. Even in the developed West, secularists and religious folk cannot see things from the same point of view. The secular age is well advanced, its ideas stemming from the Enlightenment. Some developed nations are now experiencing a religious backlash. "The battle for God was an attempt to fill the void at the heart of a society based on scientific rationalism ... It lacked the compassion which all faiths have insisted is essential to the religious life and to any experience of the numinous" (Armstrong 2001, p. 370). In developing countries there are added dimensions to the tension between secularism and communities of faith. The faith communities in the developing world experience modern secular Western culture as invasive, imperialistic and alien with respect to their faith. In the minds of many the dictates of such cultural imperialism should not be adopted lock, stock and barrel. "Studies reveal that cross-group friendships typically yield large reductions in prejudice. This effect is particularly strong when the assessment is based on behavioural measures (Pettigrew and Tropp 2011, p. 129). This effect can be seen in this thesis from its focus group dialogues.

The notions of culture and communication are integral parts of international relations, allied with new technologies of communication. Their impact on the political, economic and cultural aspects of international relations and the concept of communication as a process of interaction and dialogue is addressed by Mowlana (Mowlana 2004, p. 11). Within international interaction and dialogue, however, events are metaphorically distant and outside normal experience hence individuals can become morally detached. "Being routinely presented with images and information and events remote from our local life-world, and over which we have no control or possibility of intervention, means that we inevitably experience ourselves as, in a certain sense, outside them" (Tomlinson 1999, p. 175). Tomlinson thus suggests that people need to engage in dialogue at home as well as internationally.

Communication and dialogue are essential for survival. Willet (1989) explains that "life is characterised by its intrinsic capacity to send and receive messages to and from the different parts that make up an organism, as well as between the organism and its environment." More than this, Willet argues that it is through the ability to communicate that "human beings assure their psychological survival and define their personal identity."

Dialogue occurs through global and local forms of communication, enhanced over the past 50 years by new technologies. One of the major goals of dialogue in intergroup settings is peace. The modes of communication in the twenty-first century are therefore essential to the peace movement and to the creation of new memories of history to replace old destructive memories. Modern communication helps new and old Australians to keep in touch with the values and memories of countries of their origin. For recent settlers, this can lead to identity confusion and territorial claims for second generation children, thus the creation of new memories or the reinforcement of old ones[4].

Themes

This project draws on relevant literature from the social sciences, NGOs, and religious records to explore on the notion of survival through peaceful dialogue. It explores social scientific literature under four inter-connected themes:

---

4   An example of the tensions between new and old memories is to be found in the 2005 ethnic clashes at Cronulla Beach, NSW, between people the media tagged as Lebanese and Australians. The media reported that the Government would spend $440,000 over three years on cross-cultural experiences for young people from Sydney's Sutherland Shire district and Lebanese communities. The federal minister for Multicultural Affairs at the time, John Cobb, was quoted to have said that "Australians of ethnic background will be encouraged to become lifesavers" and will be educated about "how things work on the beach" (ABC Online). The message was that the Lebanese would retain their ethnic identity but would be encouraged to be part of, and integrated with, the Australian lifesaving culture. Public policy such as this, sparked by media coverage, can signal the creation of new memories to replace old destructive ones. Essential for conflict resolution in the Cronulla beach riots were the modern media.

a. Human needs
b. Ethical communication
c. The role of forgiveness
d. Processes of peace construction.

The four themes have been selected because they are foundational to the knowledge bases of different religious traditions. Mowlana (2003, p. 33), an Iranian American social scientist belonging to the Islamic faith, explains that he devised "a transcendental dimension of a communicative ethic as the horizon opened in-between the proximate other and the Wholly Other" by establishing "lines of communication between philosophy and religion". Gunaratne, a Sri Lankan American social scientist belonging to the Buddhist faith, developed a variation of world system theory that drew on Buddhist insights as a framework for research in international communication (Chitty 2007). Gunaratne's goal was to merge world systems analysis with the theory of dissipative structures to develop a "theoretical framework combining physics and historical social science with eastern philosophy" (Gunaratne 2007, p. 34). Common to both thinkers is the desire to develop perspectives that linked philosophy and religion and ultimately established a holistic outlook on social reality. The present study similarly seeks to establish links between social science and religion in order to gain better understanding of issues in the current religious conflicts. Insights from the inquiry on faith communities may also feed back into the fabric of social science.

Broadening of approaches is good for social science. Schaefer (2005) has a broad outlook when he argues that the dimension of relationship also is fundamental to human identity. He asks, "How can we imagine identity other than as globes, as closed spheres? We said: as a network ... the network is open. Its borders have no hem, no seam. They can link to new experiences" (Schaefer 2005).

The four themes identified above constitute the focus of the present study. They establish the broad contours of the questionnaire that will be the basis for the focus interviews to be undertaken in the present study. The themes identify the interpretive categories that enabled the exploration of focus group discussions and facilitated analysis of the interview data. Finally, as will be argued in subsequent chapters, the four themes constitute the key dimensions of what has been called in this study the language of peace.

Peace building in a globalised world is a human need and an urgent task. Bachika (2002), in Japan, has worked in the field of sociology on values that underpin ethics. Religion could, in the future, construct and propagate a common creed of core values. "The corner stone of both individual and collective well-being seems to be valuation. Individual happiness appears to be a matter of integration of personal values" (Bachika 2002, p. 214).

Globalisation is defined by Tehranian and Lum (2006, p. 5) as a "fragmenting process in rapid development, movement, and exchanges of people, goods, money, and information." Lum considers that "at the core of individual and collective group identities are philosophical and/or religious beliefs and values that define the perspectives that persons take in understanding their society" (ibid., p. 3). The closer different cultures come together, old histories of persecutions and vendettas can move to the surface. There are local possibilities of exacerbations of intergroup misunderstandings. To move to peaceful solutions, first there has to be an intention, a primary move, towards truth and reconciliation, and hopefully, "forgiveness". "Forgive; stop being angry or bitter towards somebody or about something; stop blaming or wanting to punish" (Cowie 1989, p. 483). It is the memories that are transferred to each new generation that impede the moving towards forgiveness – and the unwillingness to say "sorry."

In an ideal sense communities are collectivities of friends. Sherif, whose research centers on leadership, explains that "The adequate study of man and his relations requires taking into account his intimately felt motives, yearnings, aspirations, and the workings of his cognition in the context of his affiliations with other people and the sociocultural setting of which he is a part" (Sherif and Sherif 1964 in Sherif 1967, p. 53). The person who gathers up the yearnings of his community can lead them in many ways.

The irresponsible leader of a destructive mob or the demagogue moved chiefly by personal gain holds sway when no segment of society takes responsibility for the consequences of its actions, and none can set forth goals that can unite the dissident group. Members of groups in conflict may see wisdom in avoiding alternatives that offer only destruction and counter destruction ... there are possibilities of superordinate goals in various spheres of activity. If the efficacy of such goals is to be tested, they must be based on conditions in which all groups ... desire objectives that require contributions from all according to their resources and potential effort (Sherif 1967, p. 106-7).

Such a superordinate goal is a must for people who do not want violence but it is also one for a society that wishes to survive. These goals will be linked to the issues of the time. Bainbridge's research shows that "we will continually see that each particular religious phenomenon is inextricably tied to others and to the phenomenal of the secular world" (Bainbridge 1997, p. 55).

Research Objectives

The objectives of the study are to record and examine the views of members of interfaith groups in Sydney, Australia in order to throw light on intercultural communication and approaches to conflict among people from the three Abrahamic religions.

The core research question is: How are people of the three Abrahamic faiths that are implicated in a geopolitical confrontation able to cooperate within interfaith organizations at the local level?

Focus groups are employed in order to collect data in this regard. The analysis of data is set in a framework drawn from the literature of conflict and cooperation at international and intra-group levels, including discourses of peace, forgiveness, and ethical communication looking at conflict resolution in historical contexts. The study will draw conclusions about the roles of personal and collective memory in the construction of peace.

To examine this process, this research concentrates on the Abrahamic faiths.

Structure of the Thesis

This thesis will consist of this introductory chapter and seven other chapters.

Chapter 2 will examine the literature of conflict and cooperation at international and intra-group levels. It begins with a discussion of these antonymic concepts in realistic and constructivist International Relations, then in the field of International Communication before expanding on these concepts in international and inter-group contexts. It also discusses the notion of forgiveness as a key bridge, for consideration, between conflict and cooperation in the Abrahamic tradition.

Chapter 3 will discuss social science, humanities, religious and NGO discourses on peace as a human need, forgiveness and ethical communication – as an expansion of the pivotal notion of forgiveness that was introduced in chapter 2.

In chapter 4 a comparison is undertaken of three scenes of protracted conflict: South Africa, Ireland, and the Middle East. The chapter examines the histories and peace initiatives in those three conflicts. In considering the extent to which interfaith organizations engender reconciliation among individuals from different Abrahamic groups, this section tackles the assumption that peacemaking is difficult because of Middle East politics and the geopolitics of the Christian-Muslim-Jewish relationship. It is necessary therefore to examine the pathways Israel is taking towards Arab-Israeli conflict resolution and also to analyse the other contrasting cases. To examine the various pathways to resolution, this thesis draws on social scientific literature and on the economic, psychological, cultural, religious, and other factors relevant to the resolution process.

Chapter 5 will discuss the methodology employed for answering the research question. Beginning with a methodological discussion it will then deal with the method to be employed in field research before discussing the approach that will be taken in analysis of data.

The research findings will be reported in Appendix 1. The findings will report on the focus groups, reducing 80,000 words of transcribed speech into 17,000 words and organizing the selected quotes under basic analytical rubrics. Representative dialogue of the four groups on forgiveness and peace construction is presented unedited under common, different and noteworthy themes to allow the reader to 'be present' and 'listen' to the peace process.

Chapter 6 will go further in describing the focus group activity, detailing the individual participants in the focus groups and the Findings, (Appendix 1) record the dynamics of the focus groups. The purpose of the Findings is to observe how participants engage in dialogue in a controlled setting to discuss forgiveness and develop friendship in steps towards the construction of peace.

Chapter 7 will connect the focus group dialogue to the multi-disciplinary theory discussed in chapters 2 to 4, seeking to understand the peace construction in interfaith groups at a deeper level. It will examine the various ways the processes of forgiveness and the construction of peace which have emerged in the dialogues in the focus groups. This chapter will also contain an Open Coding Analysis and Neal's "Values and Interests in Social Change." as well as a discussion of findings in terms of literature. It is hoped that a sequence of actions from conflict to peace will emerge from the interrogation.

A final evaluation of the project will be undertaken in chapter 8. It will evaluate whether and how the research question will have been answered in the thesis. It will also undertake a critical self-reflection and then discuss future prospects for peace construction.

Summary

In this chapter the background to the problem of interfaith group cooperation has been enunciated; a theoretical approach, research question and method have been identified and the structure of the thesis outlined. The next chapter will discuss intercultural communication and conflict.

Chapter Two
Intercultural Communication and Conflict

Introduction

As stated in the previous chapter the core research question is 'how are people of the three Abrahamic faiths that are implicated in a geopolitical confrontation able to cooperate within interfaith organizations at the local level?' Confrontation and cooperation at two levels, world systemic and local organizational are therefore key theoretical areas in this study. Whether and why the world is one of conflict or cooperation is an age old question in political philosophy. This introduction is therefore followed by a discussion on the nature of the world drawing first on Hobbes and Machiavelli who may be viewed as realists in International Relations to Onuf and Pettman whose constructivist approaches are more compatible with contemporary International Communication. The field in which this study is set is the interdisciplinary one of International Communication. However, it goes further than International Communication in being interdisciplinary. The next section draws on conflict and cooperation in the literature of International Communication.

Following this the chapter goes on to discuss conflict and cooperation at international (Galtung 2007, Huntington, Sheriff 1997, White 1984) and intra-group levels (Goulet 1971, 2006, Sherif 1967). The work of Huntington on clash of culture, Ralph White (White 1984) on diabolical enemy imagery, Juergensmeyer (2000) on terror in the mind of God, Galtung (2007) on peace theory, Scheff (1997, 2002) on shame and revenge theory as well as the work of Lindner (2006) on treating people with dignity, are discussed under international cooperation and conflict. At the intra-group and organizational level Musafer Sherif's (1967) realistic conflict theory and Goulet's (1971, 2006) ethical theories are discussed along with Pope Benedict's theory of reason and faith, and Nathanson's (1992) theory of roles and personal involvement, and also D. Shriver Jnr's forgiveness in politics, an ethic for enemies.

The notion of forgiveness is addressed as it is important to discuss in the context of Abrahamic religions as a bridge between a moment of conflict and a moment of peace, cooperation and friendship. Reconciliation, the final outcome, has to be learned in community.

The Nature of the Human Being in the World

Conflict and cooperation are fundamental to the human experience. Intercultural cooperation is harmonious communication among people from different backgrounds, people who speak different languages and carry different pictures in their heads that shape their constructions of reality. Under these conditions, people are more likely to disagree than to agree. Love is perhaps the perfect motivator for cooperation as hate is for war. It is a challenge for mankind to take the value of love, and put it into practice with "the development of "head", perception and thought, "heart", emotion, and "hand", action" (Phillips & Christner 2011) and develop new ways of thinking, speaking and acting at a much deeper and more cooperative level. "At decisive points the ordinary language and conventional understandings fail and must be transcended" (Gouldner 1972, p. 16) and from this transcendence could evolve a world culture of peace.

European theorists of the early modern period speak of conflict and war. For Machiavelli, conflict was a result of the human desire for self-preservation and power. For Hobbes, the three 'principal causes of quarrel' in an anarchic state of nature were competition, insecurity and upholding of honour. For Hume, the underlying conditions for human conflict were relative scarcity of resources and limited altruism. For Rousseau, the 'state of war' was born from the 'the social state' itself (Ramsbotham et al. 2005, p. 79). All these are largely secular perspectives arising from European philosophical discourse.

Since the Enlightenment, in secular universities, theoretical approaches to the resolution of conflict have not drawn on religious knowledge. Religious approaches to conflict resolution in the family among Jews, Muslims and Christians can be traced back to Abraham. The issues then, and now, concern the acceptance or non-acceptance of one another, with non-acceptance being both caused by and leading to profound ignorance. But there are huge contradictions in the real world. For instance in January 2011, while Muslims were killing Christians in Iraq and Egypt, it was reported that "Muslims turned up in droves for the Coptic Christmas mass Thursday night offering their bodies, and lives, as 'shields' to Egypt's threatened Christian community" (Ecumenical and Interfaith Commission, EIC).

As this kind of religious issue has high visibility in world politics, social scientists and scholars in the humanities, especially philosophers, are considering the problem of this gap of religious knowledge in our understanding. Dialogue has begun within religions themselves and also occurs between religions and academics of many scientific backgrounds seeking holistic perspectives. This thesis, too, endeavours to make science and religion complementary in order to enhance the dialogue of peace.

Marshall McLuhan provides an explanation for the intellectual processing of conflict and cooperation, or war and peace. We are to construct something new. He says that comprehensive awareness comes from the right and left brains working together in apposition or complementary, fashion. Western societies have relied on their left brain hemispheres, while Eastern societies rely more on the right hemisphere (McLuhan and Powers 1989). According to this theory, to have a greater understanding of the world's cultures requires a conscious use of both sides of the brain together. .

McLuhan thought that the human being was becoming discarnate because of modern communication technologies. McGilchrist sees it another way – we are becoming virtual because the left hemisphere of the brain has become dysfunctional because of misplaced rationalism. Both agree that a properly functioning brain is going to be essential in the 21st century. There can be only one unified field of consciousness (McGilchrist 2010, p. 220). The two sides of the brain have to co-operate if we are to be consciously aware of what is happening, and want to communicate this to ourselves, and others. McGilchrist would have it that we could have two wills, formed by two desires, one in each hemisphere of the brain. He also suggests that "the core of the self is affective and deep lying: its roots lie at the level below the hemisphere divide, a level, however, with which each cognitively aware hemisphere at the highest level is still in touch" (ibid., p. 221). When we come to think about the "will" and the ability to "communicate" an action into the present day experience, we literally sometimes have two minds about it. We have to think through, and negotiate our way with our self, to express what is, possibly, some deep lying survival mechanism. This is why a change of mind, as expressed through Neal's (1965) method of analysis, involving change, or no-change, in values and interests, will be deep seated and history making.

"The brain creates its own projections in the outer world, which in turn help to influence the workings of the brain in a mutually reinforcing and self-perpetuating way. This would suggest that the nature of the modern Western urban environment may be exaggerating the tendencies that the left hemisphere has projected there as well as suggesting one reason why the natural environment is felt to have such a healing influence" (McGilchrist 2009, p. 456). The organizations in the world that the human brain has conceived are both local and intercultural. Most societies organize themselves at both local and international levels. Much of the theory on conflict and cooperation also reflects these two dimensions: The local dimension for routine functions and the global network to connect with others for an understanding of the global picture. Space travel illuminates this concept. When humans travelled into space, they looked back and saw the Earth as one entity. We can describe this as the notion of oneness. Those seeking strategies for international peace have considered the meaning of oneness, and at the same time trends in international communications are contributing to the oneness of humankind by providing new mechanisms for interaction.

International Communication

The field of International Communication (IC) came into being in the USA as a distinct field of study in the aftermath of the war of 1939–1945 though research on international propaganda had been undertaken by Lasswell, Lerner and others between the two wars. "Founders of the field, Harold Lasswell and Daniel Lerner, were preoccupied with the 'dark side' of political propaganda and the 'light side' of the propagation of modernity respectively" (Chitty 2005). The Cold War unlocked further government funding for research on the possibilities of psychological operations (a descendant of propaganda studies) and the role of communication as an engine of modernisation (Brown).

Mattelart, one of the earliest international communication scholars, argues that communication serves first of all to make war. Not many have connected war with communication, but Mattelart points out that this blind spot obstructs the fact that "war and its logics are essential components of the history of international communications and of its doctrines and theories, as well as its uses" (Mattelart 1994, p. xiii). In the context of international communication, propaganda and disinformation are weapons. The information age colonizes the mind. Therefore, freedom of expression through the media is a nebulous concept. Political freedom under such conditions requires more than the right to exercise one's will in accordance with information from mass media; it requires also a sifting of that information in order to make decisions. This can be described as informed decision-making.

> *Unless we abandon the well-established belief that the fate of democracy resides completely in the media, we can scarcely hope to begin answering the question left up in the air by Deleuze regarding the 'gradual and diffuse institution of a new regime of domination' and the uncertainty concerning forms of resistance. (Mattelart 1994, p. 229)*

Without an exercise of will, democracy fails. The will can now be informed by modern communication technologies, but it is in each local community where the truth must be sought out and acted upon.

Frederick, another International Communication scholar, identifies global patterns in media politics. One interaction pattern is the appeal to world public opinion. "Antagonists take their dispute to the global public as a means to force change ... Amnesty International has used this tactic for years" (Frederick 1993, p. 228). He defines global communication as:

> *[a] field of study that encompasses many issue areas, including culture, national development, foreign policy and diplomacy, conflict and conflict resolution, technology, news flow, national sovereignty, ideology, comparative mass communication systems, regulation and policy, human and civil rights, ideological confrontation, war and peace, and propaganda and influence. (Frederick 1993, p. 47)*

Expanding global interconnectivity means that "information and power are increasingly intertwined ... and this information is influencing people's behaviour as well as government policies and strategies" (Arquilla and Ronfeldt 1999, p. 8). A noosphere, a realm of knowledge and wisdom, is now evident. Global interconnectivity is generating a new fabric for world order, Noopolitik. "The development of cyberspace, the infosphere, and the noosphere, make noopolitik possible, and information strategy will be its essence" (ibid., p. 28). Under this new system, power and military might not necessarily coincide. Power occurs more in terms of knowledge and information. "Noopolitik is foreign policy behaviour and strategy for the information age that emphasizes the shaping and sharing of ideas, values, norms, laws, and ethics through soft power" (ibid., p. 46). An inverse relationship exists between the newness of technology and the oldness of war.

Instead of culture driving political clashes, technology is now enabling a "host of positive tools, such as those provided by the fields of intercultural communication and inter-religious dialogue, as well as conflict resolution and negotiation skills, and a commitment to various forms of peace building" (Goff in Tehranian and Lum 2006, p. 10).

The state of the world is of human making. Humans have a capacity for communication through language. This capacity is largely reliant on speech, or speech surrogates like signing. Language is significant for the study of conflict and cooperation, because communication is significant for conflict and cooperation.

I start with language because I start with words. With these words I will make an account of world affairs, and of how they have been crafted, and this account in turn will help to make a particular kind of world affairs ... The power of language makes possible both memory and imagination – the capacity to recall the past and to anticipate the future. (Pettman 2000, p. 31)

The foundations of knowledge are ancient and durable in the Western philosophical paradigms. "They were laid in Classical Greece, and they are used today to erect conceptual frameworks and construct theories" (Onuf 1989, p. 35). In the words of Onuf, "[c]onstructivism begins with deeds. Deeds done, acts taken, words spoken – these are all that facts are" (ibid., p. 6). Onuf sees language as the connection with the divine. His dictionary tells him that "Logos", the word, is the rational principle that governs and develops the universe and the divine word of reason incarnate in Jesus Christ. He considers "the triumph of epistemology finds the 'rational principle' as a permanent home in the mind, and in so doing satisfies several presumptions, namely, that humans as language users are uniquely affiliated with the divine, that cognitive activity is pulled toward reason, that the mind finds, or makes, the order in the world" (ibid., p. 39). Language is universal and has rules. "We can easily enough construe rules as an important, perhaps even constitutively decisive agency for the realization of human intentions and thereby an indispensable part of what human beings need to take into account to be able to "carry on" in a socially constructed world" (ibid., p. 51).

On empirical grounds, reasoning, like language, is universal. "Speech acts are instances of applied reasoning. To proceed from a whole to its parts is what one normally describes as deductive reasoning. To proceed from parts to whole is inductive" (ibid., p. 99). And "[i]f cultures mix rules, differentiated by category, in different proportions, then people, differentiated by gender, culture, life circumstances, and material conditions, resort to categories of reasoning in different and ever changing proportions" (ibid., p. 126).

People are human before they are intercultural, and they all have the capacity for intention. Shanta Nair-Venugopal equates intention with success. "The successful outcome and character of any intercultural communication encounter ... depends just as much on the extent to which human intention has been successfully negotiated in that specific context of interaction as it does on other factors" (Nair-Venugopal 2003, p. 20).

It is necessary to clarify the use of the terms intercultural and cross-cultural communication.

> *The terms cross-cultural and intercultural communication are often used interchangeably, yet they are somewhat different in terms of area of inquiry, depth of analysis and scope. Cross-cultural communication studies began with an examination of the impact of technology and mass communication on culture and the interaction between so-called 'developed' and 'developing' nations ... Intercultural communication was an*

expansion of cross-cultural communication studies as scholars considered what happens when different cultures interact on a more interpersonal level, not only between but also within nation. (Weaver 2003)

Implicit in this chapter about communication is conflict. In some respects people are connecting. But there are disconnections. The next section considers aspects of conflict and cooperation, in turn, that arise at the international level.

INTERNATIONAL LEVEL

Conflict at the International Level

Sociologists have deeply investigated conflict, and their conclusions can be judged by our own experience of life, both at home and abroad.

The defining characteristic of any society, from a conflict perspective, is inequality. (Conflict Theory Sociology UK). It can also be said that the struggle for control, using emotional production, underlies the power of religion and makes it an important ally of the state. 'Why is there conflict? Above all else, there is conflict because (of) violent coercion ... being coerced ... calls forth conflict in the form of antagonism to being dominated.' (Collins 1974, pp. 56–61)

Living in a period where the people of the world are very conscious of one another through worldwide media, extreme poverty and violent coercion erupts into violence. This violence in its own turn flickers onto worldwide television immediately and has global consequences. "Both poverty and violence are caused by the exercise of power by elites in the cause of perpetuating their privileged position" (Crutchfield and Wadsworth 2003, p. 68). Today, for instance, when viewers watch Syrians being killed, they explain in solidarity "we are all Syrians."

Huntington warns of a clash of civilizations. The West will increasingly have to accommodate non-Western modern civilizations whose power approaches that of the West but whose values and interests differ significantly from those of the West. In order to achieve harmony, the West will develop a more profound understanding of the basic religious and philosophical assumptions underlying other civilizations and the ways in which people in those civilizations see their interests. "It will require an effort to identify elements of commonality between Western and other civilizations. For the relevant future, there will be no universal civilization, but instead a world of different civilizations, each of which will have to learn to coexist with the others" (Huntington 1993, p. 49).

There is no shortage of theories commenting on conflict. Thomas Scheff, a sociologist who specialises in emotions, has identified some of the roots of conflict. In mediation, when a solution or compromise can't be reached, the problem may lie hidden in the emotional/relational world. Status, prestige, honour, and glory could be reasons for conflict, but intractable conflicts are also fuelled by non-material as well as material concerns. "Hitler's motivation provides an example. In his writing and speeches, he provided a material motive for German aggression ... But there is a powerful subtext in the same writing and speeches, revenge for the humiliations that the Germans had suffered, which he thought would restore community and pride to the German national" (Scheff 1994).

The Nationalist Catholics in the Northern Ireland conflict have still not found a way of acknowledging their feelings of shame after 600 years of humiliation by the English. Alienation or emotions alone do not cause protracted conflict, but their denial by the participants does. In Western societies, Scheff sees individualism as the dominant theme of all relationships.

> *This focus disguises the web of personal and social relationships that sustain all human beings. The myth of the self-sustaining individual, in turn, reflects and generates the suppression and hiding of shame and pride .... Shame is the master emotion because it has many more social and psychological functions than other emotions, and it is the key component of conscience, the moral sense, since it signals moral transgression even without thought or words, and signals trouble in a relationship. (Scheff 2002, pp. 268–9)*

Hidden shame triggers anger spirals between the two people who are communicating. Scheff defines shame "as a class name for a large family of emotions and feelings that arise through seeing oneself negatively, if even only slightly negatively, through the eyes of others" (Scheff 2002, p. 266).

Narratives about shame in the Holy Wars Theory – the Crusades of the 12th century – linger in Abrahamic memory. "In Christian Western Europe co-existence with Islam was increasingly denied. Christ's supposed enemies must be defeated and destroyed – 'truth' was to be proved by the sword (Nicholson, Nicolle 2005, p. 6), and the Crusades began. "The loss of Jerusalem to the Crusaders had actually increased the city's importance to Muslims. Saladin unified Islamic territory and "the concept of jihad as war against the infidel was revived by 12th century Sunni Muslim scholars. Jihads became organized campaigns to recover the Holy Land, just as Crusades had been to conquer it. "Saladin succeeded in defeating and almost destroying the Crusader's Kingdom of Jerusalem ... the idea of the overriding importance of tawhid or "Unity" took such deep root that it remains to this day" (Nicholson, Nicolle 2005, p. 196).

Hitler mixed shame, blame, and Martin Luther's ideas, when he said that he was "acting in accordance with the Almighty Creator: by defending myself against the Jew, I am fighting for the work of the Lord" (Lindsey 1989, p. 2). Here, in part, is a tract written by

Luther, late in life, when speaking for Christians although he had left the Catholic Church, in A.D. 1543:

> *What then shall we Christians do with this damned, rejected race of Jews? First, ... set fire to their synagogues or schools and buy and cover with dirt whatever will not burn, so that no man will ever again see a stone or cinder of them. This is to be done in honour of our Lord and of Christendom ... Second, I advise that their houses also be razed and destroyed. (Rausch 1990 in Lindsey 1990, pp. 23–24)*

After Hitler's attempt at genocide of the Jews came the UN resolution of the division of Palestine into the State of Israel and an Arab State and subsequent conflict and terrorism. In a video, bin Laden warns "this terrorism is an obligation in Allah's religion" (Ruthven 2002, p. 209). "What America is tasting now is something insignificant compared to what we have tasted for scores of years. Our nation (the Islamic world) has been tasting this humiliation and this degradation for more than 80 years" (Osama bin Laden version 1, Oct. 7, 2001, p. 2). In a tape broadcast by Al-Jazeera TV from Dubai on December 27th 2001, Osama comes back to his centre point: "our terrorism against America ... seeks to make America stop its support for Israel" (Osama bin Laden, 2001, p. 4).

As a psychologist, Sherif understands why parties in conflict want to establish who is to blame for hostility and violence. The human intellect is capable of studying events to analyse human responsibility, and as a solution to intergroup conflict, the assessment of blame is never more than a first step. Without mutual agreement on this step, the query "Who's to blame?" invariably leads to a vicious circle of recriminations that intensify conflict. Sherif points out that "if conflict is intense and prolonged, ways of learning about or communicating with the other group become limited" (Sherif 1967, p. 109). Stereotyped images arising during prolonged intergroup conflict are typically descriptions that both assign blame to the group and vindicate the motives of one's own group. It is when the other is dubbed "the enemy" that the assignment of blame becomes hopelessly entangled with these images. "As long as two or more groups within an intergroup system are in dispute and stick exclusively to their in-group premises in dealing with the adversary, tension, strategies for conflict, casting blame, and complacent self-righteousness on each side will continue" (Sherif 1967, p. 173).

Another theorist who is relevant is Ralph White. He asks us to examine the images we hold in our head about people we would consider to be enemies. In his book "Fearful Warriors", psychologist White argues that a rational approach is insufficient to explain the arms race. He turns to psychological analysis to examine the psychological fallacies which underlie the arms race. These include,

1. The image of the enemy as an inhuman monster
2. The belief that one's own country is always morally justified in any of its actions
3. The beliefs that inaction will cause the worst possible outcome to occur, but decisive action will prevent that outcome
4. The tendency to underrate the opposition that will result in questionable beliefs about the territory

White's thesis is that the fundamental cause of these incorrect perceptions is fear (Miceli 1985). Enemy images can affect any groups, whether they are racial, ethnic, economic or international. "Enemy images lead people to selectively attend to and remember negative aspects and actions of enemies. Enemy images lead people to pay attention to and remember criticism of enemies more than they attend to and remember statements supporting enemies" (Psychologists for Social Responsibility).

The news media construct frames for conflict by fitting the information they are receiving into a package that is culturally familiar. Enemy images can be put into the frame of "bad guys". The news media changed the balance of power between Israel and the Palestinians during the intifada, which was a "struggle over world opinion" (Wolfsfeld 1997). By writing Palestinian "victim" narratives, the news media placed the Palestinians on a more equal footing with

Israel. "The entire Middle East conflict is a struggle over who is the bigger victim" (Wolfsfeld 1997, p. 119).

This chapter deals with organization cooperation and conflict. It is here that the ideas of Mark Juergensmeyer could give us a deeper understanding of terror in the mind of god. His focus is on the ideas and the communities of support that lie behind violent acts rather than on those who commit them. His "goal was to understand why these acts were often associated with religious causes and why they have occurred with such frequency at this juncture in history" (Juergensmeyer 2000, p. 7).

"Peace talks with Palestinians constituted a 'betrayal', Jewish activists in Israel asserted, during the unsuccessful Wye River negotiation" (ibid., p. 45) in the year 1998. There was the tragic assassination of Israel's Prime Minister Yitzhak Rabin in 1995 by Yigal Amir. In talking with Israeli religious activists, it became clear to Juergensmeyer that what they were defending was not only the political entity of the state of Israel, but a vision of Jewish society that has ancient roots (ibid., p. 46). For instance, the Messiah would come only when the Temple was rebuilt. It was regarded as heretical by activist Yoel Learner "to give up the least of the biblical land – by which he means all of the West Bank, to Arabs and their Palestinian Authority" (ibid., p. 47).

When Yigal Amir aimed his pistol and shot the Israeli Prime Minister Yitzhak Rabin at point blank range he said he had "acted alone and on orders from God" (ibid., p. 48). He was not the only assassin.

Abd al-Salam Faraj, tried and executed in 1982 for his part in the assassination of Anwar Sadat of Egypt, argued that the Qur'an and the Hadith were fundamentally about warfare. "The duty" that has been profoundly neglected is precisely that of jihad and it calls for "fighting, which means confrontation and blood" (ibid., pp. 82–83).

The postmodern religious rebels, these small but potent groups of violent activists have represented growing masses of supporters and they have exemplified consensus of thinking and cultures of commitment that have risen to counter the prevailing modernism – the ideology of individualism and skepticism (ibid., p. 232).

These guerrilla nationalists have dreamed of revolutionary changes that would establish godly social order in the rubble of what the citizens of most secular societies have regarded as modern, egalitarian democracies. Their enemies have seemed to most people to be both benign and banal: modern secular leaders such as Yitzhak Rabin and Anwar Sadat, and such symbols of prosperity and authority as the World Trade Center and the Japanese subway system. "The logic of this kind of militant religiosity has therefore been difficult for many people to comprehend. Yet its challenge has been profound, for it has contained fundamental critique of the world's post Enlightenment secular culture and politics (ibid., p. 232).

COOPERATION AT THE INTERNATIONAL LEVEL

Just as there is a multiplicity of theorists who explain their version of conflict, so also there are those who concentrate on cooperation. In the following section we examine their theories. Once again we try to present a representative number of theorists.

For sociologist Galtung, the first focus is on peace, not security. "Compatible goals lead to ever higher levels of peace, conviviality, and incompatible goals, conflict, are handled peacefully" (Galtung 2007, p. 14). Peace is a culture of unity of human beings, (with) the way of identifying legitimate goals by mutual inquiry; in other words, by dialogue, and diversity as a source of mutual enrichment. There would be a preference for a structure of equality, and a culture of practice of a non-violent countervailing power, based on a strong identity, high level of self-reliance and much courage" (Galtung 2007, p. 24).

The decisive encounters in disputes between communities or groups are, sooner or later, confrontations of their respective spokesmen. We can see this happening in Muslim/Christian/Jewish groups. It is good to remember that the leader of a group is part of the group, not outside it. He/she is not immune to the corrective sanctions applied to any member who steps out of the acceptable bounds of outlook and the developing trends in his group. The Abrahamic religious spokesmen are dialoguing. If a leader is to negotiate effectively, he or his delegate must remain a part of his community or group and prepare the ground before taking steps toward expanding intergroup commitments. Sherif vocalises the ultimate superordinate goal for all peoples in all places that leaders can cultivate within the bounds of any human system of living. It is the goal of human survival. The role of leadership in this distinctly modern situation should be clear: to prepare and cultivate the ground within their groups toward human survival. Preparing the ground requires more from leaders than just making decisions and entering agreements for their people. It requires leaders to see that people are informed about the decision-making and about the means they have at their disposal to implement decisions. "The details of the grim consequences of pursuing armed conflict in the modern world should be frequent topics at meetings of parents, of teachers, of writers. Education in the modern world should include, as an integral part, the realities of modern arms and the means of transporting them" (Sherif 1967, p. 142).

Pontifical Communication

Pope Benedict quoted a critical text from the 13th century in Regensburg. "Show me just what Muhammad brought that was new, and there you will find things only evil and inhuman, such as his command to spread by the sword the faith he preached." This became a conflict narrative in the press. Violence is incompatible with the nature of God and the nature of the soul, he argued. God is not pleased by blood – and not acting reasonably is contrary to God's nature. "God acts with logos. Logos means both reason and word – a reason which is creative and capable of self communication, precisely as reason." He says that

> "the modern concept of reason is based, to put it briefly, on a synthesis between Platonism (Cartesianism) and empiricism, a synthesis confirmed by the success of technology." He argues that, firstly, only the kind of certainty resulting from the interplay of mathematical and empirical elements can be considered scientific. Hence the human sciences such as history, psychology, sociology and philosophy, attempt to conform themselves to this canon of scientificity. By its very nature this method excludes the question of God, making it appear unscientific or a prescientific question. And joining the global dialogue of ethics, he says that attempts to construct an ethic from the rules of evolution or from psychology and sociology end up being simply inadequate. His attempt at a critique of modern reason from within (has) the intention to broaden our concept of reason and its application. Reason and faith come together in a new way if we overcome the self-imposed limitation of reason to the empirically falsifiable, and if we once more disclose its vast horizons. "Theology is an inquiry into the rationality of faith. Only thus do we become capable of that genuine dialogue of cultures and religions so urgently needed today. Listening to the great experiences and insights of the religious traditions of humanity ... is a source of knowledge, and to ignore it would be an unacceptable restriction of our listening and responding" (Papal address at University of Regensburg).

One hundred and thirty-eight Muslim Scholars responded to the Papal address with their own message to the Christian Church, entitled A Common Word Between Us and You. They warn that without peace and justice between Christians and Muslims, who together make up more than 55 per cent of the world's populations, there can be no meaningful peace in the world. They say that "The basis for this peace and understanding already exists. It is part of the very foundational principles of both faiths: love of the One God, and love of the neighbour. These principles are found over and over again in the sacred texts of Islam and Christianity" (138 Muslim Scholars). They also focus on the forgiveness of God in Islam (God is Forgiving, Merciful: Aal 'Imran 3,31), saying that the relationship between Muslims and Christians is

> "the most important factor in contributing to meaningful peace around the world. If Muslims and Christians are not at peace, the world cannot be at peace. With the terrible weaponry of the modern world, with Muslims and Christians intertwined everywhere as never before, no side can unilaterally win a conflict between more than half of the world's inhabitants. Thus our common future is at stake. And to those who nevertheless relish conflict and destruction for their own sake or reckon that ultimately they stand to gain through them, we say that our very eternal souls are all also at stake if we fail to sincerely make every effort to make peace and come together in harmony" (138 Muslim Scholars).

The new axis for the world will be those who believe in One God or No God. The debate about whose law to use has begun. The Archbishop of Canterbury has suggested that the introduction in Britain of some aspects of Islamic law was unavoidable" (Croft 2008, p. 7). There are now more Muslims than Catholics, but according to the Vatican, Christians are now 33 per cent of the world, with Muslims 19.2 per cent, making the combined figure of Muslims and Catholics 52.2 per cent of joint world population (Kington 2008, 10). Another indication, quoted from 2009 figures, shows that the Muslim population is growing to 23 per cent (Muslim population). This would make the combined figure of Muslims and Christians over half the world population at 56 per cent.

In reply, the President of the Pontifical Council for Interreligious Dialogue, Cardinal Tauran, presented a Message for the end of Ramadan 'Id al-Fitr 1428 H. /2007 a.d. "Christians and Muslims: called to promote a culture of peace." It raises religious freedom, and renunciation of violence, which can never be motivated by religion since it wounds the very image of God in man, and then it brings up the subject of education:

> Religious authorities ... have a duty to pay attention to the spread of a just teaching. They must provide everyone an education appropriate to his or her particular circumstances, especially a civic education which invites each young person to respect those around him or her, and to consider them as brothers and sisters with whom he or she is daily called to live, not in indifference, but in fraternal care. It is thus more urgent than ever to teach the younger generations those fundamental human, moral and civic values which are necessary to both personal and community life.

He concludes: "To achieve this, I appeal to you with all my heart to heed my words, so that, by means of encounters and exchanges, Christians and Muslims will work together in mutual respect for peace" (Cardinal Tauran 2007).

The following is an account about the Pope's missive to Muslim religious leaders:

> Vatican City, Nov 29, 2007. On October 13, for the occasion of the end of the Muslim month of Ramadan (Eid al-Fitr), a group of 138 Muslim religious leaders sent an open letter to the Holy Father Benedict XVI and to other Christian leaders. The letter was entitled: A Common Word between Us and You.
>
> The Holy Father has replied with a letter of his own, signed by the Cardinal Secretary of State and addressed to Prince Ghazi bin Muhammad bin Talal, president of the Aal al-Bayt Institute for Islamic Thought and one of the signatories of the original letter. In expressing his thanks and appreciation for this significant initiative by the eminent group of Muslim figures, the Holy Father reaffirms the importance of dialogue based on effective respect for the dignity of the person, on objective knowledge of the other's religion, on the sharing of religious experience, and on joint commitment to promoting mutual respect and acceptance.

> *The Secretary of State's reply also mentions the Holy Father's willingness to receive Prince Ghazi and a delegation of the signatories of the letter, and it also highlights the readiness of the Pontifical Council for Inter-religious Dialogue, in collaboration with other specialized pontifical institutes, to organize a working meeting. (Ecumenical and Interfaith Commission)*

Evelin Gerda Lindner[5], a medical doctor and a psychologist has, I believe, an interpretation of what is happening to the world at the present moment that is a true and accurate account. She insists that we have to treat each person with respect, not humiliation. She examines the history of the human being as a hunter gatherer and then an agriculturalist – with this change meaning that the land had to be defended against the greed of the neighbour. She brings in the normative world of honour to the discussion. Honourable domination/submission could be regarded as an adaptation to the fear of attack, because the land, the resource of most of humankind, was by definition not expandable. A knowledge society like ours today resembles the hunter-gatherer model because the pie of resources – knowledge – appears to be infinitely expandable, lending itself to win-win solutions. Rigid hierarchical structures move toward the open network of our earliest hunter-gatherer ancestors. Negotiation and contract replace command lines, and coexistence is the primary strategy. "A global knowledge society entails the potential to liberate both masters and underlings, from having to force everybody into a ranked system. All are called upon to throw their creativity into the task of forging better ways to protect our shared home, planet Earth, and build a world where all can live dignified lives" (Lindner 2006, p. 3-5). Lindner defines humiliation as enforced lowering of

---

5   Dr. Evelin Gerda Lindner is known tome. She is the founder of the Human Dignity and Humiliation Studies and her thinking is focused around equality in dignity.

a person or group, a process of subjugation that damages or strips away pride, honour, or dignity.

> In the new world, belonging requires individual proactive action. Reaching out to the neighbour and creating a relationship that provides the sense of belonging requires skills that our forefathers rarely needed. Humility is a precondition of these new skills ... warmth, loyalty, solidarity, mutual recognition, dialogue, and humble acknowledgement of equal dignity – this is friendship. (Lindner 2006, pp. 147–8)

The human individual mind has a visualising centre that utilises synaesthetic combinations of image, sound and smell to create a mental holograph for imaginative 'visualisation'. In other words, the global visualisation space can perform the same function for a global 'mind.' According to communication scholar Aldridge, "a collective vision is worked out in the communications system; such a scenario presupposes the presence of interactivity in the system, that is, the global computing network is turned into a kind of 'democracy machine' where every constituent element has the ability to interact with the total system and affect its outcome" (Aldridge 1997).

Conflict at an Organizational Level

From his many years of research, Sherif recognizes that intergroup hostility arises from conflicts over vital interests, and this hostility can be changed when the groups are directed toward superordinate goals. "Relationships within and between human groups, which form the context for frustration and associated aggression toward others because of their group membership, set limits for the degree and targets of aggression and chart the direction of what is desirable, or even ideal, in intergroup action" (Sherif 1967, p. 59).

Realistic group conflict theory was recognized in the 1960s. It was a time when a more individual-level approach, authoritarian personality theory (Adorno et al. 1950), was dominant. With the insight of social psychology, it became evident that it was the structure of the situation, not personal characteristics of the individual (or an aggregate of individuals), that determined human behavior (Sherif 1966). "According to the theory, intergroup conflict is caused by an incompatibility of goals regarding material resources. It is the struggle over such structural resources as land, oil, gold, and labor that is the source of intergroup conflict, not personal characteristics like a prejudiced personality" (Liu 1999).

Social identity theory emerged in the 1970s and became by the 1990s the most important theory of intergroup relations in psychology. Sherif, whose major research centered on groups, demonstrated that mutually incompatible goals were sufficient to create intergroup conflict. Lieu disagrees, quoting Tafel, Billig, Bundy, and Flament (1971). "In the minimal group paradigm (Brewer 1979), the only thing necessary to create prejudice and discrimination between groups is a relevant and salient self-categorization, or social identity. Just the awareness of belonging to a group that is different than another group is enough to create prejudice in favor of the in-group against the out-group" (Liu 1999).

While mainstream social psychological theory furnishes an overall understanding of the processes involved in intergroup conflict, it can be criticized for falling short of explaining the psychological bases of protracted and difficult-to-resolve conflicts between ethnic and national groups, like those in Northern Ireland or Israel. Continual fighting can merge into a culture of conflict. Researching such conflict and its resolution, social psychologists have developed ways to approach the operationalization of culture relevant to intergroup relations. "One such approach is to study social representations of history, because such popular representations center on intergroup conflict (Liu 1999). The representations ... limit the ways in which groups can make favorable social comparisons against one another" (Liu 1999).

Edward T. Hall introduces us to the fact that culture is not innate but learned. To cooperate we need to know each other's way of thinking.

Today, constantly in the position of interacting with strangers, and not knowing what other people are going to do next, means that the next step for humankind is to "transcend his culture" (Hall 1981, p. 16). We will need models for this to happen.

Man is the model-making organism. We take into ourselves our culture and communication from the moment we are born, and then we act what has been modelled for us. Mead, as a philosopher, asks us to look at the child. "There are two stages which present the two essential steps in attaining self-consciousness, that of play and that of game. In play in this sense, the child is continually acting as a parent, a teacher, a preacher, a grocery man, a policeman, a pirate, or an Indian ... it is the period (when) the child is acquiring the roles of those who belong to his society" (Deegan 1999, p. 18). In the process they learn the "rules" of living. In the instance of learning what rules say, stages are observers' benchmarks in the growth of children's mastery of the propositional content of rules. "Children grow in competence to deal with socially constituted reality" (Onuf 1989, p. 112).

There are many roles in community, and often we have more than one to play.

> Given a new role, we tend to change our person both for ourselves and for other people ... each role assumed, each personality essayed, involves (among other things) some specific pattern of affect display ... each role or cultural stereotype involves a different pattern of affects damped or magnified – what Tomkins calls 'the differential magnification of innate affect. (Nathanson 1992)

As an intercultural communication scholar, Jandt says that comparative cultural patterns in Arabian and Western Cultures show that the Muslims' dominant cultural pattern is different from the Western one. Muslims question the relationship between God and humankind, the role of morality in human affairs, and the role of technology and modernization (Jandt 2001, p. 268).

As well, experience shows that personal space varies in diverse cultures (Jandt 2001, p. 108). Even the concept of time has cultural difference. Time, as a measurement of change, moves to time as a commodity, in the United States. "When time is considered a resource, it becomes something to be managed and used responsibly" (Jandt 2001, pp. 240-1). Conversely, Saudi accounting of time shows a strong relationship to the cosmos. "The traditional system of accounting time during the day is tied to the rising and setting of the sun. They also do many things at once, in polychromic time, a characteristic of Latin America and the Middle East" (ibid., p. 269). In the West there is an 'individualism' framework, as opposed to the collectivism of the Arabian cultures (ibid., pp. 244–45).

Cooperation at an Organizational Level

One recurrent theme is that cooperation to bring about a chosen, positive goal helps relieve conflict. Cooperative endeavour between groups toward superordinate goals alters the significance of other measures designed to reduce existing hostility between them. Intergroup contacts in the course of striving toward superordinate goals were used in research by Sherif for developing plans, for making decisions, and for pleasant exchanges. "Information about the other groups became interesting and sought after, rather than something to be ignored or interpreted to fit existing conceptions of the out-group" (Sherif 1967, p. 93).

"Combatants for Peace" is a group of Israeli and Palestinian individuals who were actively involved in the cycle of violence. The Israelis served as combat soldiers in the Israeli Defence Forces, and the Palestinians were involved in acts of violence in the name of Palestinian liberation. They now say:

We no longer believe that the conflict can be resolved through violence.
We believe that the bloodshed will not end unless we act together to terminate the occupation and stop all forms of violence.
We call for the establishment of a Palestinian State, alongside the State of Israel.
We will use only non-violent means to achieve our goals and call for both societies to end violence. (Combatants for Peace)

Palestinian and Israeli religious leaders from the Council of Religious Institutions of the Holy Land hope to counter extremism by facilitating dialogue among the region's modern voices. They work closely with the political leaders of Israel and the Palestinian authority to support current peace initiatives. Rabbi David Rosen is a member of the Israeli delegation. He said: "One of the reasons that peace processes have not succeeded in the past is their failing to engage the religious leaderships constructively" (Elshinawi 2007).

Still on the subject of religious leadership, Hervieu-Leger, a French sociologist, believes that religious leadership is important. She also argues that religion exists when the authority of tradition supports the act of believing. "As our fathers believed, and because they believed, we too believe ... Seen thus, one would describe any form of believing as religious which sees its commitment to a chain of belief it adopts as all-absorbing" (Hervieu-Leger 2000, p. 81).

In the UK, the British Metropolitan Police present an 'Understanding Islam' Course. It creates a foundation for understanding, mutual respect and constructive engagement, and teaches students new skills to affect more positive interactions, whether they are conducting business in an Islamic country, teaching Islamic students, or working with Islamic people (Jones Knowledge Group).

Stress and coping paradigms, especially those incorporating social cognition, are an understudied aspect of intercultural competence. Stress and coping paradigms that examine the positive and negative consequences of stressful events at different levels of analysis (physiological, cognitive, affective, behavioural, social, cultural) as well as development and ecological factors, would seem to match the complexity of the intercultural competence phenomenon (Alwin and Stokols 1988, Dinges 1996, pp. 120–1).

Putman takes for granted that "one literate person knows approximately the same things as another and is aware of the probable limits of the other person's knowledge. That second level of awareness – knowing what others probably know – is crucial for effective communication" (Hirsch 1989, p. 16). Cultural literacy is the oxygen of social intercourse … (it) lies above the everyday levels of knowledge that everyone possesses and below the expert" (ibid., p. 19).

We also have to be concerned with ethics. Goulet acknowledges that development is more than a straightforward process. It is much more than that, "involving fundamental value changes in areas such as policy planning, selection of priorities and the allocation of resources, as well as the determination of tolerable costs – human, environmental and cultural" (Goulet 2002).

Ethics are based on the belief that intercultural training is a transformative form of education. "Ethics may be thought of as principles of conduct that help govern the behaviour of individuals and groups" (Paige 1996, p. 35). As Goulet (1973, pp. 331–332) explains, ethical theories represent a community's perspective on what is good and bad in human conduct and lead to norms (prescriptive and concrete rules) that regulate action. Ethics represent what ought to be and help set standards for human behaviour. Ethics may be referred to as universalistic when the behavioural standard is accepted by virtually all societies (e.g. human rights), particularistic or culture specific when they are adhered to by a given cultural community but not by others. "No action is ethical if it harms persons affected, and the action that benefits affected persons accumulates ethical quality" (Paige 1996, p. 37).

In the Jewish-Palestinian Living Room Dialogue Group, Libby and Len Traubman ask people to widen their identification to include the whole of humankind, even our "enemies". "Realizing that we are neighbours forever with a shared, yet diverse, humanity, we can begin building our common future" (Traubman 2007). Our personal faith and our identity comes from our primary socialization[6] and the clash of idealist (love thy neighbour, turn the other cheek, forgive them their trespasses) and realist (an eye for an eye) outlooks from the New and Old Testaments respectively leaves many of us tilting less to the idealist than the realist side.

Huntington's perception was of 'closed' civilizational cultural identities ("closed hermetic globes"). Pierre Bourdieu had a more fluid concept of habitus – a structure of the mind characterized by a set of acquired schemata, with a dependency on history and memory. Schaefer, on the other hand, describes habitus generated open dynamic identity networks as cognitive, emotional and corporal dispositions acquired by individuals and collectives through socialization that allows persons, groups or even whole civilizations to be operators of a practical logic in negotiating the world. The upshot of all of this is that these networks do not clash as do globes. They express similarities. The characteristics of networks are as follows:
- The network is open.
- The network's structures are dense, where the cultural knowledge is "thick" and detailed. Where the knowledge is

---

6 I attended the 4th Annual Conference of JCMA (Jewish, Christian and Muslim Association) in July 2007 at Pallotti College, Milgrove, Victoria. At the first theme session on the Clash of Civilizations Dr. Paul Gardiner talked about religious culture. I specially asked his permission to quote him and recorded the following words spoken by him in hand:

> "Our personal faith has been largely shaped through our individual interactions with a religious culture, in most cases (but certainly not all) the culture of our parents and grandparents. 'Culture' is a broad term that includes our sacred texts, the translation and interpretations of those texts, the stories that we are told at home, school, place of worship and through the media".

"thin" and the practice irrelevant, the dispositions are wide or even nonexistent (a hole in the network).
- The network comprises all the fields of action that are significant for an individual, a group or a culture.
- The dispositions operate not only cognitively but also as emotions and states of the body.
- The network comprises individual and collective dispositions.
- The network model visualizes the fact that changes of certain attitudes never happen in an isolated manner but always exert effects upon many other dispositions that they are linked with (Schaefer 2005).

While Schaefer does not speak here directly of electronic networks, electronic networks are extensions of social networks, distending them spatially and contracting transaction times. There is now an international gathering together of interfaith groups. They share their dialogue via the internet. Yehuda Stolov[7], in the Palestine-Israel Journal 2005, explains his Interfaith Encounter Association's work in the Middle East thus:

Prejudices and fears, mistrust and even hatred exist between Jews and Arabs, or as we prefer to look at them, between

---

7   Yehuda Stolov sends me emails of the result of each encounter, which allows me to understand the full breadth of his work, with the young, the old, women's groups, and three day encounter groups. He makes the comment that most of the people he works with have never met the other before, and nearly all their knowledge about the other comes from the media. I recognize this, as in my own previous research new information about human sexuality was mostly obtained by my respondents through the media. A media mind is a mind formed by those who control the agenda – the gatekeepers of the information to be shared.

Jews, Muslims, Christians and Druze. Yet regardless of other factors that are probably very important when analyzing these phenomena, the main factor that makes it possible for these negative attitudes to prevail is ignorance – both in the sense of knowing very little, if at all, about the 'other' and in the sense of ignoring the 'other'. Consequently, getting to know each other in a deep and positive manner is the way to prevent the possibility of these phenomena. (Stolov 2005)

The process of the Interfaith Encounter Association is composed mainly of interactive interfaith dialogue.

It is important to stress that in the case of IEA, interfaith dialogue is not our goal but our vehicle to achieve the goal of true coexistence .... As an alternative to political discourse – which very often tends to be very superficial and divisive – we offer the interactive inter-religious discourse, which gives a lot of space for relaxed exchange between participants and is very effective in supplying the deep and positive interaction that is needed to overcome the attitude of ignorance. It invites its participants, religious or not, to come to the conversation from a deeper place in themselves. It reveals many similarities between the different traditions, which creates a basis for a sense of connection. But perhaps most important: it allows for a sincere joint conversation about the differences, and in this way its participants train themselves to accept the other as "an other" – someone who is different. In this way we promote our ability to develop friendships that are not conditioned by agreement. (Stolov 2005)

During 2011, according to the Data Sheet 2011 of the Interfaith Encounter Association, there were 199 encounters and events. It is estimated that over 4,000 people participated in these events or meetings (IEA Data Sheet).

Yehuda Stolov is a visionary leader who, with humour and happiness, invites Jews, Muslims and Christians to such happy gatherings as pressing olive oil together, and sharing food. In Australia, Cahill researched the entire multi faith society of Australia and reported that "Leadership roles are conceptualized differently from faith to faith" (Cahill et al. 2004, p. 64). According to Cahill religion "aims at personal transformation and conversion" (ibid., p. 69), and he continues that "the evidence suggested that religious leaders generally play a positive role in defusing hatreds and hostilities brought to Australia" (ibid., p. 90).

It needs to be said here that this present research is only concerned with the people of the one God, the Abrahamic religions. As the research interviews come from Jews, Christians and Muslims who are fully committed, it is argued that they are already transformed, and making the world a better place, each in their own way. In interfaith, they come together to co-operate with one another. The transformation of identity, from prejudice to co-operation, is a social process. The Jews, Christians and Muslims were in the process of reinterpreting themselves from "one image to another", that is, from the image of an enemy to an image of a friend, (Berger 1963, p. 121). They are all role models for leadership of remediation, reconciliation and peace that rests on hospitality and the open heart and hand. Leadership is changing according to local influences. This is explained by Bouma:

> World events such as 9/11 have changed the way religion is perceived; religions are globalised, which raises new issues and alters existing ones. One salient aspect is the dynamic nature of issues. Such issues are never fixed or stagnant; they ebb and flow according to local, national and international influences. (Bouma 2011, p. 87)

"In a stable society, most action follows directly from the norms. The norms prescribe what is to be done in given situations and action follows almost automatically without any questioning being raised explicitly as to the meaning of the action" (Glock & Stark 1965, p. 72). The Abrahamic role models in this thesis make it clear that their primary commitment is to their religion/faith, and that the norm for them all is to respect each other and begin the journey of cooperation and friendship. This norm rests on a common religious text to love God and neighbour.

A common-sense assessment comes again from Bouma:

> For most people, religion is a communal and public commitment, underscoring the fact that the person is not simply an isolated, autonomous individual but a person in solidarity with others. This solidarity is underscored also in other communities – locality, school, business, and cultural and sporting activities, and most particularly in the family (Article 16). In such communities people keep faith with the allegiances that give meaning to their lives. Respect for human rights requires the protection of the communities and associations by which a culture of human dignity flourishes. (Bouma 2011, p. 33)

A theological understanding about the overall area of interfaith comes from Jesuits Jacques Dupuis, Daniel Madigan and Thomas Michel, along with Paul Knitter.

Jacques Dupuis, in Christianity and the religions, from confrontation to dialogue, 2002, sets out to open up the Kingdom of God. The Word of God was present in the world before it became incarnate in Jesus Christ. Dupuis informs that, "the emphases of Wisdom literature are not missing in the Christology developed in the Prologue to the gospel according to John, though the author of the Fourth Gospel has privileged the concept of the Word of God to explain who is the one "with God" of whom he is speaking, and who became man in Jesus Christ. What is to be seen here is the Prologue's affirmation of a universal action and presence of the Word of God already in human history before the incarnation, as also the permanence in this action of the Logos as such after the incarnation of the Word and the resurrection of Jesus Christ" (Dupuis 2002, p. 142).

He continues: while the Kingdom of God is present in a special way in the church, it extends beyond the limits of the church, "and the adherents of other religious traditions can belong to it, provided they live its values and help to spread it in the world" (ibid., p. 199).

The values of the kingdom are love and justice (ibid., p. 201).

He then discusses an internal Catholic dialogue about dialogue and evangelisation[8]. Vatican Council II (1962–65) did not see dialogue with other religions as evangelisation. The documents after Vatican Council II did. The document 'Dialogue and Mission' (1984) "further explains that interreligious dialogue as a specific task of evangelisation – which 'finds its great place in the great dynamism of the church's mission' (30) – can itself assume various forms." (ibid., p. 20). There can be these dialogues:
1. The dialogue of life
2. The dialogue of common commitment to works of justice and human liberation
3. There is intellectual dialogue which scholars engage in as an exchange about their respective religions, with an aim of promoting communion and fellowship
4. Sharing of religious experience and prayer and contemplation (ibid., p. 220).

As will be seen in the focus groups, evangelisation of Jews and Muslims by Christians is a very sensitive issue. It has been experienced as aggressive and hurtful. The intention of a person in an interfaith group can cause unease if evangelisation becomes apparent, and not dialogue between equals. This also seems to be the opinion of Dupuis, "dialogue, it is observed, can only be sincere if it takes place on an equal footing between partners" (ibid., p. 228).

Dan Madigan, SJ, 2001, The Qur'an's Self Image, Writing and Authority in Islam's Scripture, explains to us another, completely different culture. Muslims take an almost entirely oral approach to their scriptures. 'Qur'an' means 'recitation' and refers to the actual words Muslims believe were revealed to Muhammad by God. Madigan reveals a semantic analysis of the self-awareness of the Qur'an. This self-awareness is ongoing as it responds to people and circumstances.

---

8   Evangelise – preach or spread the Christian gospel with the aim of converting. (Cowie 1989, p. 411)

Thomas Michel, SJ is a member of the Indonesian branch of the Jesuit Society and has been involved in Muslim-Christian dialogue throughout his career. His volume of essays "A Christian view of Islam. Essays on Dialogue" contains three sections, with the first titled "Interreligious Dialogue: Encountering the 'Other'". For us, in this thesis centering on hospitality and help as a remediation, it is the essay where Michel recalls how a Muslim neighbour asked him not to lock his door that is important. He complied, and left his house open. When he came home at night, he would find some food on his table (Michel 2010).

Brendan Hill, Paul Knitter and William Madges' book Faith, Religion and Theology, a contemporary Introduction is divided up into faith, religion and religious pluralism. Hill defines faith as "personal in that it can be a commitment on many levels: intellectual, emotional, volitional, and even physical, imaginative, and aesthetic. Human faith involves not only knowledge, but also feelings, decisions and actions. Faith is a "walking with" an" intimacy toward" a basis for our hopes and dreams." (Hill, Knitter, and Madges 1997 p. 9). These ideas are reflected in the stories of faith and commitment in the research.

Knitter gives voice to young Catholics. They say "if you want to get ahead in this world, if you want to be a success in business, if you want to survive in the international market, you just can't be a nice guy like Jesus and Buddha." This echoes the Western individualistic culture spoken of by Charles Taylor in the next chapter. With regard to loving your neighbour, the young people saw no difference in those who went to church. "They spend an hour in church singing God's praises and proclaiming their love of neighbour, and then in the parking lot curse the guy in the blue Pontiac for cutting in front of them" (ibid., p. 137).

Abdullah Saeed is a proponent of modern Islamic thought. In his book "Islam in Australia" he explains the basic beliefs, values and institutions of Islam, while highlighting the experience of Muslims in Australia. Muslims are one of the most ethnically diverse religious groups in Australia. More than 36 per cent of Australian Muslims are born and bred in this country and their experience of Islam is within the Australian context – many are converts to Islam from European and other backgrounds, while others are second, third and even fourth generation Muslim Australian (Saeed 2003).

Anna Halafoff and David P. Wright Neville, in Terrorism and Social Exclusion, Misplaced Risk, Common Security, continue the story of remediations that are to be found in this current Australian research. It is indeed the elevated perceptions of terrorism-related risks that are having a deleterious impact on many societies, exacerbating feelings of exclusion among individuals and groups. The remediations offered are social inclusion, participatory and deliberative measures. Inclusive counter-terrorism policies unite rather than divide multicultural societies. This book addresses underlying causes of social tension, and presents studies from Western and non-Western Societies such as Algeria, Australia, Russia and the United Kingdom (Halafoff and Neville 2010).

James Jupp, 2001, "The Australian People. An Encyclopedia of the nation, its peoples and their origins" is a comprehensive survey about citizenship and multiculturalism in Australia. We are learning to live in a multicultural Australia, therefore dialogue is particularly important to enable us to live together peacefully.

THEORIES OF FORGIVENESS

Thus far in this chapter we have gone from conflict to cooperation. A missing factor in the move from conflict to cooperation is forgiveness. We examine forgiveness as a bridge between conflict and cooperation.

Forgiveness, which is taught in all three Abrahamic religions, releases the person and the organization from revenge. The very essence of effective healing is forgiveness. If the world is to work for a hopeful future to provide sanctuary for a wise people, we need to forgive all those who have intentionally or unintentionally hurt us during our life. DeGrandis warns that "unforgiveness can block the arteries of life, the channels of love" (DeGrandis 1986, p. 14). And indeed "[t]o forgive completely is divine action needing the help of Jesus" (ibid., p. 13). When I asked the Catholic Bookshop in Melbourne for a book on forgiveness the only one they had was on penance by Hahn (2004). This confirmed the need for information on forgiveness in the Catholic community. On penance, Hahn reminds us that it is hard to say sorry. "Like his parents Cain can muster a range of emotions – fear, shame, defensiveness, self-pity – but he won't say he's sorry" (Hahn 2004, p. 17–18).

A Protestant minister and scholar, Showalter, has asked pertinent questions of Christians with regard to forgiveness. He addresses the reality of trauma and hurt. Showalter disagrees that a Christian should always try to forgive and forget. He feels it important for the sake of healing to remember a serious injury. By remembering, we face the injury and can eventually decide we want to forgive. Showalter agrees that it is good to forgive, even if the person who hurt us does not repent. Making our forgiveness dependant on another's repentance is not very helpful. It sets us up to be a victim, not just once, but twice. By making our forgiveness so dependent, we hand considerable power over our lives to the one who injured us.

Showalter disagrees that we should always be willing to be reunited with the person he/she forgives, as if the injury never happened. Reconciliation takes two people, the forgiver and the injurer. For true reconciliation to take place the injurer must usually take responsibility for the injury and desire reconciliation. I see being reunited as a step beyond reconciliation, a step some but not all reconciled persons will choose to take (Showalter, December 19th, 1997).

Showalter believes that true forgiveness is a process of inner healing and it cannot be rushed. We are to abandon all ill will toward the person we forgive. Admit the existence of those who have hurt us, strive to resolve the issues, and move beyond them in a realistic and constructive way through forgiveness. It requires an initial decision that we want to forgive (ibid.).

> *No one, not even God, can turn back the clock. What we can do – with God's help of course – is seek to forgive so that our present and our future can be redeemed from the bondage and pain of the past (ibid.).*

Rabbi Simmons agrees with the necessity to "know" the reality of the hurt. He says:

> *In Western society...pop psychology has done all it can to remove [the] whole concept of 'guilt' from our lexicon. It's much easier to rationalize our mistakes away. And it's unhealthy to feel guilt, they say, 'Suppress it!' On one level this suppression is unhealthy. When we refuse to admit, it is depressing and paralysing. The regret stays inside and festers. On another level, this suppression is downright dangerous. Because the more one repeats an inappropriate act, the more he will eventually come to rationalize it as proper. The Nazi Himmler wrote that in his own personal experience with killing Jews, the turning point came when he was able to fall asleep at night without any guilt.*

The Artscroll Machzor explains:

> *As an intelligent, thinking, imaginative being, man has all sorts of thoughts flashing constantly through his mind ... For his thoughts to have lasting meaning, he must distil them into words, because the process of thought culminates when ideas are expressed and clarified ... the person who wrenches from himself the unpleasant truth, 'I have sinned', has performed a great and meaningful act. (Rabbi Simmons)*

The importance of forgiveness in Islam is captured by Ali.

> *God the All Knowing, has the knowledge of everything including whatever a person thinks but does not express in words or deeds. An offence may be against (a) a person, (b) a group of persons or society, (c) other creation of God such as animals, plants,*

land, atmosphere, bodies of water and the life therein, and (d) God, Allah. Muslims understand that an offence against the creation of God is an offence against God. To receive forgiveness from God there are three requirements: Recognizing the offence itself and its admission before God; Making a commitment not to repeat the offence; Asking for forgiveness from God. If the other three conditions are met in sincerity, forgiveness from God is assured. (Ali)

The philosopher, Derrida, says that when we talk about forgiveness, we need to address repentance as well.

The scene of repentance and forgiveness seeking is today becoming globalized, presented on a worldwide state. Enigmatic though the concept of forgiveness, in the strict sense, remains, the scene, the form, and the language that people attempt to adjust to it belong within a religious heritage, which we may call Abrahamic, in order to group together Judaism and the various forms of Christianity and Islam. (Derrida 2001)

Other scholars are looking afresh at forgiveness.

Cambridge scholars Murphy and Hampton found a connection between forgiveness and remorse. "The act of forgiveness involves a refusal to blame. However, the relationship of forgiveness to both contrition and punishment is imprecise: the possibility of forgiveness appears to make remorse possible" (Honderich 1995, p. 284).

Judith Thompson talks about those truly human moments when two people recognize each other's pain; the perpetrator as the author of the pain, and the victim's acknowledgment of the perpetrators "suffering" as a result of remorse. Thompson invites others "[t]o join me in the soul-searching and heart leaping task of unlocking the bondage of denial, shame, hurt and anger in our own country and transforming our legacy of violence into mutual liberation which will have a global impact" (Thompson 2005, p. 13).

Finally, forgiveness in politics. "Forgiveness begins with memory suffused with moral judgment" is the uncompromising belief of

Shriver. He teaches all to "remember and forgive." To him, forgiveness begins with a remembering and a moral judgment of wrong, injustice, and in injury. It will not do to just go around "forgiving" people, as "alleged wrong doers are wary of being told that someone 'forgives' them. Immediately, they sense that they are being subjected to some moral assessment, and they may not consent to it" (Shriver 1995, p. 7). There has to be a preliminary agreement between two or more parties that there is something from the past to be forgiven. Consensus on the wrongs that human beings may have inflicted on the other may take a very long time. "Logically forgiveness goes from wrong-sufferers to wrongdoers, but in human societies, and most of all in political conflict, it may have to go both ways" (ibid., p. 7).

Forgiveness, in politics, or any other human relation, does not require the abandonment of all versions of punishments but it does require the abandonment of vengeance. "Forgiveness in a political context, then, is an act that joins moral truth, forbearance, empathy, and commitment to repair a fractured human relation. Such a combination calls for a collective turning from the past that neither ignores past evil nor excuses it, that neither overlooks justice nor reduces justice to revenge, that insists on the humanity of enemies even in their commission of dehumanizing deeds, and that values the justice that restores political community above the justice that destroys it" (ibd., p. 9). Here it is, all put together neatly in a package by Shriver, but, in practice, so hard to do. Forgiveness gets its real start under the double impetus of judgment and forbearance from revenge. Forbearance opens the door to a future that will not repeat the old crimes. Unaccompanied by forbearance in its very beginning, moral judgment often fuels new enmity. Empathy should be distinguished from sympathy. The moral stance of forgivers usually precludes sympathy with the enemies' cause and their methods of pursuing it, but on the other hand, the understanding of the humanity of enemies is another step towards entertaining the possibility of living with them as fellow human beings. The reality is that the forgiver must be prepared to begin living with the enemy again. There has to be some kind of co-existence.

Signs of Reconciliation

Reconciliation is a "word best reserved, perhaps, for the end of a process that forgiveness begins" (ibid., pp. 8-9). Shriver says that forgiveness has to be learned in a community: that seems basic to the ethical teachings of Jesus. Hannah Arendt saw this clearly and credited him and his imitators in the early Christian movement with the "discovery" of the indispensable role of forgiveness in processes of social change (ibid., p. 35). It is the putting of forgiveness into practice, it is this change of behaviour that brings back our common humanity.

Where barriers of social custom or a history of hostile relations have stood in the way of a consent to turn back and start anew, the mere joint presence of the alienated, now around the same table consuming the same food can be a powerful symbol of the beginning of negotiations on the way to reconciliation (ibid., p. 40).

This kind of beginning is often seen in the interfaith communities, who invite people to share food, music and stories.

These are the activities related to forgiveness. Forgiveness is the doorway through which a diversity of humans – many of them alienated by social custom from each other – can come together to form a new community. Instead of people continuing to blame themselves for their suffering, they were freed for a resumption of a productive, cooperative life in their communities (ibid., p. 39). The act of sitting down to eat is a human gesture of consent to human company. These signs are especially important when they depict men, women and children from different conflicting cultures taking time off to listen to one another and eating together and laughing together.

And lest we forget, there are recent instances where the violent acts have been overturned into peace. "There have been instances, however, where the power accrued through terrorist acts was converted into bargaining chips for negotiated settlements and where formerly terrorist organizations were forged into effective political parties. An example of this process, which may be called the domestication of violence, was the negotiated peace settlement in Northern Ireland and the emergence of Sinn Fein as an effective force in local elections. Public support for a compromise solution may isolate perpetrators of acts of violence, and their continued terrorism may undercut their public support" (Juergensmeyer 2000, p. 239).

While Juergensmeyer has chosen a violent disruption over land and country with some religious content to give us hope, the results from the four focus groups would say that it is very difficult to reconcile with religious fundamentalists. We have to try harder they say, and hope that they will deepen their faith.

In short, to repair broken social relations, forgiveness has to be learned in a community (Shriver, p. 35). All the four focus groups came to the conclusion that the imperatives surrounding the command to love God and neighour had to be taught, and are at the present moment, not being taught.

Forgiveness and its fullness, reconciliation, ensure "the continued existence of a fractured human community" (ibid., p. 35).

Summary

This chapter has examined conflict and cooperation at different levels of social organization by examining relevant scholarly literature. The scholars who have been drawn on represent a multi-cultural collection and their collective approaches may be viewed as characterising them as theoretically multi-disciplinary theorists, who give us both local and global input, open wide the subject of conflict, cooperation, and the bridge that allows dialogue, forgiveness and the fullness of forgiveness, reconciliation. This chapter provides the foundation for the next six chapters, where the identified concepts will be explored further and deeper, and used in the analysis of data collected later from the four focus groups comprised of Jews, Muslims and Christians. The next chapter will introduce peace education and the work of the NGOs in this area.

Chapter Three
Peace, Forgiveness and Ethical Communication

Introduction

While the previous chapter explored conflict and cooperation at international and organizational levels and went on to introduce the concept of forgiveness as a bridge between a moment of conflict and a moment of peace, cooperation and friendship, the present chapter will discuss social science, humanities, religious and NGO discourses on peace as a human need, forgiveness and ethical communication – as an expansion of the central concept of forgiveness that was introduced earlier. The frame of reference that arises from this discussion will be essential to understanding how co-operation and friendship can flourish in interfaith organizations despite the geopolitical turbulence around the Abrahamic faiths and their adherents. Such cooperation overcomes inter-racial prejudice generated by histories and by larger contexts of violence and mediated violence. People achieve peace through expressed or tacit acts of forgiveness.

It comprises an examination of (a) social science, humanities, organizational, religious and non-government discourse on (b) viz. human needs, ethical communication, the role of forgiveness, and processes of peace construction. Sections of category (a) follow this introduction and each contains sub-sections on topics from category (b).

The social science section's discussion of human needs includes reference to Maslow[9], Neal, McLelland, Burton, Sites, Clark, Fisher, Mitchell, Nudler, Scimecca, Friedman and Kelman. Its discussion of ethical communication includes reference to Mowlana, Hamelink and Habermas. The social science discussion of forgiveness includes reference to Pettit, Worthington and Enright. And the discussion of peace construction at the intra-organizational level includes reference to the intercultural theorists Weaver, Hall, Hofstede and Trompenaar, and to the conflict theorists Burton, Galtung and Azar.

In the humanities section, the discussion of human needs includes Dewey and Mead. The discussion of ethical communication includes the rhetoric of Simons, Artistotle, McLuhan, Back and Camilleri. The discussion of forgiveness includes Derrida, Taylor, Haber, Kolnai, Hieronymi, Rawl, Pettit, Worthington, Enright, Murphy, Downie and Rawls. And the discussion of peace construction at the intra-organizational level includes Nancy Nyquist Potter, Alison Bailey and Paula J. Smithka.

The sections on religious and non-government discourses focus on the three Abrahamic religions as they are portrayed in the film Encounter Point, as well as on the work of Zivetz, Hudock, and Sambal, the ICRC, Amnesty, and the International Medical Corps. The latter is in keeping with this thesis' non-traditional approach of drawing on some measure of media of different form to scholarly publications, in a quarantined form, though the preponderance of sources are scholarly publications.

The sections on various discourses are followed by a discussion of a frame of reference and then a summary is provided.

---

9   These are all referenced below when discussed.

Social Science Review

The Social Science of Human Needs

Conflict resolution is concerned with the nature of conflict as a generic human problem and with techniques to end conflict. One theory of conflict resolution is the Human Needs Theory, developed by John Burton and his colleagues. They address the power of human needs and the role of the individual in political processes. In the past, the individual was expected to change in order to fit into societies ruled by elites. Now it is time to change the society to suit the human needs of the individual (Burton 1990). Needs are related to values. People value what they need. Self-esteem "is perhaps the most pervasive of any of the needs in humans" (Sites 1990, p. 19). Mary E. Clark extends this idea further to include the sacred. "We are still only at the beginning of developing the skills needed for understanding the role of social meaning in creating "sane" societies – societies wherein the sacred social vision invites the bonding of the creative individual with the social enterprise, thus fulfilling the deepest, most human of all our needs: those for social attachment and psychological purpose" (Clark 1990, p. 36). Fisher argues that conceptualizations regarding the essential needs of human beings, such as Maslow's Hierarchy of Needs, specify the basic positive motives that underlie human behaviour. Self-actualization tops the hierarchy of Maslow's needs, followed by needs for esteem, aesthetics, cognitive experiences, social relationships, safety, and physiological balance. Fisher criticizes Maslow's list as being more equated with material satisfiers than with non-material satisfiers, (Fisher 1990, p. 90). In opposition to Clark's social attachment, Maslow describes the individual thus: self- actualizing people are propelled by growth motivation, not deficiency motivation. Basic need gratifications can come only from without, but "once these inner deficiencies are satisfied by outside satisfiers, the true problem of individual human development begins, i.e. self-actualization" (Lowry 1973, p. 188).

Neal's work is centered on social change, and she has chosen values and interests as the two functions that might be the starting point of changing from one kind of behavior to another. "One possible explanation of the function of values and interests in the process of social change assumes that decision makers tend to make choices either in value or interest terms" (Neal 1965 p. 8). For people of the Abrahamic faiths to be meeting together in dialogue all over the world is a historical moment in time, so we will frame this research dialogue with some analysis on values and interests. We know both the values, and also the interests, of the participants in the four focus groups from their family histories.

The Historical Situation

Social change is a process. Values and interests are used as choice determiners by people facing change in the historical situation in which they play significant parts. The authorized leaders of the Abrahamic faiths in Sydney responded to pressures to change that were currently institutionalized in their community life. The pressures are "characterized by an orientation to change or non-change" (Neal 1954, p. 17).

On September 11th, 2001 there was a crisis, when the U.S.A. were attacked by Muslim hijackers, who piloted passenger planes and used them as fire bombs. Response to crisis, an occasion for change, has a long history of eliciting opposite interpretations. The direction that Abrahamic leaders made in Sydney, Australia, was to call Jews, Christians and Muslims to gather together and pray for God's help. The crisis continued when Australians were killed in two separate Muslim bombing attacks in Bali, and Muslim men, both in Sydney and Melbourne were jailed for intention to bomb.

Neal maintains the main variable found in theories of social change is the value-interest dimension. "Values refer to widely shared conceptions of the good; societal values refer to conceptions of the good society. Interests refer to desires for special advantages for the self or for groups with which one is identified. Interests refer to short term desires to protect or to maximize institutional positions of the individual or the group" (ibid., p. 9).

Then, in any given situation facing change, four types of responses can be distinguished among the actors depending on their definitions of the situation:

1. A value-change orientation
2. An interest-change orientation
3. A value non change orientation
4. An interest non change orientation (ibid., p. 11)

These matters will be taken up again in the Methodology chapter 5, and the analysis in chapter 7. Glock and Stark remind us, before we move on, that "value orientations exist only as they are believed and acted upon by groups of men" and shall we add, as well, women (Glock & Stark 1965, p. 12).

Mitchell defines a genuine resolution of a conflict as a complete, acceptable, self- supporting, satisfactory state for all parties, a state in which the parties are uncompromising, innovative, and uncoerced (Mitchell 1990, p. 150). Nudler takes the idea through various stages, from primitive conflict to resolution. The primitive is where each party represents the other in negative terms. Coexistence is when they accept the other's right to exist. Dialogue follows, and restructuring is the final stage, when a new frame is constructed to meet needs and transcend the conflict (Nudler 1990, p. 197). Scimecca takes a different and new view of human needs. He says the two basic human needs are: self-consciousness, which can only be derived from self-reflexivity (the ability to think back and reflect upon one's actions); and the need for freedom, the only condition that enables self-reflexivity to develop fully. He states that nowhere in the laws of physics, nor in the laws of derivate sciences, is there any reference to consciousness of mind (Scimecca 1990, p. 208). Friedman (Burton 1990, p. 259) concentrates on knowledge:

> Knowledge is not stored information; information is the raw material of knowledge. Knowledge is realized through a process called "insight": everybody has it, but with many people it stays latent and unproductive. This insight is a particular ability within individuals similar to a creative instinct. As insight is the key to knowledge and as insight is strictly personal, people try to develop it through training and through persuasion. The effect of that development is to form a process. All religions, political ideologies, scientific and educational processes try to create a method to reach insight, to keep insight from automatically following a predetermined path. (Friedman 1990, p. 259)

It could be said that personal insight enhances information into knowledge that has greater possibilities. Kelman considers the workshop setting, where participants are encouraged to talk to each other and to listen to each other, not in order to discover the weaknesses in the other's arguments but in order to penetrate the other's perspectives. The discussions are not orientated toward assigning blame but toward exploring the causes of the conflict and the obstacles to its resolution (Kelman 1990, p. 284).

The Social Science of Ethical Communication

Contemporary movements around the world, whether in groups, communities, or nations, are constructing more humane, ethical, traditionalist, antibloc, self-reliance theories of societal development. "It is the quest for dialogue that underlies the current revolutionary movements around the world." (Mowlana 1996, p. 96). The ultimate ethical power of communication institutions within this context is to serve the public, and the zenith of serving that public is reached when a communication entity succeeds in raising a group, a community, a public, or a world to a higher level of understanding and insight, (Mowlana 1996, p. 98).

When we engage in dialogue, interactions are communicative when participants coordinate their plans of action consensually, with recognition that the claims of others are valid. "Those claims are claims to truth, claims to rightness, and claims to truthfulness, according to whether the speaker refers to something in the objective world (as the totality of existing states of affairs), to something in the shared social world (as the totality of the legitimately regulated interpersonal relationships of a social group), or to something in his own subjective world ....in communicative action one actor seeks rationally to motivate another by relying on the illocutionary binding/ bonding effect of the offer contained in his speech act" (Habermas 1990, p. 58). Hamelink argues that moral standards cannot any longer be authoritatively imposed upon all members of pluralist and multicultural societies. In dialogue the participants explore which 'minima moralia' societies can find basic and common agreement. Ethical reflection should not focus on identifying the single correct solution but rather on the due process of the moral argumentation. "The ethical dialogue does not depart from a consensus on fundamental moral values but seeks those solutions to moral dispute that optimally accommodate the parties' interests and principles" (Hamelink 2000, p. 5). Hamelink suggests a confrontation between the human being and the humanoid digital system, which he calls the 'cyborg'. A cyborg presupposes a development by which digital electronics is deployed within the human body and human brainpower is lined to cybernetic systems. He asks: "Can we design new moral codes in consultation with them?" (Hamelink 2000, p. 34)

The Social Science of Forgiveness

Forgiveness is a process. Robert Enright 's work in forgiveness education is based on the conviction that forgiveness can reduce anger and that a decrease in anger leads to less depression and anxiety and to stronger academic achievement and more peaceful social behaviour. Enright's position is that it is a choice to forgive. His study has found that when people successfully complete the forgiveness process, they have reduced or eliminated negative feelings toward the offender, negative thoughts toward the offender, and negative behaviours toward the offender.

Forgiveness is the offering of compassion, benevolence, and love at an appropriate time. The person who forgives has no fear of risk or injury. "Forgiveness is a process. You can start small – very small. And you don't necessarily have to make personal contact with the person you are forgiving. For example, you might make a deliberate decision to refrain from disparaging remarks about him or her to others. If you are religious, you can offer benevolence by saying a prayer for the offender. If not, you can try to think about him or her in a context broader than the one in which he or she inflicted hurt on you. Isn't the person more than that one act or series of acts against you?" (Enright 2001, p. 35) To complete a forgiveness agenda is to find or recover a sense of life and purpose (Guy Pettit). Everett Worthington opens the way to determine the psychological, social, and even physical mechanisms of forgiveness. It is to study the differentials of forgiveness: event, relationship, and personality. It is also to discern the social processes that occur in forgiveness within ongoing relationships. Forgiveness is defined as: the emotional replacement of hot emotions of anger or fear that follow a perceived hurt or offense; or, the emotional replacement of 'unforgiveness' that follows ruminating about the transgression, by substituting positive emotions such as unselfish love, empathy, compassion or even romantic love. If these positive emotions are strong enough and last long enough they contaminate the unforgiveness so that it can never be experienced in the same way again. Through this process, emotional replacement occurs. We experience forgiveness (Worthington 2001, p. 35). His own mother was murdered, and he used his own forgiveness process to help him to recover from this agony. Worthington was able, after a considerable time, to have compassion on the person who murdered his mother. This person had smashed every mirror in her house, so disgusted was he with his own countenance. However, this does not mean that there were not deep wounds held by Worthington's family. The sight of their mother's blood under the carpet, congealed there as she bled to death, left painful memories.

The Social Science of Peace Construction

Azar, when speaking of the Middle East conflict, talks about complicity, including complicity among economically interested parties. He reminds us that without imported armaments, the conflict would be less destructive and less violent or devoid of violence (Azar 1973, p. 72).

To this, add the emergence of the ethnic identity movement. Throughout the world, members of cultures and subcultures adversely affected by colonialism and racism have struggled with questions of identity and the consequential asymmetrical power relationship. The core issue is often the nature of communication between groups. Many scholars agree that inquiry ought to begin by using a contrast and comparison approach, whereby differences are identified, and then by moving on to consideration of similarities. The greater danger is in assuming perceived similarities, thereby trying to explain another culture in terms of one's own and at the same time denying the very existence of different cultures (Weaver 2003, pp. 76-7).

Peace construction grows when there is a shift from considering others as the enemy to engaging in dialogue with them, to seeing their needs and treating them with dignity. Edward T. Hall expresses this same idea as to "make a friend" from a different culture and to model peace (Sorrells 1998). Johan Galtung suggests opening up to the idea that there is God in everybody. He calls for communication scholars, in particular, to explore causes of protraction and escalation. He also identifies war journalism and the role of war reporting in perpetuating violence (Galtung 2007, p. 26). War reporting constructs messages about conflict in such a way as to overvalue violent responses and undervalue nonviolent ones (Lynch and McGoldrick 2007, p. 258).

Geert Hofstede researched theories that could be applied universally to people across cultures. Instead of territories of thought, as in communication theory, he suggests "mental programmes" that are inherited biologically or developed and reinforced socially via family, institutions, and culture (Hofstede 1984). This is important, because in the final analysis, according to Trompenaar, culture reconciles dilemmas between the individual and the group. "Since we are stuck with the structure of language, it is as well to consider how language achieves reconciliation. It does so by using the ladder of abstraction and putting one value (or horn of the dilemma) above the other, that is, by using both an object language and a meta-language and allowing them to dovetail (Trompenaar 1997, p. 205).

Humanities Review

Human Needs in the Humanities

John Dewey presents knowledge as necessary for the human being. "Knowledge as an act is bringing some of our dispositions to consciousness with a view to straightening out a perplexity, by conceiving the connection between ourselves and the world in which we live .... Since democracy stands in principle for free interchange, for social continuity, it must develop a theory of knowledge which sees in knowledge the method by which one experience is made available in giving direction and meaning to another" (Dewey 1916).

Knowledge comes from reflective thought, Dewey suggests, and like the French sociologist Hervieu-Leger, Dewey speaks of reflective thought as a chain. Hervieu-Leger's chain is a chain of authoritative messages; Dewey's chain is one of reflection, which:

involves not simply a sequence of ideas, but a con-sequence – a consecutive ordering in such a way that each determines the next as its proper outcome, while each outcome in turn leans back on, or refers to, its predecessors .... Each phase is a step from something to something – technically speaking, it is a term of thought. Each term leaves a deposit that is utilized in the next term. The steam or flow becomes a train or chain. There are in any reflective thought definite units that are linked together so that there is a sustained movement to a common end. (Dewey 1933, pp. 4–5)

He is another scholar who describes insight as that process of acquiring our own knowledge from information. "The ideal of a system of scientific conceptions is to gain continuity, freedom, and flexibility of transition in passing from any fact and meaning to any other; this demand is met in the degree in which we lay hold of the dynamic ties that hold things together in a continuously changing process – a principle that gives insight into mode of productions or growth" (Dewey 1933, p. 164). Dewey also worked on the significance of play and playfulness. It is the human child who has to incorporate the significance of experience and language.

When things become signs, when they gain a representative capacity as standing for other things, play is transformed from mere physical exuberance into an activity involving a mental factor ... When children play they are manipulating the things they play with – they are not living with the physical things, maybe a stone for a table, a leaf for a plate – no, they are living in the large world of meanings, natural and social, evoked by these things... In this way, a world of meanings, a store of concepts, so fundamental in all intellectual achievement, is defined and built up (Dewey 1933, p. 209).

In Mind, Self and Society (1934), Mead, who was influenced by Dewey, analyzed human experience from the standpoint of communication as essential to the social order. He saw the development of the human self, and his self-consciousness within the field of his experience, as social. Social process is prior to the structures and processes of individual experience.

All human beings wherever they come from, whatever their cultural values, have a value in themselves. Taking up the value of the human being, we begin with the child. The act of play, according to George Herbert Mead, is a fundamental process that allows for the development of all social behavior. It is necessary for the genesis of self-consciousness, and it is a pathway connecting inter-subjectivity and emotions. Play generates and is generated by the mind, self, and society" (Deegan 1997, p. xviiii).

Mead offers the following about dialogue:

> *The attitude that we characterize as that of sympathy in the adult springs from (the) same capacity to take the role of the other person with whom one is socially implicated ... Sympathy always implies that one stimulates himself to his assistance and consideration of others by taking in some degree the attitude of the person whom one is assisting. The common term for this is 'putting yourself in his place.' It is presumably an exclusively human type of conduct. (Deegan 1997, p. 83)*

In social psychology, Mead starts out with a given social-whole of complex group activity, into which he analyzes as elements the behavior of each of the separate individuals comprising that social whole. This thought could be used to analyze the focus groups that work on conflict resolution in the Abrahamic religions.

Ethical Communication in the Humanities

Aristotle had two main philosophical projects. These were, first, the clarification of the nature, scope, and possible results of the activity that he, following Plato, called dialectic, and second, the defence of the logical coherence of the notion of change and thus the possibility of a genuine science of nature, including the science of man. Dialectic comes from the ordinary Greek word for conversation (dialogos), and it is concerned with the critical scrutiny of those terms that are both philosophically significant and naturally occurring in non-specialist discussions of difficult topics. The dialectic in the academy has evolved out of Socratic techniques of cross-questioning. The assumption is that culture comes from the praxis of experiencing and reflecting, a thinking exercise, and from an acceptance of the fact that a persuasive message or experience can affect the thinking experience (Grayling 1995, p. 400).

McLuhan provides a later thought, electronically based, in which he considers that television is aimed at the right side of the brain, therefore the aim is to centre ourselves in the area of interplay between the two modes of perception and analysis, from left and right sides of the brain, thereby producing a comprehensive awareness, which he describes as "the projection of consciousness, consciousness being the sum interaction between one's self and the outside world" (McLuhan 1989, p. 52).

If we look again at McGilchrist's later work on consciousness, he says "we are first and foremost aware of ourselves through feeling states that lead to action in, and engagement with, the world as embodied beings" (McGilchrist 2009, p. 222). He quotes Panksepp "Consciousness is not simply a sensory, perceptual affair, a matter of imagery, as the contents of our mind would have us believe. It is deeply enmeshed with the brain mechanism that automatically promotes action readiness" (McGilchrist 2009, p. 222). This is another way of explaining communication in action. For our purposes, understanding comprehensive awareness is essential to gathering up Eastern and Western stories to make a new World story that we can live together.

This comprehensive awareness is enhanced rhetoric, the art of knowing what your audience knows and speaking to this knowledge and extending it to include the information you want to give the audience. It is both communication and performance. Two functions of communication – transmission and influence – both complement and hinder each other. "Using available cues, the audience makes assumptions appropriate to the prevailing function and tries to distinguish those aspects of the message that are designed to influence from those that function as transmission. "Although its principal purpose is persuasion, rhetoric also professes the aim of truth and aesthetic value" (Back 1989, p. 130).

Rhetoric is very political. Professor of International Relations at La Trobe University Melbourne, Joseph Camilleri, studies citizenship in a globalizing world. He refers to the dialogue of civilizations and the profound understanding of the relationship between politics and humanity, between the public and the private. To be truly human in ancient times, life had to be lived inside the polis. Citizenship meant participation in the life of the community and in the decisions that vitally affected its future. While it inherited the Greek legacy of citizenship, Rome substantially modified citizenship, shifting the understanding of the person into the domain of religion and metaphysics. The corollary of this shift, implicit in Augustine's doctrine of the two cities, was that the profane should be ultimately subordinate to the sacred. Secular power would be subservient to papal power. But Thomas Aquinas argued that human law can be perverted if the intention of the lawgiver is not fixed on true good, understood as the common good regulated according to divine justice. "Aquinas had foreshadowed the decisive shift in human reason as the governing principle in the ordering of human affairs" (Camilleri 2006, p. 18).

Extending further these historical principles, wherever persuaders are dialoguing, they should make their position clear and be receiver-oriented rather than source-oriented. Thus the intention to direct the audience's thoughts and actions has integrity. Co-active persuasion

is a method of bridging differences, of moving toward persuadees psychologically in the hope that they will be moved in turn to accept the persuader's position or proposal. It consists of five components:
- Communicating on the message recipient's terms;
- Reaching out in warm message tones rather than in impersonal tones;
- Combining expressions of interpersonal similarity with manifestations of expertise, knowledge of subject, and trustworthiness;
- Building on shared experiences;
- Using the yes-yes, yes-but and other such techniques in building from shared premises.
(Simons 1986, p. 138).

Forgiveness in the Humanities

Derrida argues that true forgiveness consists in forgiving the unforgivable, a condition all the more acute in this century of war.[10] He speaks of crimes against humanity which require self-indictment, repentance and forgiveness. He thinks that ultimately the only justification for the concept of crimes against humanity lies in the sacral nature to be found in Abrahamic memories, especially in Christian interpretation of neighbour and fellow man (Derrida 2004). "The Abrahamic moral tradition, in which forgiveness is a central concept, and which is at the basis of the three god monotheisms, has globalised itself in a more or less secular form" (Derrida 2001, p. xi).

---

10   The late Derrida was speaking of the 20th century when he spoke of the century of war. To forgive the unforgiveable would include the holocaust of six million Jews.

The "individual", ungodly form of Western civilization is an issue in today's world. Charles Taylor takes this concept and tries to open our eyes to the desperately narrow focus of an "individual" cast on life – where a more open community view could present new opportunities. The research from the four focus groups argues for a more open community and acceptance, but they dialogued about accepting everything. The issue of accepting everything was tackled by a Christian woman and a Jewish woman in the second focus group. In their dialogue, they agreed that we had to know the difference from the good and the wrong. We are to accept the good, and recognize the wrong.

There are some things that are intolerable, although the bearer of the wrong was not irredeemable. So the moral position is to know what is good, rather than to accept another's values without any form of reasoning out the end result of an action. Other people's values are their own, and we need to respect people, but we are also responsible for our family, our neighbor and our country. Taylor sees that not challenging another's values is a relativism which is "partly grounded in a principle of mutual respect. In other words, the relativism was itself an offshoot of a form of individualism" (Taylor 1991, p. 13).

Taylor continues "This individualism involves a centering on the self and a concomitant shutting out, or even unawareness, of the greater issues or concerns that transcend the self be they religious, political or historical. As a consequence, life is narrowed or flattened" (ibid., p. 14). And to make no mistake about his own belief he says "I think the relativism widely espoused today is a profound mistake, even in some respects self-stultifying" (ibid., p. 15).

The Moral Ideal

The moral ideal behind self-fulfillment is that of being true to oneself, and in a strange way, this moral ideal has changed what is admired in the community. "Survivalism has taken the place of heroism, as the admired quality" (ibid., p. 16). Having laid the groundwork for his argument, Taylor then moves on to describe what this all means in the everyday life of the people of our Western communities. He talks about putting one value in front of another, sacrificing love relationships and the care of children in the pursuit of careers. In fact, he says that "Today, many people feel called to do this, feel they ought to do this, feel their lives would be somehow wasted or unfulfilled if they didn't do it" (ibid., p. 17).

Taylor wants us to reason things out. Today "moral positions are not in any way grounded in reason or the nature of things but are ultimately just adopted by each of us because we find ourselves drawn to them (ibid., p. 18).

He wants us to have to believe three things
1. That authenticity is a valid idea;
2. That you can argue in reason about ideals and about the conformity of practise to these ideals;
3. That these arguments can make a difference (ibid., p. 23)

In a way, this is what participants do in interfaith. They share information, in the present day context, of ancient teachings that have been remembered and communicated for thousands of years from generation to generation. In a time of godlessness, it is helpful to have this kind of dialogue. We discover ourselves from dialogue, Taylor implies. Human life has a "fundamentally dialogical character" (ibid., p. 33). So we have a deeper understanding of ourselves and others through dialogue. "A person who accepted no moral demands would be as impossible to argue with about right and wrong as would a person who refused to accept the world of perception around us be impossible to argue with about empirical matters (ibid., p. 32).

Some of this argumentation, this dialogue, has to do with what is right and what is wrong.

In the words of Taylor, in the eighteenth century "the notion was that understanding right and wrong was not a matter of dry calculation, but was anchored in our feelings. Morality has, in a sense, a voice within (ibid., p. 26). The researcher would add, yes, a person has a conscience, an inner voice, but this conscience has to be formed, in the Christian sense, from the teaching of Jesus Christ.

What Taylor is calling 'the displacement of the moral accent' comes about when being in touch with ourselves takes on independent and crucial moral significance. It comes to be something we have to attain to be true and full human beings (ibid., p. 26). So, as I understand this, the displacement of the moral accent has to be attained by individual achievement, not by what your culture or belief tells you is right or wrong. Taylor swiftly comes in for his conclusion.

"Your feeling a certain way can never be sufficient grounds for respecting your position, because your feeling can't determine what is significant. Soft relativism self-destructs (ibid., p. 37). The lived lives of the participants in the focus groups can shine more light onto Taylor's theory.

When examining what happens during the dialogue of the four focus groups it can be seen that a person can only define their identity against the background of things that matter. Things that matter have to include history, nature, society, the demands of solidarity, and for these participants, the authentic messages they have received from their religious communities.

Only if a person exists "in a world in which history or the demands of nature or the needs of my fellow human beings, or the duties of citizenship, or the call of God or something else of this order matters crucially, can I define an identity for myself that is not trivial. Authenticity is not the enemy of demands that emanate from beyond the self; it supposes such demands" (ibid., pp. 40–1).

The four focus groups ask for recognition of difference. When you ask "What is involved in truly recognizing difference?", Taylor replies, "this means recognizing the equal value of different ways of being" (ibid., p. 51). But what grounds the equality of value? Taylor replies:

If men and women are equal it is not because they are different, but because overriding the difference are some properties, common or complementary, which are of value. They are beings capable of reason, or love, or memory, or dialogical recognition." (ibid., p. 51)

The combined message from the four focus groups was the necessity to respect difference. Taylor defines what this is. "To come together on a mutual recognition of difference – that is, of the equal value of different identities – requires that we share more than a belief in this principle; we have to share also some standards of value on which the identities concerned check out as equal. There must be some substantive agreement on value, or else the formal principle of equality will be empty and a sham.

We can pay lip service to equal recognition, but we won't really share an understanding of equality unless we share something more. Recognizing difference, like self-choosing, requires a horizon of significance, in this case, a shared one" (ibid., p. 52). The shared value of the three Abrahamic faith communities, Jews, Christians and Muslims, is the common religious text to love God and neighbour. It is their belief, and their practice.

To be more specific about my position with regard to forgiveness and reconciliation, I bring forward the focus group material into the main body of the thesis, I have to say that they have answered all my questions in a clear and concise way. For all three Abrahamic groups, an Abrahamic person has to love God first, and then neighbour. The same is for forgiveness and reconciliation. The ancient Abrahamic groups (some of the younger Protestant groups are still thinking through the ritual of this) have to say sorry to God first, and then to neighbour, with the intention and actuality of movement towards behavioural change. It generally comes down to sharing, and treating one another with dignity and respect. Sharing is the first and most important lesson human children have to be taught. As for reconciliation with an organization that is committed to non-sharing, and disrespect, it is not possible to continue to allow these things to happen. There needs to be articulation of what is not good, and a change of behavior. Alex Boraine left his position in the Methodist Church to become a politician and give voice to the black people in South Africa. It is a matter of conscience. Pope Paul quotes from the Vatican II document Gaudium et Spes

> *In the depths of his conscience, man detects a law which he does not impose upon himself, but which holds him to obedience. Always summoning him to love good and avoid evil, the voice of conscience when necessary speaks to his heart: do this, shun that. For man has in his heart a law written by God; to obey it is the very dignity of man; according to it he will be judged. (9) Conscience is the most secret core and sanctuary of a man. There he is alone with God, Whose voice echoes in his depths. (10) In a wonderful manner conscience reveals that law which is fulfilled by love of God and neighbour. (11) In fidelity to conscience, Christians are joined with the rest of men in the search for truth, and for the genuine solution to the numerous problems which arise in the life of individuals from social relationships. Hence the more right conscience holds sway, the more persons and groups turn aside from blind choice and strive to be guided by the objective norms of morality. (Pope Paul Dec.7th 1965, speaking from the "Pastoral Constitution on the Church in the Modern World, Gaudium et Spes", from Vatican Council II)*

Glock & Stark understand conscience as "the authority of self". "It does not seem to be arbitrary to say that the individual conscience can exercise authority and is capable of rewarding and punishing" (Glock & Stark 1965 p. 179).

Joram Haber presents moral absolutism as the theory that certain kinds of actions are absolutely wrong. Conversely, ethical relativism is a theory of universal truths that transcend provincial concepts of right and wrong. Kant argues that to be truthful, meaning honest, in all deliberations is to hold to a sacred and absolutely commanding decree of reason, limited by no expediency" (Haber 1994, p. 2).

Aurel Kolnai, a Jewish convert to Christianity, speaks about moral consensus, but with the warning: "A disintegration of the moral universe of discourse would gravely affect the business of life, and the breakdown of society as a far-expanding medium of communication would tend to render our moral experience and judgements singularly weightless and pointless if not vacuous" (Kolnai 1977, p. 146). He explains how he would feel if someone else felt differently from him about the wrongness of lying. "I would feel shocked in a unique fashion, and feel smitten with a sort of helpless wonderment as if the ground were being knocked out from under my feet" (Kolnai 1977, p. 147). Moral codes and traditions crystalize consensus, thus indicating enlightenment and support for people who adhere to those codes. Without them, moral certitudes would vanish or become tenuous.

Any philosophical account of forgiveness must be articulate and must allow for forgiveness that is uncompromising. So argues Pamela Hieronymi in Articulating an Uncompromising Forgiveness. She opens her argument with three interrelated judgments: the act in question is wrong, a serious offence worthy of moral attention; the wrongdoer is a legitimate member of a moral community and therefore can be expected to avoid such acts; and the one who is wronged ought not to be wronged. Wrongdoing then stands as an offence to another person. She concludes that an apology brings about a change in view or revision of judgment, a process that undermines resentment. "The account articulates the judgment on which resentment is grounded and then articulates one condition under which it would be rationally undermined. Resentment is grounded not on the three judgments that must be maintained, but on a fourth judgment which, other things being equal, the three imply: that the event makes a threatening claim. This fourth judgment can be rationally undermined by an apology, without requiring the abandonment or revision of the other three" (Hieronymi 2001).

John Rawls (2005) in A Theory of Justice presents conditions of justice that would preclude many occasions needing forgiveness. His is a human needs perspective. His priority rule is the priority of liberty. This rule concerns the right of each person to extensive liberty compatible with the liberty of others. His second rule is the priority of Justice over the efficiency and welfare. This rule says that justice precedes the principle of efficiency so that social and economic positions are to be to everyone's advantage and open to all. A key problem for Rawls is to show how such principles would be universally adopted, and here the work borders on general ethical issues. He introduces a theoretical veil of ignorance in which all the players in the social game would be placed in a situation which he calls the original position. Having only a general knowledge about the facts of life and society, each player is to make a rationally prudential choice concerning the kind of social institution they would enter into contract with. Denying the players any specific information about themselves forces them to adopt a generalized point of view that bears a strong resemblance to the moral point of view. "Moral conclusions can be reached without abandoning the prudential standpoint and positing a moral outlook merely by pursuing one's own prudential reasoning under certain procedural bargaining and knowledge constraints" (Academic Dialogue on Applied Ethics).

Dr Pettit's forgiveness process begins with a progressive ability for a person to observe themselves and others more compassionately. There follows a progressive ability to know and communicate needs in a wiser manner. The next step is to train the will in wiser and more skilful ways. Then comes the development of a progressive ability to make better contact with, and increasingly to identify with, what Pettit calls a person's higher self, that part of the human psyche that is the source of love, strength, wisdom and creativity. Also included in the forgiveness process, according to Pettit, is a progressive ability to understand and balance the energies of both love and will. This leads to an increased sense of wholeness and an increased ability to give to the community and to become "for-giving" in a new and deeper sense (Pettit).

Worthington's studies of forgiveness derive from his clinical work with couples and families. From a health point of view, he suggests, 'unforgiveness' is a heavy burden to carry. Resentment, one of the core elements of 'unforgiveness', is like carrying around a red hot rock with the intention of someday throwing it back at the one who caused the hurt. It tires people and burns them out. Worthington says people are healthier if they forgive rather than if they stew in 'unforgiveness'. A large body of evidence suggests that hostility causes cardiovascular difficulties. Also, chronic stress is related to poor immune system functioning (Worthington 2001, pp. 8–9).

In Dimensions of Forgiveness (Worthington 1998), McCullough, Exline, and Baumeister (1998) present an annotated bibliography on forgiveness research. Robert Enright (2001) and his colleagues at the University of Wisconsin define forgiveness from a cognitive developmental perspective.

Forgiveness is the overcoming of negative affect and judgment toward the offender, not by denying ourselves the right to such affect and judgment, but by endeavouring to view the offender with benevolence, compassion, and even love, while recognizing that he or she has abandoned the right to them. The important parts of the definition are as follows; a): one who forgives has suffered a deep hurt, thus showing resentment; b) the offended person has a moral right to resentment but overcomes it nonetheless; a new response to the other accrues, including compassion and love; c) this loving response occurs despite the realization that there is no obligation to love the offender. (Subkoviak et al. 1992, p. 3)

Jeffrie G. Murphy in Getting Even, Forgiveness and its Limits proposes that vindictive emotions such as anger, resentment, and the desire for revenge actually deserve a more legitimate place in the emotional, social, and legal lives of individuals than researchers currently recognized, while forgiveness deserves to be more selectively granted. In the philosophy of criminal law and its related issues getting even is a conflict issue. Vindictiveness, temptation to revenge and struggle to handle or even overcome these passions are always on the table. The justice of the rule of law is being perverted by such practices as the presentation of highly charged and angry victim impact statements – statements that cloud reason and may emotionally sway judges or juries toward harsher sentences than some criminals deserve. "Making forgiveness contingent on repentance by the wrongdoer might in part be justified, not merely by the self-respect benefits that such a strategy sometimes conveys on the victim, but also by the role that such a strategy might play in the rebirth of the wrongdoer" (Murphy 2003, p. 80).

Reconciliation in Family Life

Forgiveness is unilateral, reconciliation is bilateral. In family life, as in the life of organizations and politics, the way back to relationship, leading onto living together again, needs some change in behaviour. In marriage, sometimes this is not possible. A marriage can break down, new relationships are made, and the children have to accommodate. In the four focus groups these issues were brought up in the family histories. Not everyone's journey was without sorrow. Articulation and acceptance of the new situation was a necessity, and the energy to create a new life for themselves was found in their religion. It was discovered that without a person accepting that they had hurt you, there was not a full reconciliation. "Reconciliation, which in some form is the desired goal on the part of the injured party who has forgiven the wrongdoer, is not possible unless the wrongdoer accepts that forgiveness, and acceptance, in turn, requires repentance for the wrong" (North 2000, p. 29).

The issue of forgiveness never really goes away because, even when reconciliation may be inadvisable, forgiving helps the person who has been hurt to move on with his or her life (Coleman 1998).

Family therapy and also marriage mediation has many facets. Forgiveness is a process, and doesn't happen overnight.

"Sometimes family members may pressure an individual to forgive before he or she is ready or able to consider the possibility, or will expect forgiveness to occur within a shorter timeframe than is reasonable. In contrast, family members may sometimes prefer to sweep transgressions under the rug, so to speak, because they would rather not deal with the broader implications of or the fallout from the harm that has been caused. In other cases, family members may choose sides, supporting the offender

and perhaps blaming the injured party. Sometimes they may actively discourage forgiving, e.g., in situations involving acts of infidelity, in the case of bitter divorces" (Forgiveness).

In a family the effort to overcome deep hurt and betrayal often involves a desire for reconciliation on at least one member's part. Forgiveness is not reconciliation. It is possible to forgive without reconciling, without coming together again in love and friendship, but it is not possible to reconcile truly without forgiveness. (Coleman 2000, p. 78)

The family therapists who deal with injured party experiences, try to work towards empathy for the offender (McCullough, Worthington, and Rachal 1997). The aim is to reframe the hurtful event as a means of separating the offender from his or her hurtful actions. The injured party also needs to have humility, (Cunningham 1985; Worthington 1998) and all need to reach the understanding that everyone needs mercy and forgiveness; being forgiven requires being willing to forgive.

So, reconciliation is the end result of the forgiveness process. Forgiveness has a history in marital and family therapy. Only five studies on forgiveness appeared prior to 1985, a number that has since increased by over 4,000% (Fincham, Jackson, & Beach, 2005). The slow infusion of forgiveness in counseling (DiBlasio & Proctor, 1993) may reflect an aversion to the religious origins of the construct (e.g., Rye et al., 2000) or the fact that many of the early models of forgiveness had limited utility for clinicians (McCullough & Worthington, 1994). However, the importance of forgiveness for mental and physical health has now become widely recognized (e.g., Harris & Thoresen, 2005; Toussaint, Williams, Musick, & Everson, 2001). The capacity to seek and grant forgiveness is seen as one of the most significant factors contributing to marital longevity and marital satisfaction (Fenell, 1993). Further, marital therapists note that forgiveness is a critical part of the healing process for major relationship transgressions such as infidelity (Gordon, Baucom, & Snyder, 2005) as well as dealing with everyday relationship hurts

(Fincham, Beach, & Davila, 2004) (Fincham, FD, Hall, J and Beach Steven RH 2006). Finally, a word on creation. "Conflict is a crisis that forces us to recognize explicitly that we live with multiple realities, and must negotiate a common reality. That we bring to each situation different, frequently contrasting stories and must create together a single strand story with a role for each and for both (Augsburger DW 1989, p. 11). In a sermon by M. Augsburger, "God-kind of love always takes the initiative. You do not stand by passively. You move into the experience of the difficulty. You become involved in the problem." (Augsburger M 1985)

Intra-Organizational Peace Construction in the Humanities

Associate Professor of Philosophy at the University of Louisville and executive board member of Philosophers for Peace, Nancy Nyguist Potter, edits a book in which the authors examine militaristic language and metaphor, effects of media violence on children, humanitarian intervention, and political forgiveness to identify problem polices and identify better ones. What we think of as knowledge is at least partly determined by our conceptual schemes. Our perceptions of the world are always mediated by our various ideologies and belief systems (Potter 2004).

The work of teacher Allison Bailey concerns children who are struggling with literacy. Her studies show that when provided with resources and guidance and when encouraged to pursue multiple paths of change in their students, teachers too can develop greater conceptual understanding of subject matter, thus greater forgiveness and acceptance. (e.g Borko et al., 2000) (Heritage and Bailey 2006:174).

Paula J. Smithka joins with Allison Bailey to present a vision of a multicultural community that emphasises differences over sameness. Diversity enables a sharing and peaceful reconciliation of conflicts. Dialogue is the means to achieve this goal. The philosophical starting point is the idea that group-based social movements and writings associated with identity have positive implications for the politics of peace (Bailey and Smithka 2002).

RELIGIOUS DISCOURSE REVIEW

Religious Discourse on Human Needs

With regard to the need for food for the inner man, St. Augustine wrote:

> I came to Carthage where a whole frying-pan of wicked loves spluttered all around me. I was not yet in love, but I was in love with love, and with a deep seated want I hated myself for wanting too little. I was looking for something to love, still in love with love. I hated safety and a path without snares, because I had a hunger within - for that food of the inner man, yourself, my God. (Blaiklock 1983, p. 58)

In Milan, with the help of Bishop Ambrose, a man of persuasive rhetoric, St Augustine came to the following conclusion about God: "A closed heart does not shut out your eye, nor can man's harshness push away your hand. In mercy and in judgement you open it when you will and nothing can escape your warmth" (Blaiklock 1983, p. 103).

Today, an echo comes from Bishop John Heaps. "When forgiveness has been given and accepted, the power of sin is broken; its force for destruction no longer exits" (Heaps 1998, p. 39). Like the aforementioned scholars, he also talks of the process of forgiveness. The beginning for him is to admit the need for help. Then the sacraments and wisdom of Jesus, and his presence, are essential in the process.

Religious Discourse on Ethical Communication

It is by "[e]stablishing the lines of communication between philosophy and religion, from within the abysmal centre of the western philosophical tradition, I conceived of a transcendental dimension of a communicative ethics as the horizon opened in-between the proximate other and the Wholly Other" (Mowlana 2003, p. 33). Mowlana goes on to write that "the transcendent dimension of a communication ethics is of the sublime imperative and demand which, disclosing the limits of reason alone, opens the critical reflex to its movement beyond its self. Responding to the call of the other … is nothing other than an ethics of communication" (ibid., p. 18). This idea leads to a related concept: the limits of reason as the horizon itself, which in turn opens up thoughts about the formerly in-appropriable other. "Does not the concern with the other broach the boundary between philosophy and religion? Does not an ethical limit of reason broach the boundary between philosophy and religion?"(ibid., p. 19). The concept of religion as a horizon yet to be opened, and the notion of a gap haunting the history of international communication, is the poetic way Mowlana presents the problem.

The question haunts contemporary societies, where the border between philosophy and religion is ripe for revision. "Conceived in reference to the call of the other and the transcendent dimension of a communicative ethics, the philosophical significance of religion, and the religious significance of philosophy, is of a border which has yet to be crossed" (ibid., p. 19).

Religious Discourse on Forgiveness

Faith is weak. It is stifled by a world that is a stranger to it, turning the gift of God to its own advantage. Selfishness then gains ground over love. Immersion in the gift of God is the opposite to loss of faith. In the words of Jeremiah, renewal of trust in the unfailing faithfulness of God is to beg him to "bring us back, let us come back" (Jeremiah XXXI.18.) The plea involves a process of conversion. To turn towards God is to turn from ourselves and from whatever forms an obstacle to the gift of God. It is to ask God's pardon for actual offences. Then God forgives. That is to say, he renews the gift he has made of himself. He recreates us, puts new life into love, and purifies it a little more of its selfish traits. It is then that we "attempt to look to other people with the attitude of love Jesus has for them, and in this way, to purify our judgement of them" (Teams of Our Lady - Equipes Notre Dame - Rome Pilgrimage, 1982, pp. 6–7). Related to that concept is a resolution never to go to sleep without asking God's forgiveness for our faults and without forgiving one another.

Religious Discourse on Peace Construction

> To set the theme for this section of the thesis, I present a particularly clear statement from the US Catholic Bishops in 1983. "At the centre of the Church's teaching on peace and at the centre of all Catholic social teaching are the transcendence of God and the dignity of the human person. The human person is the clearest reflection of God's presence in the world; all of the Church's work in pursuit of both justice and peace is designed to protect and promote the dignity of the human person." (US Catholic Bishops 1983)

The Equipes Notre Dame, a French Catholic movement for married couples, known in Australia as Teams of Our Lady, construct peace in marriage. Couples in the Teams deepen their religious knowledge to discover the extent of Christ's demands on them, in order to live up to such demands at all times. They pursue this aim in common with the members of their team. The word team has been chosen in preference to any other because it signifies that those who belong to the movement have a specific aim, which is jointly and vigorously pursued (Teams of Our Lady - Charter of Equipes Notre Dame International).

The 'family clusters', as Margaret Sawin has developed the model, is a group of four or five complete family units who contract to meet together periodically over an extended period of time to share educational experiences. They provide mutual support for each other, learn skills to enhance living within the family, and celebrate their beliefs and lives together. The most important area of family life is the development and continuation of self-worth, members of this group believe. A growth curriculum for families deals with awareness of the total self, awareness of others within the family system, and awareness of how God operates within family relationships. Because each family system has its own way of interacting, the interpretation of these 'awarenesses' differs among families. Sharing the meanings of life's experiences is the prime purpose for interacting. The manner in which people interact is related to how they share in verbal and nonverbal communication. We cannot share meanings until first we communicate effectively (Sawin 1979).

The following is an open letter entitled "A Call to Peace, Dialogue and Understanding between Muslims and Jews" published by Muslim scholars from the Centre for the Study of Muslim-Jewish Relations on 25/2/2008:

> *Many Jews and Muslims today stand apart from each other due to feelings of anger, which in some parts of the world, translate into violence. It is our contention that we are faced today not with 'a clash of civilizations' but with 'a clash of ill-formed misunderstandings.' Deep-seated stereotypes and prejudices have resulted in a distancing of the communities and even a dehumanizing of the 'Other' ... We must strive towards turning*

ignorance into knowledge, intolerance into understanding, and pain into courage and sensitivity for the "Other'...As a pillar of our faith (Iman), we (Muslims) are expected to believe that the author of the Torah (Tawrat) and the Qur'an is the same one God (Qur'an 5:44)...It is important to be honest about the level of anti-Jewish and anti-Muslim/anti-Arab sentiment that translates into conflict within and between the two communities. At this moment there is no challenge more pressing than the need to bring to a closure some of the historical and long lasting estrangements between the Jews and Muslims. Because of the increasing polarisation, many feel forced to choose between dialogue and violence as a response. Most Muslims would hope that the sufferings that Jews have experienced over many centuries would make them more sensitive to the sufferings of others, especially the Palestinian people ... While the purpose of this letter is to generate dialogue and understanding between Jews and Muslims, it reflects the need for a wider dialogue between all faiths and communities. We must keep talking – especially when we do not agree." (Muslim scholars from the Centre for the Study of Muslim-Jewish Relations)

A Jewish call from the International Jewish Committee for Interreligious Consultations for Muslim-Jewish Dialogue follows:
Seek peace and pursue it. (Psalm 34:15)

As Jewish leaders we write this letter with the hope it reaches those with whom we might fulfil the words of the prophets "to do justice, to love kindness, And to walk humbly with God." (Micah 6:8) We are fully aware that both of our religious communities have a robust tradition of varying interpretations of sacred text and religious principles, often yielding competing understandings. We call to dialogue all of those who affirm that our mandate as leaders is to guide our communities in accordance with values which benefit all of human society and the world at large. Judaism and Islam have historically shared much in common, and it is instructive for both of our religions to continue to export how our respective religious understandings have evolved, often in relationship to one another .... Those of us who are informed by and are leaders of our respective religious communities have a particular mandate to highlight the common repudiation in Judaism and Islam of murder, violence, injustice and indignity. Further we must seek to reaffirm the commandments in our respective Faiths to pursue peace and to affirm the dignity of the other ... As believers in the One Creator and Guide of the Universe, referred to in both our Traditions as the Merciful One, who demands mercy and compassion of us all, it is essential to recapture and develop the spirit of Jewish-Muslim dialogue and mutual respect. True love of God demands this dialogue. (Seek Peace and Pursue it: a Jewish Call to Muslim-Jewish Dialogue)

NON-GOVERNMENT ORGANIZATION DISCOURSE REVIEW

Non-Government Organizations and Human Needs

ACFID, The Australian Council for International Development, is the umbrella organization for Australian NGOs. The NG0s work inside overseas countries and also in their own countries, and they lobby the Australian Government for change. Amnesty, Greenpeace, and the Jesuit Refugee Services have been set up to bring change, whereas the evangelisation and development groups work with local communities, supplying their human needs such as common pots in Chile, education, and hospitals in Papua New Guinea. These endeavours in themselves can lead to change, making people aware of their human rights. NGO's also work toward structural transformation, for example by acting to empower the weaker side in a conflict situation (van der Merwe, 1989; Lederach 1995; Curle, 1996; Ramsbotham, Woodhouse, Miall 2005, p. 170). On the other hand, The Red Cross charter is apolitical, and so the organization supplies health needs, compassion, and sympathy but does not engage in political issues. Overall, there is a lot of sharing of information and knowledge. At the time of writing, Kenya is suffering violence. The International Medical Corps Newsroom connects the rest of the world with this suffering and shows that in the middle of such trauma something new can grow: connections between tribes. Pastor Joseph John Dmanyo "has spent the church funds on food and blankets and asked the congregation to donate more food. 'For me it is a blessing, he says, we have people from all tribes staying in the church and I counsel them and ask them to live together in peace" from "Providing Primary Health Care while Revenge and Violence Continue", January 31, 2008, (International Medical Corps Newsroom).

"NGOs such as the African Centre for the Constructive Resolution of Disputes (ACCORD), the Berghof Research Centre for Constructive Conflict Management, the Carter Centre, the Community of Sant'Egidio, the Conflict Analysis Centre at Kent, and the Harvard Centre of Negotiation have gained experience in working in conflict, (van Tongeren 1996; Serbe et al. 1997). They use a variety of approaches, including facilitation (Fisher and Ury 1981), problem solving workshops (de Reuck, 1984; Burton 1987; Kelman 1992; Mitchell and Banks, 1996) and sustained mediation" (Ramsbotham, Woodhouse, Miall 2005:169).

Mediators from NGOs have contributed to transformation at key moments, usually in conjunction with governments and international organizations.

Non-Government Organizations and Ethical Communication

Ethical communication is truthful communication. In a tribute to Onesta Carpene, a former Caritas staff member who worked for more than 20 years in Cambodia as a representative of international Catholic aid agencies, Caritas News wrote the following: "Her insistence on working closely in partnership with the people and making decisions based on their expressed needs was renowned. Onesta had a remarkable ability to communicate at all levels – with Cambodian people in the villages and in the government. Through her dealings with the local people she had an extraordinary sense of what was best for Cambodians" (Caritas 2007).

In South Africa there was a strong civil society. "A great deal of innovation, energy and passion had gone into the development of a strong civil society, with one of the largest numbers of non-government organizations in the world" (Boraine 2000, p. 264). Of these NGOs, there were those who focused on legal issues, others were in education, and some were caring for the victims of apartheid, to mention a few. They were also useful in another way. Many people in the Truth and Reconciliation Commission had worked with these members of the NGOs, and some were available to work in the Commission itself. Indeed, it was the NGO, Justice in Transition, that created opportunities for conferences, workshops, discussion and debate about the Truth and Reconciliation Commission.

The life of an NGO is, however, not easy. As they work with the conqueror, NGOs are tolerated and, for the most part, embraced as partners of development. Yet many NGOs hesitate to become politically active. They often adopt what one analyst has phased a bypass strategy. Their ability to link the empowerment of the powerless with the development of a democratic society and polity is limited (Dicklitch 2002, p. 25). But the growth of the NGOs represents a profound development in international relations that transcends the creation of political community within specific issue areas. "NGOs have been effective in shaping the practices of multinational corporations, particularly in the area of child labour and environmental protection" (Sambal 2002, p. 258).

Zivetz's analysis of NGOs lays out sequentially the history, philosophy, organizational structure and staffing, funding and expenditure, development projects, relations with other non-government organizations, relations with government, and development education of many of the well-known organizations in Australia. "Two million Australians give some 100 million dollars a year through non-government organizations. The agencies that operate as a channel for these voluntary contributions represent a diversity of constituencies within the Australian public...in the 1960s and 1970s, the NGO community began to focus on longer term developmental strategies designed to address basic human needs" (Zivetz and Ryan 1991, p. 98).

Ann Hudock says:

[A]s NGOs struggle to represent the interests of the poor and the marginalized, they provide politicians and international agencies with an opportunity to gain favourable publicity by responding to the needs of these groups once the NGOs have made them public. As NGOs and governments clarify their relationships and work together, governments' concerns that NGOs represent a political threat may lessen, and as many authoritarian regimes are replaced by new democracies, the new regimes may be more open to NGO involvement. (Hudock 1999, p. 55)

Non-Government Organizations and Forgiveness

A letter from Amnesty International, Australia, highlights a lack of forgiveness. "Atefeh Rajabi Sahaaleh was publicly hanged on 15th August, 2004. According to eyewitnesses, as she was taken to the crane set up for her execution, this terrified young girl repeatedly cried out to God for forgiveness, even as the executioner was tying the noose around her neck. She was just 16 years old." Atefeh was hanged in public for crimes against chastity, and her father wasn't told that his daughter was to be executed. Father and daughter were cruelly denied the chance to say their final goodbyes. The letter asks for monetary help to end these human rights abuses. "Since 1990, Iran has executed 25 child offenders, with 17 of these children hanged in the last three years" (Amnesty International Australia 21st November, 2007).

Non-Government Organizations and Peace Construction

The Levantine Cultural Centre and the Raoul Wallenberg Institute of Ethics, along with NGOs whose South Californian members work on peace and interfaith issues, are presenting the film Encounter Point. The film features everyday heroes, both Israeli and Palestinian, working together to make co-existence and reconciliation a reality (Levantine Cultural Centre).

One of the larger humanitarian organizations, the Swiss-based International Committee of the Red Cross (ICRC), employs some 12,000 people in 80 delegations around the world. Formed in 1863, it is the founding body of the International Red Cross and Red Crescent Movement. "The ICRC's principal mission is to assist and protect victims of war," says head of the ICRC regional delegation for the Pacific, Jean-Luc Metzker, "But we're just as active during peacetime to prevent conflict." In the Pacific, for example, ICRC activities include visiting people detained in relation to internal unrest and violence, cooperating with regional and national Red Cross societies, encouraging states to ratify treaties relating to international humanitarian law, and advancing international humanitarian law and humanitarian ideals (Focus 2007, p. 19).

Frames of Reference

This section builds on the analysis of the literature throughout this chapter, using the three frames of reference to highlight comparisons in the literature and to tackle the central question of the thesis: How are people of Abrahamic faiths, faiths that are implicated in a geopolitical confrontation, able to cooperate within religious organizations? The frames of reference are knowledge, dialogue, and speech.

There are two kinds of knowledge: the "because of what" (propter quid) and the "what something is" (quod aliquid sit). When these two kinds of knowledge are compared with each other, Friedman states, it is a question of which of them comes first. "The reply is that knowledge of what something is comes first, since first principles are learnt in this way and these should be known first in any faculty" (Friedman 1990, p. 193). First principles can be established in four ways: by induction, by sense, by familiarity, or by some other way. Induction, according to Cicero, is arriving at a conclusion through the comparison of many similar things, or, as Aristotle and the logicians said, once many instances have been collected together it is possible to draw a universal conclusion.

So our first comparative frame of reference will be knowledge of what something is. This will be knowledge of people of the Abrahamic religions and their human needs.

A process of self-preservation that has to satisfy the rationality conditions of communicative action becomes dependent on the integrative accomplishments of subjects who coordinate their action via criticisable validity claims. Communication reason cannot be subsumed without resistance under a blind self-preservation. It refers neither to a subject that preserves itself in relating to objects via representation and action, nor to a self-maintaining system that demarcates itself from an environment, but to a symbolically structured life-world that is constituted in the interpretive accomplishments of its members and only reproduced through communication (Habermas 1981, Vol. 1, p. 38). Therefore our second frame of reference will be the interpretive accomplishments of truthful dialogue.

Communicative reason does not simply encounter ready-made subjects and systems; rather, it takes part in structuring what is to be preserved. The utopian perspective of reconciliation and freedom is ingrained in the conditions for the communicative socialisation of individuals; it is built into the linguistic mechanism of the reproduction of the species (ibid., p. 398). The third frame of reference for comparative analysis will be the role of speech in the reconciliation process.

Explanations for peace construction have been attempted by many scholars. Habermas's theory of communication action holds that two people can use language to come to some kind of "action" together. Or in his own words:

> *There is then a fundamental connection between understanding communicative actions and constructing rational interpretations. This connection is fundamental because communicative actions cannot be interpreted in two stages – first understood in their actual course and only then compared with an ideal-typical model. Rather, an interpreter who participates virtually, without his own aims of actions, can descriptively grasp the meaning of the actual course of a process of reaching understanding only under the presupposition that he judges the agreement and disagreement, the validity claims and potential reasons with which he is confronted, on a common basis shared in principle by him and those immediately involved. At any rate, this participation is imperative for a social-scientific interpreter who bases his descriptions on the communicative model of action. (ibid., pp. 116–117)*

An appropriate comparison is between the individual and the group. The scholars address the power of human needs and the role of the individual in political processes. In the past the individual was to change to fit into societies ruled by elites. Now it is time to change the society to suit the human needs of the individual (Burton 1990). Individual needs are related to value, self-esteem, material and non-material satisfiers, self-actualization, freedom, insight, reflective thought, chain of thought, and sympathy for the 'other', all symbolic of a hunger within to feed the inner man. There are diversity needs, as well as common needs.

Group needs are for sane, secure societies, for being part of a workshop to reach group consensus, and for democratic development of a theory of knowledge, all of which make one person's experience available to another. In times of war, and of NGO intervention, different tribes take shelter together. Films then can be made to show that warring groups can co-exist if individuals adopt a model of reconciliation.

In the case Maslow presents, the individual is divorced from needing his group any more when he reaches material self-actualization. Conversely, Clark would say that we always need one another. No such contradiction exists for knowledge. Knowledge is needed both for the individual and the group, and it is gained by insight from personal experience as well as from sharing. The internet is the device people use today to share knowledge. Individuals find ways of adding their own perspectives to blogs and journals. Thus public discourse works as a force for change.

The Interpretive Accomplishments of Truthful Dialogue

Contemporary movements around the world, whether in groups, communities, or nations, are constructing more humane, ethical, traditionalist, antibloc, self-reliance theories of societal development. "It is the quest for dialogue that underlies the current revolutionary movements around the world" (Mowlana 1996, p. 96). Here Mowlana is agreeing with Burton: society is going to be changed to meet human needs by truthful dialogue.

Interactions are communicative action when participants coordinate their plans of action consensually with regard to validity of claims. "Those claims are claims to truth, rightness, and truthfulness" (Habermas 1990 p. 58). Dialogue does not depart from consensus on fundamental moral values. "Culture comes from the praxis of experience and reflection, a thinking exercise" (Grayling 1995, p. 400). A persuasive message can affect the thinking process, but you need to be critically as well as culturally moved. Human life exists in the polis and its quality depends on it being receiver-oriented. Habermas goes on to makes his points abundantly clear. "In the claims to truth or rightness, the speaker can redeem his guarantee decisively, that is, by advancing reasons; in the case of claims of truthfulness, he does so through consistent behaviour. (A person can convince someone that he means what he says only through his actions, not by giving reasons) (ibid., p. 59).

What are the ramifications of the thought of Habermas when applied to the four focus groups?

In dialogue, the focus groups ask us to know the right, and also recognize that which is wrong. Thinking of Abrahamic communities, we are barely able to speak to one another, (BJA (F) tells us that most people have never met a Jew), let al.one do we understand one another. From a distance point of view, the far has become near, be it for family reasons, for business, or for purposes of refugee asylum. Now, all of us have to begin the task of reasoning things out, and making a decision about the validity, truthfulness and rightness of our dialogue partner's reasoning. The question to ask is "Do the reasons given in dialogue carry on into subsequent behaviour that 'lives out' the reason". In other words, do the reasons truthfully match up with the consequent behaviour (Habermas 1984)? If our dialogue brings good fruit, understanding, forming trust, and positive cooperation, we can look forward to universal beginnings, perhaps, of a world democracy. Habermas thinks that this kind of basis for democracy is his most important contribution to the world.

Put another way, Habermas "thinks that practical issues of the social life of modern (postmodern) society, including the issue of social conflicts, can be solved by the rational discourse among people ... it is necessary to develop universal communication ethics and establish adequate democratic procedures among people and social groups" (Mitrovic 1999).

Becoming part of the communicative action of the Abrahamic communities is a privilege. It is a precursor to world peace, as the Abrahamic communities, Jews, Christians and Muslims, make up 55% of the world's population.

However, how do we come to understand people who are both culturally and religiously different from ourselves? And how do we recognize right from wrong? These are some of the issues talked through in dialogue in the focus groups. Jurgen Habermas has an answer to this most pressing question. His answer is encased in his understanding of lifeworld. Lifeworld is the rationalization of free and open interpersonal communication. You ask questions, you give answers, you give reasons for your positions; there is a cognitive dimension to democracy.

The process of reaching an understanding between world and lifeworld. The lifeworld, then, offers both an intuitively pre-understood context for an action situation and resources for the interpretive process in which participants in communication engage as they strive to meet the need for agreement in the action situation. (Habermas 1990, p. 136)

So, we have two or more people wanting to use language to express their feelings and their perspectives and understanding of the lifeworld, with a goal of coming to some common meaning, some common understanding, whereby they can made the language "live" in a common communicative action.

Thus "agreement in the communicative practice of everyday life rests simultaneously on the inter-subjectively shared propositional knowledge, on normative accord, and on mutual trust" (ibid., p. 136). That trust, of course, will be shattered if one of these participants in communicative action fails to convince the other(s) that his language is truthful, that it is right, and that what he is proposing is valid.

> *Relations to the world and claims to validity:* "A measure of whether or not participants in communication reach agreement is the yes or no position taken by the hearer whereby he accepts or rejects the claim to validity that has been raised by the speaker. In the attitude orientated toward reaching understanding, the speaker raises with every intelligible utterance the claim that the utterance in question is true (or that the existential presuppositions of the propositional content hold true), that the speech act is right in terms of a given normative context (or that the normative content that it satisfies is itself legitimate), and that the speaker's manifest intentions are meant in the way they are expressed.
>
> When someone rejects what is offered in an intelligible speech act, he denies the validity of an utterance in at least one of three respects, truth, rightness, or truthfulness. His "no" signals that the utterance has failed to fulfil at least one of its three functions (the representation of states of affairs, the maintenance of an interpersonal relationship, or the manifestation of lived experience) because the utterance is not in accordance with either the world of existing states of affairs, our world of legitimately ordered interpersonal relations, or each participant's own world of subjective lived experience (ibid., p. 136–7).

Moral judgments have cognitive content. They represent more than expressions of the contingent emotions, preferences, and decisions of a speaker or action. (ibid., p. 120)

There is a structure that makes everything clearer, running from 1 to 10.

Action and language are intrinsically linked. Deeply embedded in the mind of the researcher is the biblical verse, "by their fruits you will know them" (Matthew 7:15-20.) There is the old adage, actions speak louder than words, and also the quote from James 2:26, faith without good works is dead. ("Just as the body is dead without breath, so is faith dead without good works.")

So we find that all this wisdom is reworked by Habermas, and he uses some of Willet's understanding that language is for our survival. Why?
1. Language conveys meaning
2. Meaning has to have substance
3. Meaning helps to form friendships by
4. Understanding the others' opinions and feelings
5. Because you are able to understand their source
6. You 'can reason out' if their reasons and opinions are valid
7. Every speech act has to be cognitively examined for
8. Truth (external objective world)
9. Rightness (internal objective social world)
10. Truthfulness (internal subjective world)

All this is dialogued together to come to a trusting relationship, in a course of questions and answers and evidence to bring the dialogue partners to a deeper understanding, a deeper meaning of the subject, and new thought, a new creation of both minds, a cognitive meeting place, where they can envision a cooperative action. Habermas has called this communicative action. If the dialogue partners do not agree with one another, and their trust goes, so does the communicative action fade away and die. The test of utterances and actions did not ring true.

There is basic agreement on the interpretative accomplishments of truthful dialogue. It is revolutionary. It is truthful, right, moral, and involves the whole person. It is a thinking exercise in the polis, geared to a receiver. It is social development for a new one-earth concept that calls for wholeness not fragmentation.

The Role of Speech in the Reconciliation Process

Among researchers there is contradiction in the role of speech in the reconciliation process. Murphy considers the courts of justice, where victim statements are allowed. He thinks the justice of the rule of law is being perverted by such angry statements. In this forum, making forgiveness contingent on repentance by the wrongdoer might be justified. Derrida, however, coming from the holocaust perspective, maintains that the emergence of the human rights movement requires forgiveness of the unforgivable. This notion of forgiveness comes from the Judaic/Christian justice system. It is the language of law, the Abrahamic moral tradition on which forgiveness is a central concept. A third notion is moral absolutism, as presented by Joram Haber. There are certain kinds of actions that are absolutely wrong. For instance, Kant also says to be truthful is a sacred and absolutely commanding decree of reason. All these perspectives have developed against a background of a utopian theory of justice, where Rawls sees that the right of each person is to have basic liberty and where social and economic positions are open to all. This has yet to happen. Enright's work in helping others to forgive, an empirical guide for resolving anger and restoring hope, might open the way to lift the veil of ignorance and arrive at some communicative action to enhance our understanding of justice, repentance and forgiveness.

The Reasons for Choosing Peace

Murder, violence, injustice, and indignity are reasons for choosing peace. A reaffirmation of the commandments in various faiths to pursue peace and to affirm the dignity of the other is a reason for peace. One Creator and Guide of the Universe, referred as the Merciful One, demands of us all mercy and compassion. True love of God demands this dialogue. (Seek peace and pursue it: a Jewish call to Muslim-Jewish dialogue). This statement from the Jews matches with the US Bishops' statement about the importance of justice and peace to protect and promote the dignity of the human person, who in turn reflects god. Peace construction grows from a personal movement. It begins with seeing others as the enemy and progresses to dialogue with them and to seeing their needs. This is the idea that God is in everybody. Escalation of war, particularly by war journalism, only shows up the complicity of war. War reporting dehumanizes the other. The hardware of war makes money, thereby making war seem economically necessary. Fostering self-worth and awareness of others, encouraging family groups to work together, and strengthening the educational structure to increase teacher knowledge and support will improve life (through development) rather than create death (through conflict).

Under the models discussed, creating quality of life (development) is a thinking exercise, a truthful dialogue, and an acknowledgement of the needs of others. We are to train our will to be wise. Under these models, creating quality of life remains within the traditions of the three Abrahamic religions. Their teachings and traditions are the same in core respects: love of God and neighbour, forgiveness, mercy, and compassion. Moral consensus comes from codes and traditions, justice, and fairness for all. But a new understanding can come from aspects of forgiveness, repentance and justice already present in judicial system. They present a conflict that has to be thought out, using both sides of the brain to centre ourselves in the area of interplay between the two modes of perception and analysis, from left and right sides of the brain, thereby producing a comprehensive awareness. This awareness can be shared with others to enhance information into knowledge. Dialogue education makes it possible to construct sacred and sane societies in backyards rather than in treaties. Researchers display consensus about the choice to forgive. Enright teaches children how to make a choice to forgive; Hieronymi says forgiveness must be uncompromising; Christians ask The Father to forgive their trespasses. Therein lies the potential to look at a neighbour in an attitude of love.

The question of truthful dialogue being able to construct peace seems to be absurd, considering the amount of money gun manufacturing generates, and considering the entire machinery for war. What incentive would there be to offer something else in lieu of monetary gain? The 138 Muslim Scholars who wrote "A Common Word between Us and You" would proffer the saving of the soul of the human being. But St. Augustine writes that the energy has to be found to pursue peace and allow it to embrace justice. The inner man has to be fed. There are many separate units of study in relationships, but this thesis calls on communication scholars to track the authoritative message of the Abrahamic religions: love God and neighbour. It is this message, this chain in religion, that could be developed from theory to action. In this way, the communication scholar can prepare the way for peace, because peace is in communication. In that great quest for dialogue, a revolutionary new attitude could be created.

The world faces a prudential judgement about its evolution. One way toward a sane, sacred society is to honour human needs, to allow freedom, to acquire knowledge and insight, to foster self-esteem, to show sympathy for the "other", to engage in truthful dialogue, to listen, and to accomplish deeper understanding. This means using the language of peace. It means arriving at a moral consensus. It means being truthful about personal situations and being open-minded about the situation of others. Beyond these, there is the person's will to choose. Choice, including willingness to engage in dialogue for the common good, revolves around choice to forgive, choice to give up anger and resentment, and choice to welcome diversity.

Summary

Through its discussion of social science, humanities, religious and NGO discourses on peace as a human need, forgiveness, reconciliation and ethical communication, this chapter has shown pathways to peace (or life and development rather than conflict and death). It is anticipated that these pathways will inform the thinking of members of interfaith groups who will share their views in the focus groups that will be conducted in this study. The next chapter examines conflict and peace initiatives in South Africa, Ireland and the Middle East.

Chapter Four
Communication and
Conflict Resolution

Introduction

Following on from the examination of conflict and cooperation at international and organizational levels and social science, humanities, religious and NGO discourses on peace as a human need, forgiveness and ethical communication, this chapter considers by way of comparison three scenes of protracted conflict: South Africa, Ireland, and the Middle East. The similarities are discussed below:
1. All worked for peace, (South Africa Truth and Reconciliation Commission).
2. All had introduced settlers (Ireland had 600 years of British rule).
3. All had the enemy "within" their community, not without.
4. Equal rights ("Zionism and Palestinian nationalism clashed over the ownership of the land, the right for self-determination, and statehood" (Rouhana 1998, p. 762).)
5. Lack of education, work, housing for all ("[T]heir demands cannot be met by the same resources at the same time" (Wallensteen 2002, p. 15).)
6. Deep seated experiences of being "wronged" ("[C]onflicts are carried forward by states and states-in-waiting, and are often about the control of land and resources – including people." (Kant 1795).)
7. Various violent and non-violent efforts to claim back what is lost.

8. A final understanding that everyone has to work together and the beginning of community education for peace.

Only two conflict resolutions were resolved. Assassinations of both Arab and Israeli leaders were a feature of the non-resolution in Israel so this chapter examines in turn the histories and peace initiatives in the three conflicts viz. Blacks and Whites in South Africa; Protestant Northern Ireland and Roman Catholic Ireland; and Israelis and Palestinians. In considering the extent to which interfaith organizations engender reconciliation among individuals from different Abrahamic groups, this section tackles the assumption that peacemaking is difficult because of Middle East politics and the geopolitics of the Christian-Muslim-Jewish relationship. It is necessary therefore to examine the pathways Israel is taking towards Arab-Israeli conflict resolution, but also to analyse the other contrasting cases. In South Africa and Northern Ireland, reconciliation has progressed further than it has in the Middle East, in relation to the cessation of violence. To examine the various pathways to resolution, this thesis draws on social scientific literature and on the economic, psychological, cultural, religious, and other factors relevant to the resolution process. Kant's decisive comment, "it follows that a war of extermination, in which the destruction of both parties and of all justice can result, would permit perpetual peace only in the vast burial ground of the human race" (Kant I, 1795), is a call to push ever further to renew the effort for peace.

It needs to be said that many other conflict situations with peaceful initiatives could have been chosen, mostly of British domination, say for instance in India, but in the end Northern Ireland and South Africa were chosen because of their very successful outcomes.

THE CASE OF BLACKS AND WHITES IN SOUTH AFRICA

History of the Conflict

Dutch settlers, the Boers, arrived in South Africa in 1652 to set up a way station for the Dutch East India Company. They clashed with the African inhabitants over land and livestock, with wars erupting from the mid-1700s to the mid-1800s. Based on slavery, the Dutch East India Company "bred a master-servant relationship between the Cape gentry and their slaves inside the colony" (Ohlson, Stedman, Davies 1994, p. 23). Political, ideological, and local cultural forces have played a major role in the production of structural and direct violence in modern Africa. Some African societies put up violent resistance towards the European intruders, but for the most part they engendered a permanent state of internal war as many African rulers embraced the slave trade in order to profit from it (Oholson, Stedman and Davies 1994, p. 20). Race classification underpinned all practices. The colonial power reserved 86 per cent of the land for whites and limited the education and job opportunities for blacks.

When the British seized the colony from the Dutch in 1806, the tension between settlers and colonial authorities intensified. The British wanted control of the Cape in order to secure the sea route to Asian trade. Violence soon erupted between Boer slave-holding farmers and the British, who implemented legislation conducive to the free labour market requirements of the new era. The British Colonial Government overcame minor rebellions by Boer farmers in the first three decades of the 1800s and abolished slavery in 1834. When Britain devolved a measure of self-government to the Cape Colony it insisted on a colour-blind franchise with voting restrictions limited to property or legal employment (ibid., pp. 23-24). Meeting the wartime needs of the Western allies fostered a manufacturing boom in South Africa. The increased strength of an African urban, organized, industrial work force led to growing political strength for organizations that challenged white political domination in South Africa, notably the African National Congress ANC (ibid., p. 40).

For decades South Africa's conflict has provided a framework for discussion of international conflicts between superpowers and competing socioeconomic systems. Apartheid came to South Africa when the National Party (NP) representing Afrikaner extremism won seats in the 1948 elections, amid racial separation. Most Western countries, until the mid-1980s, refused to implement economic sanctions (Lodge 1991, p. 115). The ANC gathered strength though against the "state-enforced control in a system that forces the majority of the population to provide cheap labour while it prevents their social and political mobilization" (Ohlson 1991, p. 222). The ANC predisposition toward a negotiated transition to social democracy may have derived from its own ideological traditions, including a consistent advocacy of racial reconciliation. Since 1969 the ANC has included whites in its membership, and in the 1950s, it functioned within the Congress Alliance, which brought together Indian, coloured, and white congresses as well as a multiracial trade union movement (ibid., p. 125). In 1990 when President F.W. de Klerk of the NP released Nelson Mandela of the ANC, negotiations began for the future of South Africa.

Pathways to Resolution in South Africa

South Africa has been the most embargoed nation in the world. International opposition to South Africa's policy of apartheid and to its policy of regional aggression in southern Africa has since 1963 been expressed in numerous UN Security Council resolutions concerning the trade in arms and military technology with South Africa (ibid.

1991, pp. 245–246). There were, however, internal movements for peace. The ANC had a predisposition toward a negotiated transition to social democracy. The party had its "own ideological traditions, including a consistent advocacy of racial reconciliation. Since 1969 the ANC has included whites in its membership… (and) in the 1950s the ANC functioned within the Congress Alliance, which brought together Indian, coloured and white congresses as well as multiracial trade union movement" (Lodge 1991, p. 125).

Peace Initiative: Apartheid Abandoned

In 1978, P.W. Botha of the National Party became Prime Minister and put in place what Robert Price calls South Africa's "security driven agenda". Apartheid was to be abandoned, reluctantly, to ensure continued white political and economic domination; in its place would be a program of social, economic, and political reforms aimed at drawing what state strategists dubbed "useful blacks" into a new supportive alliance. Purposeful repression would be used to lower black expectations about the extent of change and to alleviate white worries that reform would result in the majority coming to power.

Outcome

Although Botha's program made concessions to the demands and grievances of selected parts of the disenfranchised majority – for example, black trade unions were legalized and local communities were given state permission to end petty discrimination if they so desired – it resolutely maintained direct white minority control of the political system (Ohlson 1994, p. 61).

The overall historical narrative was that in the 1980s conflict resolution ideas were increasingly making a difference in South Africa. For example, the Centre for Intergroup Studies was applying these ideas to the developing confrontation between apartheid and its challengers, with impressive results (Ramsbotham et al. 2005, p. 4).

Peace Initiative: Release of Mandela

Lodge has suggested a historical process in which the principal determinants of a negotiated political transition are internal. Both sides have to understand, he suggests, that unilateral victory is impossible but that substantial gains or concessions can be extracted from a negotiated compromise. "The release of Nelson Mandela, the unbanning of the ANC and other prohibited organizations, the ANC's suspension of guerrilla hostilities, and the onset of constitutional discussion between its leaders and members of the de Klerk administration, all are developments that seem to reflect swifter and more powerful compulsions toward reconciliation" (Lodge 1991, p. 147).

Outcome

South Africa's first non- racial election held on 26 to 28 April 1994 culminated in four years of intensive negotiations. These years were filled with conflict resolution. Political adversaries across the ideological spectrum were engaged in intensive problem solving: debating, exchanging information, learning, and negotiating solutions to many South African conflicts. Political parties and interest groups as well as individual South Africans narrowed the gaps on matters such as a constitution, reduction of violence, economic policies for growth, and redistribution of the wealth. At the same time, however, political parties were engaged in a battle for primacy of power that led to a level of direct political violence unprecedented in recent South African history. "Between February 1990 and December 1993 nearly 13,000 people died in massacres, assassinations, and other forms of political violence, mainly in black townships. During that time radical rhetoric escalated, the political positions of peacemakers weakened, and the economy, in desperate need of domestic and foreign investment, continued to plunge as joblessness and poverty, already high, increased (Ohlson 1994, pp. 185–6).

A settlement among those same parties established the mechanisms for a gradual transition to democracy. Business, labour, and government formed a National Economic Forum to consult and propose solutions to South Africa's economic crisis. In the long run, however, conflict resolution in South Africa has had to rely on cognitive change or "enlightened self- interest" whereby groups "see the long term superiority of social contracts over simple contracts. That change came through learning and problem solving and established a corps of leaders in the ANC, NP, trade unions and business committed to cooperative solutions to South Africa's most intractable problems" (Ohlson 1994, p. 187).

Centuries of white domination, 42 years of apartheid, and more than a decade of war meant that negotiators would have to replace a constitution that entrenched white political and economic power and also would have to confront a state bureaucracy with a vested interest in perpetuating its own privilege.

The stability of any agreement would depend on redressing deep seated gaps between blacks and whites in wealth, income, land, and access to social services, but the ability of policymakers to narrow such gaps was constrained by a poorly performing economy. Nation building would have to overcome the centrifugal pull of narrow identities, a task made difficult by high levels of political and social violence which induce fear and breed mistrust (ibid., p. 134).

Apology and forgiveness were needed.

Peace Initiative: The South African Truth and Reconciliation Commission

"Apology and forgiveness clearly try to deal with the wrong that has been done; another form of acknowledging that wrong has been committed may be achieved through reparation or making amends in some way" (de la Rey 2001, p. 258).

The Truth and Reconciliation Commission (TRC) in South Africa came from the 1995 Promotion of National Unity and Reconciliation Act requiring the TRC to contribute to the building of a historic bridge, linking a deeply divided society to a new future of human rights. The public nature of the event, having an audience, permitted the reconstruction of private, individual trauma. "Victims and perpetrators and those who thought that they were just innocent bystanders now realize their complicity and have an opportunity to participate in each other's humanity in story form" (ibid., p. 260).

Avoiding vindictiveness on the one hand and disregarding wrongs and sufferings on the other underpinned full public disclosure of the human rights violations that had occurred since 1960. As well, "some acknowledgement of responsibility, if not expression of regret (Committee on Human Rights Violations), as well as some measure of reparation for the victims (Committee on Reparations and Rehabilitation), would open up an emotional space sufficient for accommodation if not forgiveness, with the question of punishment or amnesty abstracted or postponed" (Committee on Amnesty) (Asmal et al. 1996; Boraine et al. 1997; Boraine, 2000; Ramsbottom et al. 2005, p. 238–9).

Outcome

Truth commissions and tribunals, by establishing what has actually happened, can help to reduce violence towards the perpetrators while at the same time acknowledging victims' suffering. This then promotes healing. Affirming that the violence was neither normal nor acceptable could help victims feel safer. The punishment of perpetrators, especially of leaders, communicates to the world and to the formerly victimized group that violence against groups is not acceptable. "The truth commission in South Africa was effective in enabling some people to tell their stories and to make the actions of perpetrators public knowledge. However, some of the people who were victimized during the apartheid regime have felt deeply hurt that many perpetrators who confessed what they had done, seemingly without regret or apology, could get amnesty" (Staub 2001, p. 84).

A common assumption about deeply divided societies is that an absence of dialogue is at the source of the conflict. Communication is then presented as the antidote. But in many divided societies there is dialogue even when there is intense conflict. Thus not all types of dialogue may be useful in attaining reconciliation (van der Merwe 1993, p. 263). "Reflective dialogue, which allows disputing parties to articulate to each other and discover the meeting points in their narratives, best fits the requirements of reconciliation" (de la Rey 2001, p. 260).

Peace Initiative: Education and Cultural

The reconciliation process helps to provide an outcome of the conflict resolution when the adversarial groups must continue to live in one political system. There is a need to establish one political, societal, economic, legal, cultural, and educational system that will incorporate the two past rivals. The reconciliation process requires changes in each group's beliefs about its own goals in order to remove the cognitive foundations of the conflict. "The process of reconciliation requires the formation of new beliefs that not only describe realistically the meaning of living in peace but also present the conditions necessary for living in peace" (Bar Tel 2000, pp. 355–359). The educational system can be used to socialize the whole young generation to live in peace with the past enemy. Support in the mass media for the reconciliation process may persuade the society member of its utility and of the possibility of its actualization. Also, the voice of the cultural elite may help to carry out reconciliation. Films and theatrical plays serve as a valuable support for reconciliation (Wallensteen 2002, pp. 145–6).

Reconciliation also requires the evolution of new beliefs about the nature of peace and ways of living in conditions of peace. In South Africa, this means that "special attention has to be given to the process of reconstructing the past – with its acts of discrimination, injustice, killing, and torture … in order to foster societal healing" (Bar Tal 2000, p. 356).

Outcome

All approaches to reconciliation recognize that psychological change has to occur. In other words, there must be a transition to beliefs and attitudes that support peaceful relations between former enemies. Archbishop Tutu states: "It is crucial, when a relationship has been damaged or when a potential relationship has been made impossible, that the perpetrator should acknowledge the truth and be ready and willing to apologize. It helps the process of forgiveness and reconciliation immensely. It is never easy … in almost every language the most difficult words are, 'I am sorry'" (Tutu 2000, p. 269).

In economic performance during the 1990–94 period, South African economic woes intensified. Real GDP per capita declined every year and by the second quarter of 1993 was 13.5 per cent lower than in the second quarter of 1988. Gross fixed investment fell to 16 per cent of GDP, the number of homeless people in South Africa increased to 7.7 million, and a South African bank warned that less than 1 per cent of those who left school would find formal employment in 1994 ("No work for school leavers" Cape Times, May 27, 1993, p. 6) (Ohlson 1994, p. 182).

Evidence suggests the economic struggle continues today, despite the extent of peace dialogue. A chance encounter with a visitor from South Africa[11] who complained about the economy, and the

---

11   The visitor I had from South Africa told me that he was frightened and disturbed by the crime rate, electricity shortages and lack of trained staff in the running of his country. Two of his friends had

internet source *Economist Intelligence Unit Briefing, South Africa's Economy*, from the Economist Intelligence Unit ViewsWire, revealed in 2009 electricity shortages and a slowdown in consumer demand. According to the latest figures from Statistics South Africa, the economy grew by just 2.1 per cent in the first three months of 2008, less than half the rate of the previous quarter (5.3 per cent) and the lowest quarterly rate in six years. Mining production fell by 22.1 per cent in the January/March quarter, declining to its lowest level in 40 years. Households were cutting back on spending, and manufacturing had dropped sharply from an expansion of 8.2 per cent in the September/December quarter to a 1 per cent contraction in the first three months of the year. As well, the Purchasing Managers' Index (PMI) dropped to 49.1 in May from 54.7 in the previous month. Inflation rose to 10.4 per cent in April, the 13th successive month in which the government's 6 per cent target ceiling had been breached (Economist Intelligence Unit ViewsWire 2009)

The figures indicate there still needs to be dialogue about sharing of needs and hopes and that the progress to peace is never ending.

---

been murdered; his brother had been accosted and his arm broken. Despite his injuries his brother had not solicited the assistance of the police because he believed that they would do nothing, and that some policemen could neither read nor write.

The Case of Northern Ireland and the Republic of Ireland

History of the Conflict

Mari Fitzduff lived through the contemporary period of conflict in Ireland, the period known as "the troubles". Historically, Fitzduff sees the arrival of settlers from Britain in 1170 as the start of the conflict. By 1608, what became known as the plantation of Ulster began. To achieve dominance, the British confiscated large tracts of land and used "plantations" of settlers on the island as a means of control. This was opposed by the Irish, and in 1641 there was a Catholic-Gaelic uprising in response to the plantation and a subsequent confiscation of land by Protestant settlers from England and Scotland. In retaliation came the Battle of the Boyne in 1690. It was a victory for Protestant William II over Catholic James II. This victory is still celebrated in many parades in Northern Ireland. To compound matters for the Irish, in 1801 the Act of Union abolished the Irish Parliament and bound Ireland and Britain together as parts of the United Kingdom. The Protestants were very happy with this Union, and in 1912 the Ulster Solemn League and Covenant was signed by more than 400,000 Protestants who wanted to remain in the Union. This was not so for the Irish, hence the famous Easter Uprising in Dublin against British rule erupted in 1916. Within five years, in 1921, a treaty was signed leading to the establishment of an Irish Free State of 26 counties, with the six counties of Northern Ireland remaining British. The Balfour Report (1926) declared that Britain and the Dominions of Canada, South Africa, Australia, New Zealand and the Irish Free State were "autonomous Communities within the British Empire" (http://fourdocs.gov.au/item-did-24.html).

However, the start of the present troubles arose, in part, out of the campaign by Catholics in Northern Ireland for civil rights. Some kind of resolution appeared in 1998 with the Belfast Agreement in which every constituent had to vote to gain a cooperative future. Sometimes this is called the Good Friday Agreement. It took until 1999 for the setting up of a power-sharing Assembly in Northern Ireland (Fitzduff and O'Hagen 2000, p. 2).

O'Leary and McGarry provide another version of the troubles in Ireland. "The nationalists begin their histories of Ireland in 1169 with the first Norman invasion, and seek to persuade their audiences of uninterrupted English brutality in Ireland; while unionists begin their histories with the plantation of Ulster in 1609, and regale their listeners with tales of the survival of Protestants of British stock steadfastly withstanding barbaric sieges ever since" (O'Leary & McGarry 1996, p. 54). Ruane and Todd argue that the proximate cause of conflict comes from "two communities with conflicting economic, political and cultural interests under conditions of an uneven and changing balance of power" (Ruane & Todd 1996, p. 307).

When the British government was pressured to grant independence to the island, and the Unionists threatened to use force, there was a compromise. In 1921 "The British Prime Minister of Britain, Lloyd George, insisted that the island be portioned into two sections, the six counties in the north-east would remain part of the United Kingdom while the other 26 counties would gain independence. Each state would have its own parliament" (Fitzduff and O'Hagan 2000, p. 3).

Ireland became a full republic in 1949, and the British government gave new constitutional guarantees to the Northern Ireland Parliament of Stormont. "The British had used Stormont to suppress nationalists, but when it was destabilized by a legitimate mass democratic movement they intervened to shore up Stormont with a massive security presence, and when reconstructing Stormont proved futile, they opted for direct rule" (O'Leary and McGarry 1996, p. 154). The Anglo-Irish Agreement in 1985 removed any ambiguity about British perceptions and intentions. "The Agreement reiterated the guarantee of Northern Ireland's constitutional status, dependent on the will of a majority in Northern Ireland, but it also recognized the island-wide identity of Northern nationalists and gave the Irish government a role in policy-making and a permanent presence in Northern Ireland in the Anglo-Irish Secretariat" (Ruane and Todd 1996, pp. 134–5).

In the Belfast Agreement of 1998 the parties accepted that the constitutional future of Northern Ireland was to be decided by the people of Northern Ireland. "There would be a power sharing assembly within which the parties would allocate chairs and vice chairs on an agreed basis, and a cross community consensus would be necessary for agreement on issues of major relevance to both communities" (Fitzduff 2002, p. 15).

Pathways to Resolution in Ireland

The struggle for, and against, the union of Ireland and Britain "completed the process of welding Catholics and Protestants into two separate and opposing communal blocks" (Ruane and Todd 1996, p. 36).

Northern Ireland is the site of one fundamental cultural clash: the clash of rival political nationalisms. The central problem which must be addressed in the peace making process is for "each national community (to be) equally secure, recognized and expressed" (McGarry & O'Leary 1995, p. 264).

The British government granted limited independence to Ireland after the great war of 1914-1918. However, the Unionists of Northern Ireland threatened to use force if they were coerced into a united Ireland and began to mobilize private armies against such an eventuality.

The Case of Northern Ireland and the Republic of Ireland   133

Peace Initiative: A Compromise

In 1921 the island was divided into two sections, each state having its own parliament. "Irish nationalist leaders were divided over this suggestion, but the offer was eventually accepted by those leaders who were sent to conduct treaty negotiations with the British ... it was also accepted by the unionists" (Fitzduff & O'Hagan 2000, p. 3).

Outcome

There was however bitter civil conflict between nationalists who accepted partition and those who rejected it. The Irish Free State was formed in 1923. In 1937 The Irish Constitution adopted the title Eire (the Irish word for Ireland) for the state. The state then declared itself a Republic on Easter Monday, 18 April 1949 (Fitzduff and O'Hagan 2003, p. 3). There was, however, discrimination against the Catholics in Northern Ireland, who were inspired by a worldwide non-violent movement for civil rights to secure rights to votes, jobs, and services. "The campaign of violence and counter violence by the Loyalist paramilitaries, with attempts at containment by both the police and army, lasted until the ceasefires of 1994" (Fizduff and O'Hagan 2003, p. 4).

Peace Initiative: 1974 Power Sharing Assembly

In 1974 the government negotiated an agreement among the main constitutional parties to a form of power sharing in government (Fitzduff 2002, p. 11).

Outcome

This initiative survived for only five months before it was destroyed by the Loyalist paramilitaries (Fitzduff 2002, p. 11).

On 5th May, 1981 Bobby Sands, the IRA leader held at Maze prison dies after refusing food for 66 days. Nine others die of starvation between May 12 and August 20 1981. Many people believe them to be the struggle for independence, and around 10,000 people attend Bobby Sands funeral. The hunger strike radicalised national politics and was the driving force that enabled Sinn Fein to become a mainstream political party (Northern Ireland Hunger Strike).

Peace Initiative: 1985 Anglo-Irish Agreement

On 15 November 1985 an international treaty was signed by the Irish Prime Minister Dr Garret FitzGerald and the British Prime Minister Margaret Thatcher. This Anglo-Irish Agreement (AIA) was proclaimed as a major initiative to replace antagonism with accommodation. The official communiqués declared that the AIA would promote peace and reconciliation between the two traditions in Northern Ireland and across both parts of Ireland and that it would consolidate better relations between Great Britain and Ireland (O'Leary and McGarry 1996, p. 221).

Outcome

Backed by Britain and the Republic of Ireland, the agreement was rejected by the Unionists, who saw it as diluting the union with Britain, and by Sinn Fein, who saw it as confirming partition. But "[i]t has proved to be an extremely important key to the development of an eventual political solution, as it considerably increased the capacity of both governments to address the conflict as a joint problem" (Fitzduff 2002, p. 12).

Throughout the 1970s and early 1980s community development and community workers were funded by district councils. There was a new phase of policy making, explicitly designed to foster contact and cultural tolerance, equality, and pluralism between Protestant and Catholic. "A Central Community Relations Unit was set up in 1987, with the role of monitoring government policy for its effects on community relations" (Ruane and Todd 1996, p. 187).

Following the agreement, it became obvious by the mid '80s to many people within Sinn Fein that a continuing military campaign by the IRA (Irish Republican Army) would not necessarily achieve a British withdrawal from Northern Ireland. It was also obvious to the British army that, although it could contain the conflict, it could not, given the existing community support, defeat the IRA through military means (Fitzduff 2002, p. 12).

Peace Initiative: 1990–92 Inter-Party Talks

The Secretary of State for Northern Ireland, Peter Brooke, began a series of meetings with all political parties, except Sinn Fein, to see if any agreement could be reached between them about possible political ways forward.

A joint UUP-DUP document on 'Administrative and legislative devolution' formed the basis of their negotiating posture. "It envisaged an executiveless assembly based upon strong committees, in which the elected parties would be proportionally represented … and it also foresaw an assembly large enough to ensure that there would be no danger that Unionists lacked a permanent majority on every committee.

'Proportionality, yes: power-sharing no' was this document's code (O'Leary McGarry 1996, p. 315).

Outcome

The differences between the parties proved to be too difficult to surmount and the talks ended in summer 1992.

Peace Initiative: 1993 Downing Street Declaration

The British Prime Minister in December 1993 signed a Joint Declaration for Peace, which again allowed for the possibility of Irish unification, albeit with the consent of a majority of the electorate in the North (McGarry and O'Leary, p. 47).

The Joint Declaration for Peace gave these rights:

> *The right of free political thought; the right of freedom and expression of religion; the right to pursue democratically national and political aspirations; the right to seek constitutional change by peaceful and legitimate means; the right to live wherever one chooses without hindrance; the right to equal opportunity in all social and economic activity, regardless of class, creed, sex or colour (McGarry and O'Leary 1995, p. 410).*

Outcome

In September 1994, the IRA halted its military operations in order to achieve its aspirations through the political process. Six weeks later the Loyalist paramilitaries also called a ceasefire (Fitzduff 2002, pp. 13–14).

Peace Initiative: 1995 Framework Document

The Frameworks for the Future comprised two distinct but related documents: a Framework for Accountable Government in Northern Ireland, the responsibility of the British government, and a New Framework for Agreement, or Joint Framework Document, the joint responsibility of the British and Irish governments. "The former document describes London's assessment of the internal settlement most likely to command support across the parties in Northern Ireland ... the latter document presents the views of both governments on the relationships which should be established between

Northern Ireland and the Irish Republic" (O'Leary and McGarry 1996, p. 335-6).

The Joint Framework Document focuses on North-South and British-Irish relations. It envisages institutions which allow "greed, dynamic, new co-operative and constructive relationships" (Ruane and Todd 1996, p. 298).

Outcome

Unionists felt that these proposals represented just one more step on what many of them saw as an inevitable road to a united Ireland. But the ceasefires remained. In May 1995 the government entered into ministerial dialogue with Sinn Fein, which also committed itself to discussing arms decommissioning along with other matters of political interest (Fitzduff 2002, p. 127).

Peace Initiative: 1998 Belfast Agreement

The Belfast Agreement delivered on Good Friday 1998 was to lead to a power-sharing government between most of the political parties in Northern Ireland as well as to guarantees on issues of equality and cultural diversity for all communities. By 2001, notwithstanding the various wrangles on policing and decommissioning that were to follow the agreement, all the major political parties had together agreed on a program for government for Northern Ireland on issues such as education, health, and economic development that would be of joint benefit to all of their constituents (Fitzduff 2002, p. xiii).

In many ways, this agreement grew from the work of the Community Relations Council in Northern Ireland. Saunders (1999) offers a fine analysis of the role of sustained dialogue in attempts to transform intractable ethnic and racial conflicts (Ramsbotham et al. 2005, p. 292).

Mari Fitzduff, who lived through the violence, says the Belfast Agreement was the result of the development of many conflict resolution initiatives in the fields of equality, diversity, and security work, as well as political and community dialogue (Fitzduff 2002, p. xiii).

Outcome

The agreement was subsequently endorsed by referenda in Northern Ireland on Friday 22 May 1998. In December 1999 a legislative Assembly of both unionist and nationalist politicians was finally set up to share power in Northern Ireland, with ministers and committee members drawn from both sides of politics (Fitzduff and O'Hagan 2000, p. 2).

Implementation of the Agreement

The Independent Commission on Policing in Northern Ireland was set up as part of the Agreement reached in Belfast on 10 April 1998. In a preamble to that Agreement, the participants set out its main purposes:

1. We believe that the Agreement we have negotiated offers a truly historic opportunity for a new beginning.

2. The tragedies of the past have left a deep and profoundly regrettable legacy of suffering.

We must never forget those who have died or been injured, and their families. But we can best honour them through a fresh start, in which we firmly dedicate ourselves to the achievement of reconciliation, tolerance, and mutual trust, and to the protection and vindication of the human rights of all. (Patten Report)

The agreement came into play on 2 December, 1999. A bomb attack in August 1998 in Omagh which killed both Protestants and Catholics, the work of a dissenting Republican group, caused a great deal of shock. The effect on the political leaders was that in September 1998, David Trimble, the leader of the Ulster Unionist party and now first minister designate in the new assembly, met

Gerry Adams, the leader of Sin Fein, for their first face-to-face meeting. Gradually the various aspects of the agreement began to be implemented (Fitzduff 2002, p. 131).

In November and December 1999, the IRA confirmed that it would appoint a representative to the Independent Commission on Decommissioning. A Power sharing executive was set up simultaneously on 2 December 1999. In October 2001 the IRA announced that it had begun to decommission its weapons.

One way of making the commitment is for leaders on both sides to lock their personal political fortunes so strong to one option that they could not go down the other path without resigning. In real peace processes, confidence-building measures, agreement on procedures or a timetable for moving forward, and public commitments by leaders are among the methods of building and sustaining a peace process (Ramsbotham et al. 2005, p. 173).

And so it was in Northern Ireland. Ramsbotham also makes mention of mediation, which is important when face-to-face meetings are difficult to arrange. Mediation and back channels were used in the peace processes of Northern Ireland. "The SDLP (Social Democratic and Labor Party), Sinn Fein, and the Irish government established communications by sending secret messages through representatives of the Clonard monastery" (Ramsbotham et al. 2005, p. 168).

Much of the peace building came from community relations organizations in Northern Ireland, which built networks of people across the communities as a long term resource for peace building. "Thus the encounter between conflict resolution ideas and social and political forces can subtly transform the context of conflict (Ramsbotham 2005, p. 170). Ramsbotham defines the three phases of conflict resolution as intervention, stabilization, and normalization (Ramsbotham et al. 2005, p. 198).

Reconstruction

The term peace-building was conceived by Johan Galtung. It was meant to characterize progression towards positive peace following the ending of war.

> *The main priority of international efforts, however, has been to secure sufficient stability to avoid the recurrence of war and sometimes also to introduce a democratic system. As a result, the term reconstruction is problematic for some. For example, in Northern Ireland, Mari Fitzduff says, "'reconstruction' is a no-go term – it implies that one reconstructs society to resemble what it was like before the conflict … (this) implies going back to a past which exemplifies the very factors that created the conflict." (Austin 2004, p. 375) (Ramsbotham 2005, p. 186)*

It is generally agreed that the peace process in Northern Ireland was developed from a combination of factors.

These include a realisation by both the IRA and the British Army that the war could not be won militarily, and the decision by the IRA to develop politics, through its political party Sinn Fein, as an alternative way to fight for political goals.

Another factor was the willingness of the Social Democratic Party and the Labor Party to engage with Sinn Fein in pursuing common nationalist political goals by peaceful means.

Third, there was a changing social and economic context in which much discrimination against Catholics was addressed and in which a legal and social infrastructure to address issues of inequality and show a respect for diversity was developed.

Fourth was a willingness within society, including among business, trade union, and community groups, to actively engage in political leverage for peace.

The development of some new political parties by the Loyalists and by the Women's Coalition fed some new thinking into the political landscape.

A changing international context helped too. The United States Government, US businessmen, and South Africa too assisted in developing peace processes (Fitzduff and O'Hagan 2000, p. 6).

Finally, Ian Paisley of the DUP and Gerry Adams of Sinn Fein began power- sharing on 8 May 2007.

THE CASE OF ISRAEL AND PALESTINE

History of the Conflict

Palestine was ruled by a succession of kingdoms and empires, with the Ottoman Turks in control from the 1500s until the latter days of World War I. The present Israeli-Palestinian conflict originated with the appearance of Zionism around the turn of the previous century as a communal clash between indigenous Palestinians and Jewish immigrants to Palestine. Zionism aimed at the establishment of a Jewish state in Palestine. However, because on the same land lived Arabs who had their own national identity as Palestinians ... Zionism and Palestinian nationalism clashed over the ownership of the land, the right for self-determination, and statehood (Rouhana 1998, p. 762).

Also it has been said that "[t]he most significant division and source of internal conflict in Israel society is between its Jewish majority and its Arab minority" (Landau 1997, p. 126).

The Balfour Declaration (November 1917) was a letter sent to Lord Balfour from Baron Rothschild, the leader of the Jewish Community, stating Great Britain's commitment to "a national homeland for Jewish people". The declaration was accepted by the League of Nations in 1922 (Stand for Israel).

The post-1945 period saw the involvement of the United States of America in the Middle East as oil companies had economic domination, and it saw "the need to protect the state of Israel" (Jamieson 2006, p. 177).

In 1947, the United Nations declared the partition of Palestine into two states, one Arab and one Jewish. "After the establishment of Israel in 1948 a bitter hatred grew up between Jews and Muslims" (Jamieson 2006, p. 10). Five Arab states declared war against Israel. Israel won and expanded its borders beyond those designated by the UN resolution (Rouhana 1998, p. 762). The Palestinians who lived in the portion of Palestine on which Israel was established were dispersed as refugees.

In 1967 war erupted between Israel and Egypt, Jordan, and Syria. "In June 1967, immediately after the war, Israel annexed East Jerusalem, declaring the two parts of the city as Israel's capital and extending the status of residents (but not citizens) to its Arab population. The rest of the West Bank and Gaza remained under occupation.... Israel also began a process of establishing Jewish settlements in the West Bank and Gaza and around East Jerusalem" (Rouhana 1998, p. 762).

Armistice agreements, brokered through United Nations mediation in 1949, did not stop violence in 1956, 1967 and 1973, with an Israeli invasion of Lebanon in 1982. The United States mediated disengagement agreements between Egypt and Israel after the 1973 war and brought about the peace process that resulted in the signing of the Camp David accords. However, the Palestinian issue was excluded. Thus the Middle East conflict has moved to relations between Israelis and Palestinians. In 1987 there was the first Palestinian intifada (uprising) against Israeli occupation. After the Gulf War in 1991, the United States and Russia initiated formal peace negotiations between Israel and its Arab neighbours, with little success. In 1993, through back-channel negotiations mediated by Norwegian academics and officials, came an in-principle agreement on a transition toward self-rule for Palestinians in the

West Bank and Gaza, and a break-through of mutual recognition by the Israeli government and the PLO. Palestinians recognized the right of Israel to exist in peace and security, and Israeli recognized the PLO as the legitimate representative of the Palestinian people (Fisher 1997, pp. 64–65). It was rejected.

An attempt at reconciliation at Camp David in the USA in 2000, and a Geneva Accord in 2003 both failed. The second Palestinian intifada began in 2000. Negation of the other is a central element of each party's own identity. "Each party finds it necessary to deny the other's authenticity as a people, the other's links to the land, and the other's national rights, especially its right to national self-determination through the establishment of an independent state in the land both claim" (Kelman 2008, p. 26).

Pathways to Resolution in Israel

Peace Theorists

Reconciliation, a consequence of successful conflict resolution, appears as an issue in the post Cold War era. "Over the course of these years we have witnessed an increase in the frequency, intensity and deadliness of deep-rooted conflicts, not across national borders but between ethnic or other identity groups within a single political unit" (ibid., p. 15). It is mutual trust and mutual acceptance that have to be highlighted when we think about interaction between groups who are sensitive about their security, dignity and well-being. "Each party's need for assurances about its continued national existence is probably the central issue in the conflict and in efforts to resolve it. This issue is directly linked to what I see as the psychological core of the Israeli-Palestinian conflict" (ibid., p. 354).

Kelman believes that in the Israeli-Palestinian case the mutual denial of the other's identity has been a central feature of the conflict over the decades and that when reconciliation occurs each side must take responsibility for the wrong it has done to the other and for the course of the conflict (Kelman 2007: 313). Reconciliation assumes that the conflictual relationship between the parties will be resolved through a process of conflict resolution (Kelman 2006, p. 23). There are four kinds of impacts related to the perception of change. In the context of Israeli-Palestinian interactions they are: learning that there is someone to talk to and something to talk about; learning to distinguish between dreams and operational programs; learning that mutual concessions may create a new situation, setting a process of change into motion; and learning about the occurrence or possibility of structural changes in the leadership of the other side (Kelman 1979, p. 117).

The theorist Edward Azar in his work on protracted social conflicts shows that lack of security is at the heart of some group violence. "The prolonged, and often violent struggle by communal groups (is) for such basic needs as security" (Azar 1991, p. 93). Azar identifies more than 60 examples of a new type of conflict, which revolve around the questions of communal identity (Ramsbotham 2005, p. 85).

Peace Initiative: First Camp David, September 1978

Some conflicts can be resolved when the parties realize, perhaps with the help of a third party, that their perceptions of divergent interests are erroneous. "Once uncovered and corrected, erroneous assumptions can lead to mutually satisfactory ways of resolving a conflict, as illustrated by President Jimmy Carter's mediation leading to the Camp David Accords of 1978 between Israel and Egypt" (Fry and Fry 1997, p. 11). Carter's initial efforts were unacceptable to both sides. It was discovered however, that Israel wanted its borders to be safe, and that Egypt was interested in sovereignty. "First, Carter recounted how real progress was made after Begin and Sadat were given the opportunity to interact informally (Carter 1982). Second, the fact that Carter invited the disputants to Camp David in Maryland illustrates the utility of choosing a neutral location for mediations, and the fact that he kept Begin and Sadat isolated from the pressures and influences of constituencies and the press shows his concern to use a closed site" (Fry and Fry 1997, p. 11).

Outcome

The agreement formed the basis of a 1979 treaty between Egypt and Israel, with Israel withdrawing from Egyptian territory.

Peace Initiative: The Oslo Accords, August 1993

"The Oslo Accords were finalized in Oslo, Norway on 20 August 1993 and officially signed at a public ceremony in Washington DC on 13 September, 1993. They "outlined a set of principles that governed an interim period of Palestinian self-rule in the West Bank and Gaza, to be implemented in stages and to be followed by final status negotiations regarding the most difficult issues of the conflict: the future of Jewish settlement in the West Bank and Gaza, the status of Jerusalem, the return of Palestinian refugees, the borers between Israel and a future Palestinian entity" (Rouhana 1998, p. 763).

Outcome

This agreement was seen as a breakthrough in the Palestinian/Israeli conflict.

The accords opened the way to a self-governing Palestinian authority, mutual recognition of Israel and the PLO and final status talks on other dividing issues. Yet the failure to implement the accords and Israel's continuing subordination of the Palestinians living in the occupied territories raise troubling questions about whether it was ever appropriate to attempt conflict resolution in the first place between such unequal parties (Ramsbotham et al. 2005 p. 176).

"Ten years later, most of the provisions of the Accords were suspended, the key final status issues of the conflict remained unresolved, the violent occupation of Gaza and the west bank continued and Palestinian suicide bombers were retaliating by blowing up Israeli civilians" (Ramsbotham et al. 2005, p. 181).

Abu-Nimer (1999) gives an Arab viewpoint: "Israeli and Palestinian opposition groups have successfully blocked the peace process. On the Israeli side, the right wing and religious fundamentalists' campaign against the peace process resulted in further religious, political and ethnic polarization in Israeli society. In November 1996 the prime minister was assassinated by a fanatic religious Jew. On the Palestinian side, the Islamic movement (Hamas and the Islamic Jihad) has launched fierce suicidal bomb attacks on Israeli cities ... and (there is) economic deterioration as a result of the siege imposed by the Israeli authority in response to the suicidal bombs" (Abu-Nimer 1999, p. 133-4). The denouement of this process was the construction of what the Arabs call the apartheid wall, symbolizing the Sharon government's intention to keep the Palestinians down and out (Ramsbotham et al. 2005, pp. 181–2). Neither Rabin nor Peres was prepared at that time to accept a Palestinian state. Violence on both sides followed: the Hebron massacre attacks by Hamas and the assassination of Prime Minister Rabin. With the election of Netanyahu, the Israeli government turned away from the Oslo process.

Peace Initiative: Second Camp David, July 2006

The second Camp David summit was on 11–24 July 2000, with Bill Clinton, Ehud Barak, and PLO Chairman Yasser Arafat. The purpose was to negotiate the final settlement of the 1999 Oslo Agreement, but they were unable to come to agreement.

"At the Camp David talks in 2000, Israeli Prime Minister Barak went further than any of his predecessors in appearing to accept

Palestinian sovereignty over East Jerusalem, and being willing to return 91 per cent – but not all – of the West Bank to the Palestinians" (Ramsbotham et al. 2005, p. 182). Wallensteen suggests that when a solution was presented in July 2000 it may have been too late. The agreement involved elements of the division of functional influence, sovereignty, and guarantees, and the issue of Jerusalem was left to the last stage (Wallensteen 2002, p. 186).

Outcome

It was still not enough. Too many other matters remained unsolved, according to expectation, leaving little confidence for settling the issue. Leaving important matters to the last stages might have been counter-productive. But so probably is the opposite strategy of solving the most difficult issues first. "Difficult questions have to be tackled when confidence and momentum are at their highest" (Wallensteen 2002, p. 186). According to Barak, "The Palestinians said that I (and Clinton) presented our proposals as a diktat, take it or leave it. This is a lie. Everything proposed was open to continued negotiations. They could have raised counter-proposals. But they never did" (Morris 2002, p. 44). Barak implies that under the prodding of the intifada the revisionists ignored the shift in the Israeli and American positions between July and the end of 2000. Israel had agreed to Washington's proposal that it withdraw from about 95 per cent of the West Bank with substantial territorial compensation for the Palestinians from Israel proper, and that the Arab neighbourhoods of Jerusalem would become sovereign Palestinian territory (Morris 2002, p. 44).

Peace Initiative: Geneva Accord, October 2003

In mid-October 2003, a group of prominent Israelis and Palestinians initiated a virtual final status peace agreement (Geneva Accord 2003).

Ramsbotham states that under this peace plan, Israel would withdraw to the internationally recognized 1967 borders and Palestine would become a state.

> Jewish settlements, except those included in exchanges, would revert to Palestinian sovereignty; Jerusalem would be divided, with Palestinian sovereignty over Arab parts of East Jerusalem and the Temple Mount. In return, the Palestinian negotiators were prepared to concede the right of Palestinian refugees to return to their homes. It was a painful concession, abandoning a pillar of faith of the Palestinian struggle. (Ramsbotham et al. 2005, pp. 82–3)

Outcome

Most Palestinians rejected the Geneva Accords on this account, while the Israeli government rejected the territorial proposals out of hand (ibid., p. 183). As Kant writes: "No treaty of peace shall be held valid in which there is tacitly reserved matter for a future war" (Kant 1795).

Peace Initiative: Annapolis, November 2007

At the United States Naval Academy in Annapolis, Maryland, the conference articulated a two-state solution as the mutually agreed equal outline for addressing the Israeli Palestinian conflict. Hamas, in power on the Gaza Strip, was not present.

Outcome

This has not been ratified, and the participants are exiting: Olmert from Israel, Bush from USA, and Brown from England.

The Role of Religion

The Role of Religion in South African, Northern Ireland and Israel/Palestine Conflicts

I revisit the South African, Northern Ireland and Israel Palestinian conflicts and peace initiatives to consider the role of religion in a political situation.

To supplement the bare bones of the peace initiatives, the role of religions in South Africa bore a fruit that not only helped South African society to heal, but which was a role model for the whole world. Mandela handed out the Truth and Reconciliation Commission not to judges, but to two people who were Christian leaders. The Black Anglican Archbishop Desmond Tutu, and the Methodist leader Alex Boraine. Boraine had come to the belief that a false gospel of apartheid was being lived under South African Government policies.

Racism which is fundamentally a denial of personhood to another human being is seen in all its monstrous inhumanity of white superiority and imposed black inferiority in South Africa.... The only solution, it seemed to me at the time, was that the fire of racism had to be countered and overcome with another fire-blazing love which had at its heart justice and reconciliation (Boraine, p. 19). Boraine explains to us that "in the speeches I made in Parliament during those twelve years, the emphasis was on trying to confront the government with the bankruptcy and the horror of its policies. I little anticipated that transformation would come on a voluntary basis and that the government would move away from the heart of its policies. (ibid., p. 21)

The Report of the Truth and Reconciliation Commission was handed over to President Nelson Mandela on October 29, 1998. The five volumes of the Report contain a detailed account of gross human rights violations committed by the state, former homeland regimes and the liberation movements in and outside Africa. The wholly secular world of dealing with moral issues was put aside, for truth, mercy and compassion and some forgiveness. Justice was sacrificed for mercy and compassion. So the major factor in the role of religion in politics is the conscience of the religious person. If they really believe something is wrong, are they going to right it with a right and not a wrong? That is, if there is violence to a person or persons, the religious person will find a way to remediate the situation. Then violence will not be returned with violence.

> There is now a new kind of justice, transitional justice. It is not a 'special' kind of justice, but an approach to achieving justice in times of transition from conflict and/or state repression. It can be used to try and restore civic trust and strengthen democratic rule of law where there have been human rights abuses on a large scale. It is not only the victims who have been affected, but the society in which they live, as a whole. The State has a duty to make sure that the violations will not recur, and to reform institutions that were either involved in or incapable of preventing abuses. (International Centre for Transitional Justice)

Religion Entering Secular Politics

To begin, to open up the question, we ask "What are the ways in which religion enters into and influences human values and human action?" (Glock & Stark 1965, p. 172).

In South Africa Boraine stepped over the line from church leadership to secular politician for a religious reason, a religious value, that is, that the South African Government were putting into place a false gospel. In Northern Ireland, after 600 years of domination by the British, guns were already blazing. Where is the religious leadership here?

Juergensmeyer interviewed Tom Hartley about the religious component in the Northern Ireland Troubles.

Hartley said he basically agreed with Gerry Adams that republicans were engaged in an "anticolonial struggle that had nothing to do with religion. They simply wanted the British out" (Juergensmeyer 2000 p. 37). However, the religions had different thought processes.

Catholics were hierarchal. All Catholics in a region such as Ireland are part of a unified community, the leaders of which can generally count on the loyalty of their people. "When Gerry Adams participated in peace processes earlier in 1998, he could do so in secret, Hartley said, knowing that his party would stand behind him, even if they did not know what the terms of his agreement would be" (ibid., p. 38). Hartley is an Irish republican politician and activist. The Irish Protestants on the other hand were democratic. Protestant leadership was based not on office, but charisma.

In general Adams had much more support within the Catholic community than any single leader within the Protestant camp.

But there was more than a different way of thinking. Juergensmeyer kept on with his questions and found out, that in fact, something had happened within the Catholic Church.

"I asked Hartley ... had Sinn Fein in many ways replaced the official Catholic Church, especially in acting as spokesperson for the community and providing a moral voice for the masses? ... he acknowledged in some ways Sinn Fein had taken over the role of moral leadership that he feels the Church had abdicated. In a curious way, Sinn Fein has been pioneering in a new kind of religious community, a kind of Irish political Catholicism" (ibid., p. 43).

So even though Sinn Fein encouraged a certain Northern Irish revival of Catholicism, Ian Paisley and his political and religious organisations have stirred a revival of Protestant culture and thought within their community also.

What was very different in Northern Ireland was the input of women. The Nobel Peace Prize, in 1976, was awarded to the Northern

Ireland Peace Movement. Betty Willliams, a Protestant, and Mairead Corrigan, a Catholic, came together to work for peace in Northern Ireland and to organize their famous peace demonstrations. (Northern Ireland Peace Movement).

Also, a new political party, The Northern Ireland Women's Coalition, NIWC, succeeded in getting elected to the multiparty tasks that led to the Belfast agreement.

The Northern Ireland Women's Coalition (NIWC) was a minor political party. In 1996 it was founded by Catholic academic Monica McWilliams and Protestant social worker Pearl Sagar to contest the elections in the Northern Ireland Forum, the body for all-party talks which led to the Belfast Agreement. The party did not espouse a particular ideology and campaigned principally around the fact that it was led by women rather than men. It declined to take any position on whether Northern Ireland should be part of the United Kingdom or the Republic of Ireland, but strongly opposed sectarian violence from both sides. It attracted support from former supporters of the Alliance Party of Northern Ireland, but also the Social Democratic and Labor Party and the Ulster Unionist Party.

The party claimed credit for the inclusion of a commitment to integrated education in the agreement, as did the much larger Alliance Party.

So here is conscience again – calling Catholic and Protestant women to walk over the line and begin to work together (Northern Ireland Women's Coalition).

Extended Look at the Role of Religion in the Israel/Palestine Conflict

Earlier, we have seen that conflict theorists think that land is at the center of the conflict. However, I have approached the Abrahamic communities as family communities. All having common connections in history, and able to call Abraham their father in faith. So if we look at this conflict from an extended way – we look for the connections and commonalities:

1. Israel is a Jewish State, and the proposed Palestinian State would be Muslim.
2. Both Jews and Muslims have lived on this land for thousands of years.
3. They are genetically connected. Both have Abraham as their earthly father, in the common DNA kind of way that we find out today with gene research. The Jews are descended from Isaac and the Arab Muslims from Ishmael, both sons of Abraham, but with different mothers; Isaac from Sarah, and Ismael from Hagar. They both had life and death experiences with their father, but, eventually, buried him together in peace. (Gen. 25.9).
4. The religious role in the Oslo Accords was negative in the extreme. The Jewish peacemaker Yitzhak Rabin was assassinated on November 4th 1995 by a far-right-wing Zionist Yigal Amir from his own country, who did not want him to sign the Peace Treaty. Extreme outbursts of activism were "not just expressions of disagreement with policy, however; they were signs of frustration with a world gone awry. The dissenters' anxiety was personal as well as political, and in a fundamental way, their fears were intensely religious" (Juergensmeyer 2000–2003 p. 45).
5. Twenty percent of the Jewish population of Israel can be said to be of the religious right, under the banner of Zionism. Zionism is the national movement for the return of the Jewish people to their homeland and the resumption of Jewish sovereignty in the land of Israel (Zionism, Jewish virtual library). Historical ties and religious tradition link the Jewish people to the land of Israel. Juergensmeyer explains that "In talking to Israel's religious activists , it became clear to me that what they were defending was not only the political entity of the State of Israel, but a vision of Jewish society that had ancient roots" (ibid., p. 46).

6. There was also an 'enemy' within the Muslim camp. The Egyptian Anwar Sadat was assassinated on 6th October 1981 by fundamentalist army officers after he had negotiated a peace treaty with Israel.
7. The same negativity can be seen within the Hamas political party who is governing Gaza at the present moment. They have in their constitution a very negative religious indictment of the Jewish people. The Hamas Covenant 1988, in the preamble, states that Israel will continue to exist until Islam will obliterate it. Article 6 includes "The Islamic Resistance movement strives to raise the banner of Allah over every inch of Palestine". Article 13 includes "there is no solution for the Palestine question except through jihad (Yale Law School 1988). According to Sheik Omar Abdul Rahman in an interview shortly after the 1993 bombing of the World Trade Centre, a Muslim can "never call for violence," only for "love, forgiveness and tolerance." But he added that "if we are aggressed against, if our land is usurped, we must call for hitting the attacker and the aggressor to put an end to the aggression" (ibid.).

The Muslims, Jews and Christians in the research groups throw a light onto a common way forward for the seemingly impossible and unchangeable attitudes of family members of Abraham. They discuss from a family point of view enemies, forgiveness, and the construction of peace. The way forward is with remediations that can begin where you are living. They also dialogued about fundamentalists, hoping that they would achieve a deeper faith, and coming to the conclusion that they had to accept the good they held, while also recognizing in them what was not good. The action I speak of now is that of Boraine. He discerned and confronted the South African Government with the premise that they were living out a false gospel. So, for us, we can look at the evidence that the common commandment to love God and neighbour is not being taught in Abrahamic communities. The focus groups have reached this conclusion, that it is not being taught, and remember, it has to be taught before it can be put into practice. The focus groups have stood up and spoken with a plea for its reinstatement. As well, H. M. King Abdullah II bin Al- Hussein of Jordon, through HRH Prince Ghazi, has already stood up in the United Nations, saying that religion has to be part of any solution to interfaith harmony (Video UN Prince Ghazi). He speaks on behalf of the Hashemite Kingdom of Jordan and the 29 other co-sponsors: Albania; Azerbaijan; Bahrain; Bangladesh; Costa Rica; the Dominican Republic; Egypt; El Salvador; Georgia; Guatemala; Guyana; Honduras; Kazakhstan; Kuwait; Liberia; Libya; Mauritius; Morocco; Oman; Paraguay; Qatar; the Russian Federation; Saudi Arabia; Tanzania; Tunisia; Turkey; the United Arab Emirates; Uruguay and Yemen. On 20th October 2010, in the UN resolution A/RES/65/5, the General Assembly proclaimed "the first week in February every year the World Interfaith Harmony Week" (UN Interfaith Harmony). The UN encourages all States to support the message of interfaith harmony in the world's Churches, Mosques, Synagogues, Temples and other places of worship based on love of God and neighbour. These questions are internal questions for all religions. The 138 Muslim scholars tell us that we all will lose our soul if we do not begin to make peace (138 Muslim Scholars). In the researcher's opinion this is the articulation of the problem for the world today. Whoever listens and takes heed, and whatever happens, there is only one outcome. No one will be found to be perfect. All need mercy and compassion, and a perception that peace is possible. But it will be a peace that will include religion in some way.

Juergensmeyer talks about religious activists taking an active part in secular politics, "Few religious activists are willing to retreat to the time when secular authorities ran the public arena and religion remained safely within the confines of churches, mosques, temples and synagogues. Most religious activities ... dream of restoring religion to what they regard as its rightful position at the centre of public consciousness" (Juergensmeyer 2000, p. 241). We know, now of course, that consciousness means that our brain mechanisms will automatically "promote action readiness" (McGilchrist 2009, p. 222).

The Process of Reconciliation

The process of reconciliation depends on the following factors: successful conflict resolution; acts that reflect a desire to change adversarial relationships into peaceful relationships; external supportive conditions, such as a peaceful international climate; and the strength or weakness of the opposition to the peace process (Bar-Tal 2000, pp. 351-365).

Arab-Jewish Encounter Programs

Muhammad Abu-Nimer critiques Arab-Jewish encounter programs. These programs are run in Arab and Jewish schools in Israel, with teachers and students as participants. He concludes that they act as control mechanisms, reinforcing asymmetric power structures. Although concerned about lack of preparation and follow up, he does admit some improvement in relationships, but in his opinion, the micro structure has had no effect on the macro structure. Eliminating hatred, stereotyping, and fear at the micro level will eventually produce positive changes such as understanding, knowledge, and tolerance. This will in turn correct the micro-level problems. But, writes Abu-Nimer:

> *Those who oppose this argument claim that the intervention program organizations do not confront the root causes of the micro-level problems on which they focus their energy. Fears, stereotypes, and hatred are a result of the macro-level problems of occupation, discrimination policy against the Palestinian minority in Israel, and definition of Jewish state. (Abu-Nimer 1999, pp. 152–3)*

Abu Nimer prefers the conflict resolution approach. " ... based on the fact that there are conflicts between Arabs and Jews in Israel, and that facing and discussing these conflicts is a constructive rather than a destructive act. Currently, by avoiding discussion of the political issues and power relations issues in Arab-Jewish programs, Arabs and Jews are contributing to the escalation of the conflict in the future" (Abu-Nimer 1999, p. 167). Abu–Nimer saw that in these encounters "the dominance of the Hebrew language caused Arabs to feel inferior, insecure, and alienated from the process, while Jews were very comfortable" (Abu-Nimer 1999, p. 150).

An Educational Program for Peace

Grace Feuerverger has introduced a bilingual school for peace (SFP) workshop in Israel. The village Neve Shalom/Wahat Al-Salam was founded in 1972 as an intercultural experiment, and the first families took up residence there in 1978. SFP believes it very important to maintain personal, social and national identity for both Jews and Arabs. The participants are divided into small, mixed groups of 12 to 14 Jews and an equal number of Arabs from high schools all over the country. This educational program promotes acquaintance, understanding and dialogue between the two peoples and is especially designed to reach those who have leadership positions in their school. The use of two languages gives the message to the participants of negotiation, discussion, dialogue, and change in their search to give equal expression to their national identities (Feuerverger 1997: 17/18). A participant in the SFP said that his words "had represented a call for a shared consciousness toward building a sense of moral development and responsibility in the midst of violent conflict and enmity". Feuerverger reports that throughout the workshops she observed "the facilitator constantly attempting to empower their participants to become storytellers and to guide them as they gradually began a process of uncovering and reconstructing the meaning of their cultural and national identities" (Feuerverger 1997, p. 20-23). "Only when people learn to understand and respect each other can peaceful coexistence begin" (Fry and Bjorkqvist 1997, p. 252).

Summary

I have presented in this chapter the views of the theorists who have studied the conflicts between Black and White South Africans, Protestant Northern Ireland and Roman Catholic Ireland; and Israelis and Palestinians. It is worth noting that while religious leaders were involved in reconciliation, especially Archbishop Desmond Tutu, who influenced not only South Africa, but Ireland, and Israel as well, the fighting was more about territory and resources. In other words, power.

For almost 1,300 years Christians and Muslims have fought frequent and bitter wars, and for most of that period the Muslims had generally had the better of the struggle. However, from the seventeenth century onwards the power of Christian Europe grew dramatically. With the division of the Ottoman Empire after the allied victory in 1918, only a handful of Muslim states were not part of one of the European colonial empires. The triumph of the Christians seemed complete. Yet the sources of the power that gave the Christians victory also undermined any idea that this success was principally based on a religious commitment. The superior economic and military power of the Christian West sprang from the scientific revolution in the seventeenth century, the secular spirit of enquiry of the eighteenth-century Enlightenment, and, above all, from the nineteenth century Industrial Revolution. "Christianity may have helped to shape the conditions that gave birth to the revolutionary changes, but the wider implications of those changes challenged all forms of religious belief, including both Islam and Christianity[12]" (Jamieson 2006, p. 9).

Mediation, Not Religion, Is Practised Today

> A distinction is drawn between their roles and functions on one hand, and their techniques and skills on the other. Hence roles and functions refer to the higher level order of mediator activities ... such as creating optimal conditions for the parties' decision making and encouraging them to settle. Skills and techniques refer to the lower level order of mediation activities – their practical acts and interventions such as arranging the setting or reframing the parties language ... Judges are increasingly required to evaluate the behaviour (of mediation roles and functions). (Boulle 2005, p. 79)

But Mari Fitzduff warns: "Addressing and resolving conflicts usually needs the development of a meta-conflict approach. A meta-conflict approach is one which can address the many facets of a conflict whether these be structural (political or constitutional arrangements, legislation, economic and aid factors, etc.) or psycho- cultural (e.g. attitudes, relationships, divided histories) in a comprehensive and complementary manner (Fitzduff 2002; Ross 2000)" (Fitzduff 2004). With de Chardin we look forward to a rise in "psychic temperature" (which) should automatically accompany better social arrangement" (de Chardin 1966, p. 98). Those in the interfaith groups all over the earth could bring in a better world movement in the future. They could do it by loving God and neighbour. It is possible.

This chapter, having examined the histories of peace initiatives in South Africa, Ireland, and the Middle East and drawn on peace

---

12 Jamieson (2006) stereotypes the West as Christian, this would not be accurate today.

theory in order to build a context within which a discussion can take place, together with the preceding three chapters sets the stage for the methodological discussion that is undertaken in the next chapter.

Chapter Five
Research Methodology

Introduction

In previous chapters the commonalities and differences of the three faiths in relation to key concepts such as cooperation, conflict and forgiveness and to the real world situation of the Palestine-Israel conflict have been discussed. This chapter discusses the methodology employed for answering the research question: 'how are people of the three Abrahamic faiths that are implicated in a geopolitical confrontation able to cooperate within interfaith organizations at the local level?' It begins with a methodological discussion, then deals with the method to be employed in field research before discussing the approach that will be taken in analysis of data.

Methodological Reflections

The scientific method starts when you ask a question about something that you observe. "How, What, When, Who, Which, Why or Where? There is an attempt to minimize the influence of bias or prejudice in the researcher when testing their question. There is a procession from observable facts of experience to a reasonable explanation of those facts. Thus the framework of the methodology for this thesis, that which keeps everything in its place, is deductive. I began with an abstract, logical relationship among concepts. The concepts in this thesis will be drawn from people of Abrahamic faiths whose larger communities (at the geopolitical level) have a history of non-peace, but who overturn this history of non-peace through dialogue, cooperation and peace in religious Abrahamic organizations. The variables are identity and commitment to their religion (in Neal's (1965) terms, interests), deep listening and willingness to dialogue, values and basic understanding of forgiveness, and religious texts supporting the construction of peace. I have to show what it is that links a movement from non-peace to peace (Neuman 1997, p. 46).

An Argument for Communication

Looking at the variables, the classification as independent, or "cause variable" is ethical communication. Neal's (1965) variables of values and interests have to be added as cause variables as well.

The variables that identify forces or conditions that act on something else are the independent variables. The variables that are the effect or are the result or outcome of another variable are the dependent variables. In this case, the outcome would be the construction of peace (Neuman 1997, p. 107).

So the formal argument would be:

> This is a communication thesis, within an interdisciplinary frame, to examine the process of the construction of peace in Abrahamic communities. Without ethical (truthful) communication this is not possible. The underlying energy to attempt ethical communication, to actually meet together with a diverse group of Abrahamic people, comes from personal and group values and interests. From values, interests and communication, the process of the construction of peace begins. It grows, with individual and group effort into cooperation and friendship at the local level in

Sydney, NSW The argument shows the action from ethical communication:

The beginning of the construction of national peace in Northern Ireland and South Africa was done with community help at the local level (McDuff M 2002, and South African Truth and Reconciliation Commission).

Abrahamic interfaith groups meet at the local level in Sydney and dialogue truthfully about Jews, Christians and Muslims and peaceful cooperation.

Abrahamic interfaith groups have begun the construction of peace at the local level in Sydney, NSW This peace construction will grow to the national, and perhaps, even global level, with the help of other local and global interfaith groups, some of which are documented in this thesis.

Deductive and Inductive Research

This will be a comparative study within a broadly deductive frame of reference. The context for this research is geopolitical confrontation and in particular the war between Israel and Gaza. This conflict involves people of the three Abrahamic faiths. Examples of cooperation provide grounds for comparison and also reveal inherent difficulties. Are Jewish, Christian, and Muslim approaches to human needs, to respect and recognition, to ethical communication or dialogue, to values, and to forgiveness the same or different? And within focus groups of Jews, Christians, and Muslims, will they come to the same or different conclusions about the pursuit of peace? "As in any argumentative paper, your thesis statement will convey the gist of your argument, which necessarily follows from your frame of reference … In a compare-and-contrast, the thesis depends on how the things you've chosen to compare actually relate to one another" (Walk 1998).

The focus groups brought my core research question to an everyday level, because representatives from the three religious groupings not only engaged in dialogue with each other but also wanted to continue towards cooperation and friendship. Friendship implies a trusting relationship where cooperation is possible.

It is also necessary to speak any overflow of information that may not rest easily in a deductive framework. This may come from detailed histories of each person, their willingness to share their lives and their work may give a deeply human, and deeply vulnerable and courageous qualitative aspect to this research. The research is therefore open to inductively derived data that may help discover patterns, while the deductive analysis will most likely support the articulated patterns. In other words, by using a deductive method through the forming of a questionnaire derived from theoretic insights from the literature review I can give firm leadership to what I wanted – the background, identity, commitment, that led to understanding of self and others, and continued on to discussing forgiveness within the foundations of human life, the family, and construction of peace from the foundations of religious life, the commandment of God to love God and neighbour, (Schadewitz and Jachna, 2007). You could describe this methodology as a hybrid methodology.

The Global Theatre

In this thesis I want to bring my research into the global theatre. "Intergroup contact is universally useful in reducing prejudice across a wide range of intergroup situations" (Pettigrew & Tropp 2011, p. 60). One of the best indications of successful intergroup research is when the participants are voluntary. All the participants in this present research were voluntary. The focus groups were very successful. Affinity (Muslim Interfaith) gave me feedback which allowed that I could interview their people again.

In intergroup contact, many forms of intergroup prejudice range from stereotypes to feelings.

> *This raises the question as to whether intergroup contact influences all forms of prejudice. Our meta-analysis into 20th century research shows that contact is far more likely to influence affective components (e.g. emotions, feeling and liking) than cognitive components (e.g. stereotypes and beliefs). Affective elements of prejudice are typically more loosely related to intergroup behaviour. (Esses et al. 1993; Stangor et al. 1991; Talaska et al. 2008) (Pettigrew & Tropp ibid., p. 203)*

In the context of this thesis, it can be affirmed that the behaviour of the Abrahamic communities towards one another had been changed from prejudice to (in one instance particularly in Group F) giving up prejudice and praying for one another.

Presence of Divinity

Glock and Stark questioned people about a confirming experience of an awareness of the presence of divinity. Because this research was done in a secular institution, this question was not asked. However, the story of the participants' commitment to their religion brought forth awareness of the presence of divinity. A conversation at night with God when going to sleep as a child, a guiding light as to whether to become a minister, a search for God, who was found "within" the person themselves, could all come under the label of a "divine presence". Glock & Stark give us their emotional reaction to this kind of experience:

> *The absolute frequency of even the least intimate variety of religious experience seems something of a surprise. There are few clues in the culture which would lead an observer to predict so high a rate of supernaturalism in what seems to be an increasingly modern, scientific, and secularized society." (Glock & Stark 1965 p. 158.) "45 per cent of the Protestants and 43 per cent of*

the Roman Catholics were sure that they had experience of a divine presence" (ibid., pp. 157–8).

This will be discussed further in chapter 6.

The Fear Factor

The "fear" factor has to be addressed. Fear is an "emotion caused by the nearness or possibility of danger" (Cowie 1994, p. 443). If you are fearful you are "nervous and afraid" (ibid., p. 444). The Jewish participants reported the most accounts of fear. A Christian minister also had a very long and fearful episode in her life when she stood up against racism and prejudice. Petttigrew and Tropp called it another name, they used the word "threat". If you are accused of killing Christ, if your children are accosted in the street, if your church is invaded by a bikie this is a very real threat to your security.

Racism and Anti-Semitism are very real in Sydney. However, these threats and fears have begun to recede with new memories of kindness and hospitality, and it is hoped that this thesis will inform the Australian community of the remediating work in interfaith dialogue.

Social Change

Sociologists are very interested in "change", especially in values and interests. It has been suggested by Bachika (Bachika 2002), that you could have a common global value, with different symbols, from different religions, to make this value recognizable. In the Abrahamic communities, this is slightly easier. Instead of a global value, you could have an Abrahamic value. One also has to consider the situation. Sociologists have centered on structure, but have not been so concerned for the situation. And maybe the situation in the world today has risen to overcome the structure.

> *The persistence of alternate theories to explain the same social phenomena suggested that in different situations it may be possible to perceive either value or interest dimensions as dominating the historical process and that focus on certain moments or situations would account for the contradictions in the theories of the conflict and functional schools. This conclusion suggested the usefulness of examining both value and interest dimensions of some current situations currently experiencing noticeable pressures toward change to find out just how values and interests function in the process. (Neal 1965, p. 71)*

The Abrahamic communities are certainly facing social change as, for instance, Eastern people of the Muslim faith are now living in most parts of the world, and in Western society even though we could be said to come from the Judean/Christian background, science and money seem to have taken over from God. Perhaps it would be better to use the terms of Taylor, that the individual striving for attainment has taken over from all else. And there are groups, in every part of the world, trying to interfere in the construction, or non-construction of peace in Israel/Palestine.

Neal (1965) asks us to discover any change or no-change in values, or in interests. It can be said that most of the participants have not changed their values. Some, if you look at their family histories, have moved from exclusion to inclusion. One Jewish woman made the decision to move away from fear in the actual context of the focus group. However, there is a change from an interest in their own religion, which is unchanged, to an added interest in interfaith. To put it another way, the change is from fear to friendship, from exclusion to inclusion, from interest in an individual religion, to an interest and willingness to cooperate with Abrahamic religions in the plural.

This change, energy being directed to interfaith dialogue, has been achieved with their values. There is mostly no change in their values, not in this setting anyway. As mentioned, a Jewish woman was moved to change her mind about the Muslims, and she was open to encountering them in her area. Also a young Muslim scholar moved from prejudice to understanding difference. But in the main, their values remained the same. We can summarize as below:

> Neal (1965) maintains the main variable found in theories of social change is the value- interest dimension. "Values refer to widely shared conceptions of the good; societal values refer to conceptions of the good society. Interests refer to desires for special advantages for the self or for groups with which one is identified. Interests refer to short term desires to protect or to maximise institutional positions of the individual or the group" (ibid., p. 9).

Into this global framework, I also introduce Neal's understanding that if there is a change in either values or interests, then this could be an historical change, according to the situation.

Neal (1965) made me go back to the coding of the information achieved from the participants answering questions. Firstly, I would explain that the Findings (Appendix 1), the results of the Focus Groups, were achieved with coding from the questions answered in the questionnaire (Appendix 2). After sharing their personal history and commitment to their religion, the participants discussed questions to do with needs, dialogue, forgiveness, and peace construction. These questions elicited many themes, which included identity and fundamentalism.

The coding of the interview material constitutes the critical center of the entire research design. The content analysis should reveal any patterned or characteristic mode of resistance or acceptance of change that is typically associated with this typology. The central expectations are two:

Change or no change in values

Change or no change in interests

The change that is happening in the world is that of world tribes and communities coming together. Australia is increasing rapidly as a multicultural country. "New census data has revealed that almost a quarter (24.6 per cent) of Australia's population was born overseas, and 43.1 per cent of people have at least one overseas born parent." (Australian Bureau of Statistics 2011). As we have seen from the research by Cahill in the introduction, the leaders of the faith groupings of these residents can smooth the way for integration into the Australian way of life. This way has been described as "the fair go for everyone." However, Muslim terrorists, in the world scene, and also in Australia, different ways of dressing, stricter moral codes, and in some instances, religious "blaming" for the death of Christ, has caused pain in our communal life. Abrahamic communities can perceive one another as enemies. So if we are looking at change, yes, there has been change in the interests of the participant. Their values are the values of a person committed to God, a person serving God and making the world a better place for the good of society. Their values have not changed. However, they have acted on their values, they have actually made the world a better place with hospitality and acceptance, and you can discern from their family histories that they now have another interest – interfaith. This will be further discussed in the analysis in chapter 7.

Goal Attainment

Defining religion as entailing a supernatural referent (Glock & Stark 1965, p. 172) Glock and Stark point to the obvious "it is evident that the details of religious expression are extremely varied" (ibid., p. 19). "Attitudes and behaviour in secular areas of life can be used as measures of religious commitment only where they are grounded in religious conviction – where they follow from religious belief, practice, experience, and knowledge" (ibid., p. 21).

Into religious belief, practice, experience and knowledge we add goal attainment.

> *The value orientated person is concerned with the achieving of a goal which is in conformity with a standard of excellence. Realization of values is his primary concern. The interest orientated person is primarily concerned that the process of goal attainment afford advantage to certain people, to the exclusion, if necessary of others. (Neal 1965, p. 10)*

It is suggested, and will be argued in chapter 7, that the goal attainment is for good relations within the Abrahamic communities.

> Goal attainment entails "motivation to contribute what is necessary for the functioning of the system; these contributions vary ... a goal is therefore determined as equilibrium. It is a directional change that tends to reduce the discrepancy between the needs of the system, with respect to input output interchange. And the conditions in the environing systems that bear upon the fulfillment of such needs. (ibid., pp. 10–11)

Values and Leadership

When considering the leadership of Abrahamic interfaith groups, persons concerned with adaptation should perceive the social structure as something that can be changed through new ideas, new division of labour, new ordering of role relations.

"People concerned with goal attainment should perceive the social system as something that can be manipulated by individuals striving to realize specific goals. On the other hand, if the concern is with integration, then a person's interest should focus on social harmony, order, cooperation, and conformity" (ibid., p. 101).

It will be seen when the focus interviews are analyzed that the common values of these participants referred to widely shared conceptions of the good; generally, we are not prepared to bargain with our values. "The intention the value-oriented actor is more to bring about in time those programs, behaviours, and artifacts he believes reflect the values to which he is committed" (ibid., p. 10). "Shared definitions of what is accepted as true or real will immediately make a difference in how stimuli to change are received and interpreted" (ibid., p. 102).

Common Sense and Skepticism – A Knowing Word from Paul Grice

In all the groups, common sense within an accepting and respectful attitude, was foremost in their approach to their relationships with one another, and each other's religion. Can we say "Now I know" about Abrahamic religions?

> *The Skeptic will still refuse to admit that we can say correctly "I know" however long we continue with our test (and this goes not only for there is cheese on the table but for every other empirical proposition as well). Since, therefore the accumulation of further evidence is irrelevant to the dispute between the Skeptic and his opponent, the Skeptic's thesis must be an a priori one, namely that to say that, for example "I know that there is cheese on the table" is to assert (or try to assert) something self-contradictory or logically absurd ... the Sketpic will have to admit that 'I know there is cheese on the table' is in this sense an ordinary expression, and so, to remain a Skeptic, he will have to maintain that some ordinary expressions are self-contradictory or absurd. (Grice 1989, pp. 148–9)*

I hand over to you sacred material, presented in every day terms. The common words are self-explanatory. It is not propaganda. It is real life lived in Sydney NSW by Jews, Muslims and Christians.

Friendship Construction and Method

The concept of friendship was conceived by Aristotle, elaborated by Cicero, and understood for centuries in the context of the Christian conception of personhood. The traditional idea of friendship had three essential contents. Is there a method of construction of friendship that can inform a method of research? "Friends must enjoy one another's company, they must be useful to one another, and they must share a common commitment to the good" (Bellah et al. 1985, p. 115) and "Let us designate the first social cognition of friendship as communication ... communication is noted by mutual understanding, 'a mutual, deep knowledge, an acceptance' of your friend" (Gurdin 1996, p. 32). The method of friendship construction has to begin with a vital piece of information – 'friendship' needs to be a voluntary act. "Friendship is culturally encoded within a cognitive field which distinguishes it from other social relationships. It refers to a voluntary act." (ibid., p. 357). So we have the notions of companionship, usefulness, commitment to good and voluntary association. Friendship also has to enable one to be different. "Friendship is a relationship which encourages the preservation of its interactants' whole selves rather than their merging into a new dyadic self, toleration respect and appreciation of these ascribed and achieved statuses are the modes of recognition of these differences in true friendship" (ibid., p. 361).

So, as a researcher on conflict, cooperation and forgiveness in the construction of peace in the Abrahamic religions I needed to pave a ground of friendship where my data would be gathered. This naturally drove me to decide on a focus group type situation with a questionnaire, allowing both inductively and deductively derived data to arise. The focus groups will allow participants who share a commitment to the common good to communicate with mutual understanding and voluntarily engage in acts of friendship.

The examination of the humanities, social sciences, NGOs, and religious literature carries on from the survival needs identified by

Willet (1989). These survival needs are the intrinsic capacity to send and receive messages, which I will show can be met by peaceful dialogue. The themes from this literature appear in three categories: human needs, ethical communication, and the role of forgiveness in the process of peace construction. Peace construction, or cooperation for survival emerging globally in interfaith encounter groups, is the focus of this study. The literature review charts some of the international dialogue for truth, reconciliation, and forgiveness and peace-making in the three Abrahamic religions. The focus groups will add to this knowledge by examining the dialogues, interactions, and memories of ordinary Abrahamic people. In these groups, individuals reveal cultural values belonging to all three Abrahamic faith communities. For example, all three faiths call for belief in one God, all have a religious teaching that God is a wise "forgiving" God, and all place high value on prayer. Through their own narratives of what it is to be Jewish, Christian or Muslim, through their expressions of their own values, and through their expressions of the ways they address difficulties and disputes in their own families, the participants will reveal more information about what it is to be a Jew/Christian/Muslim in Australian society.

The Ethnographic Approach

Focus groups belong to a broad ethnographic approach. The social world of a particular culture is socially constructed as people act on understandings which give their lives and actions meaning. That meaning is upheld by the rest of their "group". "The language of ethnography refers to actors and actions, rather than, say 'subjects' and 'behaviour' and the question is always "how is it done?" What cultural resources, stocks of knowledge, routines and strategies do the actors bring to bear?" (Burns 1996, p. 301). While qualitative, these understandings will have a great deal of bearing on my conclusions, because it is expected that the results from human needs, dialogue, forgiveness and peace construction will form themselves into a language - a language that everybody spoke in the focus groups because they had learnt, spoken and acted upon it in their search for interfaith dialogue and friendship.

To make this sentence clearer, it is the researcher's opinion that these groups were more like focus/dialogue groups. "Dialogue is shared exploration towards greater understanding, connection, or possibility" (The Co-intelligence Institute). With this definition I do think they belong to the broad ethnographic approach. The human need is to be recognized, difference and all, and this is done with dialogue. It's not only language, it is the open mind, open heart and open hand. It is communication in action – it is having a more comprehensive consciousness – that consciousness that is alert and ready for action.

Ethnography is applicable because it helps me to obtain information, in their own cultural context, of the Abrahamic religious communities as a whole.

Meanings and interpretations are not fixed entities because they are generated by social interaction. Meanings may change. Identities are also subject to a process of 'becoming'. There was a definite sense of a growing understanding by the participants that they were the People of the One God during the focus groups. "There are multiple and competing definitions current in almost every social situation. The metaphor of negotiation is often used to capture the processes of interaction whereby social meanings are generated, and a precarious social order is produced" (Burns 1996, p. 301). Social meanings leading to the construction of peace were formed during the focus groups. "Individuals have interpretations based on their experiences from the unique vantage point of their life and biography. These personal interpretations include the perceptions, intentions, expectations and relevancies through which each one of us makes sense of things" (Burns 1996, p. 302).

It is my intention during the focus groups to understand the beliefs and perceptions of the three interrelated Abrahamic communities, especially those related to cooperation and friendship, and to gain knowledge of social expectations and patterns. The focus groups would be forums in which all participants are immersed in dialogue about what it was to be a Jew, a Christian, or a Muslim in Australian society.

Spatial perceptual objects can only be perceived from a point of view. In this research many points of view from a literature search were put together. The interviews from the focus groups will add to these points of view. Because of the recent war between Israel and Palestinians in Gaza, and the heavy death toll of children and civilians, the focus-groups' points of view would have to be understood from this perspective. Phenomenological truths are thought to be both non empirical and necessary; they are said to be true a priori. "Phenomenology has its own method, reflection on the essences of mental acts, and it has its own subject-matter, consciousness. Phenomenology, according to this conception, is "the study of the essence of consciousness" (Honerich 1995a, p. 660). The difficulty with this method is that consciousness has not been defined. It exists, but it resists definition. "Consciousness involves experience or awareness. Human mental life has a phenomenal side, a subjective side that the most sophisticated information-processing system might lack" (Honderich 1995b, p. 152).

To discuss consciousness is to broach deep waters, but in the world where the media stand gatekeeper over images and the academic world gatekeeper over abstractions, some information is not given to the world to evaluate. "Conscious mental states are heterogeneous in phenomenal kind. Sensations, moods, emotions, dreams, propositional thought, self-awareness all occur consciously – perhaps some of these states only occur consciously" (Honderich 1995, p. 152). Two questions follow: Does this dialogue raise my consciousness, my awareness of a situation, so that I look at it in a new way? Is there information available that is not in the media or has not been tackled by the academic community?

Focus Group Interviews

The focus group is an interview style designed for small groups. Through dialogue, researchers strive to learn about conscious, semiconscious, and unconscious psychological and sociological characteristics and processes among various groups (Basch 1987; Lengua et al. 1992). focus groups can open up the biographies and life structures of group participants. "Focus group interviews are either guided or unguided discussions addressing a particular topic of interest or relevance to the group and the researcher" (Edmunds 1999) (Berg 2004, p. 123). The moderator's job is to draw out information from the participants regarding topics of importance to a given research investigation.

In everyday terms, this study contributes to the understanding of how Abrahamic communities, many linked through their ancient heritage, make friends in Australia. The purpose of the research is therefore to find out specifically how members of Jewish, Christian and Islamic multi-faith organizations address intra-organizationally the extra-organizationally unresolved questions of reconciliation and forgiveness in local and world-wide settings. It is communication for survival. Communication as survival is explained by Willet as: "life is characterised by its intrinsic capacity to send and receive messages to and from the different parts that make up an organism, as well as between the organism and its environment. It is through this ability that human beings assure their psychological survival and define their personal identity" (Willet 1989).

The aim of the focus group methodology in this study was to enable people of the three Abrahamic religions to meet, in order to understand other faiths and their own more deeply by discovering what faith meant to others. This approach was based on evidence from the JCMA principles for interfaith dialogue conference. They hoped to understand other faiths (and their own) more deeply by starting to discover what they mean to other people who lived them (JCMA 2007). The dialogue would be put together to move from biographies to the subjects of the human need for respect and recognition, the dialogue of ethical communication, the values of faith, and the role of forgiveness and cooperation in the construction of peace.

The task of the moderator in a focus group is similar to the roles they perform in face-to-face interviews. These tasks can be made more systematic by preparing a procedural guide in advance of conducting the actual focus group. A guide requires consideration of the level of language for the focus group. It should also provide a kind of outline or staging and the sequence of what the moderator should say and do. In accordance with this scheme, the moderator's guide in this study included an introduction and introductory activities, a statement of the basic rules or guidelines for the interview, special activities or exercises, and guidance for dealing with sensitive issues.

The value of the focus group interviews is that it enables greater scope for comparison. There were grounds for comparison among the input of the Jews, the Christians and the Muslims. But there were also grounds for comparison among the four focus groups themselves. The dynamics included working in cooperation within the groups and between each individual and their group. A single person in a focus group would ask a question and the reply would be given by another member or by members of the whole focus group. This phenomenon resembles Mowlana's understanding that within communication ethics, when one person calls out, and another person answers, the horizon of both is extended to the Wholly Other (Mowlana 2003, p. 19).

Interaction within all the focus groups was harmonious. A great deal of time was taken up with the presentation of biographies, which inspired the participants. They then began to grapple with the harder questions: how they saw the other Abrahamic groups and how the other Abrahamic groups saw them. The participants found it easy to talk about values, a little more difficult to talk about forgiveness, and more difficult again to talk about peace making. Despite these challenges, everyone joined in and helped each other to think about the meaning of neighbour, and they all agreed that central to their own religion was a belief to love God and love neighbour.

The Questionnaire

The group discussion began with a history of each person's faith journey. Were they born into Judaism, Christianity, or Islam; who taught them; when did they begin to believe; in what way did this belief become a part of their adolescent life, and their mature-life decisions.

This introduction was followed by structured questions and answers reflecting the four themes: needs, dialogue, forgiveness and peacemaking. Within that structure, participants expressed their thoughts and attitudes. In the subsequent analysis, I repeat, word-for-word what the participants said, in order to avoid blurring the detail into an academic production. The intention of the study is to hear their concerns clearly in their own words. A summary of the questions is outlined in Appendix 2.

The answers to the questions in the questionnaire were coded. These issues were then used to put together the dialogue in such a way as to enable the reader to follow the different groups when they discussed those issues. So you got their thoughts, for instance, on fundamentalism and identity, among others. In the Findings (Appendix 1), this coded material was edited into 17,000 words.

The 7 hours of constant dialogue (transcribed to 80,000 words) was reduced by retaining but editing the narrative story of human beings coming from Jewish, Muslim and Christian families, who then became, themselves, committed to their religion. There was rigorous editing of the family source stories, which were long, and just a few were chosen, highlighting the commitment process, the final reduction being 17,000 words.

To continue the story, or stories, the dialogue was followed that emanated from the participants' answers to the questionnaire (Appendix 2). Firstly we can categorise these participants as:
1. 5 young, 6 middle aged and 4 old
2. 5 men and 10 women
3. All committed Jews, Christians and Muslims, well-informed and well educated
4. Most with academic degrees
5. Most were global travellers
6. 5 born overseas, 10 born in Australia
7. Most had experience in interfaith dialogue
8. Most knew and had made friends in interfaith groups with Jews, Christians and Muslims
9. The Jews and Muslims were authorized by their communities
10. The Christians were self-chosen.

These are the people who gave stories of the beginning of their family life, the process of commitment to their religion, the recognition of this by their communities, in some instances their communication with God, and in all instances, their endeavours to serve God and make the world a better place. They are well-educated and well informed.

The whole chapter, at the same time, looked at what was the same, and then what was different in the various groupings of Jews, Christians and Muslims. Endearing stories of BCB(M) looking for Jesus and finding him within will always have a place in memory, as will the understanding that there can be no reconciliation without a person saying "sorry" to the person he/she has injured. Most of all the common sense and huge experience of the participants came out when they were discussing the construction of peace. When things got difficult we were all to try harder, DMB(F) tells us we cannot love someone if we do not know them first, BJA(F) is adamant that she doesn't "believe in absolute tolerance of evil. But I think there are some things that you can say, 'This is intolerable or unacceptable.'"

However, we are to respect and exercise hospitality with an open heart and open hand. The aim of my editing was to include you, the reader, in the dialogue groups, to let you hear exactly what was said, and how it was said, and to know, by the end of the chapter, that you cannot make the peace alone, you need to have a friend to help you.

The questions asked of the participants, around the needs of human beings, their enemies, their values, their dialogue, their forgiveness and their peace construction were tailored to the articulation of who they are, and how they live and act in the present moment. We are aware of their history, because they have told us. Now, it is time to understand who is, and where is, the enemy. The enemy in this group is someone who has injured them in some way, and sometimes the injury comes from a person in another Abrahamic community. It is necessary also to understand, as they share with us their lives, the truth of these lives. Occasionally, one or two of the participants would say, "yes, I know your story", or thank a person for their input to interfaith. They know one another, and we were reminded that they are, indeed, telling the truth. This is credible testimony to the Abrahamic organizations that they come from. The process of peace has already begun. Reconciliation, Shriver has already told us in chapter 2, is the "fullness of forgiveness."

Selection of Participants

Participants in the focus groups were chosen for the diversity of their experiences, Jewish, Christian or Muslim. This representation in the sample was essential. The interfaith organizations in Sydney and Melbourne helped with the selection of people from their communities who they thought suitable. All were voluntary.

The right to speak has to be divided among the actors. "The manner in which the group functions and communicates is the responsibility of the moderator, whether a therapist or research worker, after the fashion of the sociologist" (Hamel 2001, p. 343).

Sociological intervention is described as "an intensive, in-depth process during which sociologists lead the actors from a struggle they must carry on themselves to an analysis of their own action. This process involves a series of states that constitute the history of the research (Touraine et al. 1982, p. 280)" (Hamel 2001, p. 344). In the original groups they met more than once, but the core is the same, self-analysis, which requires the active participation of social actors engaged in a collective struggle concerning political and social issues. "The goal of the sociologists' intervention in such struggle is to turn them into a social movement" (Hamel 2001, p. 345).

It can easily be argued that these Abrahamic organizations are already social movements for peace in Australian society. This study examined how they did that in these particular focus groups. Using the focus group as a research procedure gave a window to three groups of religious people sharing their faith journey and interacting on themes of need, dialogue, values, and peacemaking.

Hearing how one group member responds to another provides insights without disrupting underlying normative group assumptions. Meanings and answers arising during focus group interviews are socially constructed rather than individually created. Situations such as focus group interviews provide access to both actual and existentially meaningful or relevant interactional experiences. Such naturally arising glimpses into people's biographies are necessary for interpretive interactionalism (Berg 2004, p. 127).

Specifically Berg states that when we contact potential participants we have to convince them that their participation is important and necessary.

Gaining Access to Participants

My first introduction was to the overseas encounter groups, including one that had existed for 16 years, the Jewish-Palestinian Living Room Dialogue Group. It began in the USA to help Jews, Christians, and

Muslims talk in friendship to one another (Traubman). Another was the Jerusalem group the Interfaith Encounter Association administered by Yehuda Stolov (IEA). Stolov is tireless in his efforts in Israel to teach Jews, Muslims, and Christens to engage in dialogue and also to discuss their sacred texts. I personally had experienced this kind of interfaith encounter in Melbourne, Australia. JCMA (Jewish Christian Muslim Association) had a faith encounter meeting at Pallotti College, Millgrove, in June/July 2007, when I listened to group input from each tradition. As well as taking part in the discussion groups, I was also part of an on-going home group during the conference, which enabled me to hear about the faith journeys of others as well as speak about my own. One of the questions on that occasion was: "how many times do you pray a day?" It came from one of the young Muslim members of the group. The group had night prayers together, each Abrahamic community leading on different nights (JCMA 2007). The following year, June/July 2008, I was a member of the Common Good Conference, presented by Latrobe University at Trinity College, Melbourne University. This academic setting accommodated some disrespectful behaviour when the audience cat-called a Jewish academic twice on completion of his paper about making peace. I wrote a protest letter complaining about this and other instances of disrespectful behaviour and the inclusion at the conference of a Holocaust denier who was photographed with the group when they visited the Governor of Victoria and who had previously been in jaill in Germany for incitement to hatred. The same person was shortly to be brought to court in Adelaide for matters relating to his website "The Adelaide Institute".

These earlier experiences contributed to my understanding of individual people and the political climate in Australia. In my own study, I asked a Muslim Imam from the earlier JCMA conference whether my work would offend the Muslims. I also consulted him when I did not understand a word or a situation. He assisted regularly, for which I was very grateful. A Jewish academic, Paul Gardiner, also allowed me to use the presentation he gave to the JCMA conference 2007 (Gardiner 2007).

Gaining access and negotiating entry were both very difficult. The groups themselves, not the university, had to take responsibility for the participants. As you will see, this was a very high hurdle for me, and it actually formed the whole thesis, as I did not get a random sample, but role models, to research. I first set out to conduct the focus groups in Sydney with a Muslim Group called Affinity. In October 2008, I visited the group's conference in Sydney after giving a paper at Macquarie, and there I met Mehmet Saral, President of Affinity Intercultural foundation. I gave him a rough copy of my early draft paper on methodology, and then at the end of November I wrote to him. (Gaining Access to Respondents, Appendix 3)

Mehmet said he would cooperate but that he could arrange for me to contact perhaps only six Muslims for this work. As I needed 12 Muslims, I decided at the time, to explore the possibility of gaining the bulk of my focus groups in Melbourne where I had some previous contact with some interfaith groups. I emailed the secretary of the JCMA group, Rev. Phillip Newman, sending also a copy to the Muslim Imam who had been helping me from JCMA, Riad Galil, about the focus groups. "I have put down my name for the women's group in March, and if they accept me, I maybe with some luck could do one down there at Lower Plenty."

Thus in March 2009 I was to attend the JCMA's women's conference, Daughters in Faith, at Lower Plenty in Victoria. They would allow me, as a visitor, to ask for volunteers for my focus groups. However, as an interfaith group they were not prepared to take responsibility for these participants. I reluctantly told them that my participants could only be contacted through an organization that was prepared to send out information and consent forms, and so they made a decision not to do this. Hence I did not go. Subsequently I got in touch with Jeremy Jones, National Vice President of the Executive Council of Australian Jewry and Director of Community Affairs of the Australia/Israel and Jewish Affairs Council in Sydney, and he was prepared to help me obtain participants, not a random sample, but volunteers chosen by him. They were authorized participants to speak for the Jewish community. Rev. Mary Pearson of the Interfaith

Executive of the Uniting Church, Sydney, was very kind also in handing around my information sheets, but once again there were not enough willing volunteers for random selection. Brisbane Catholic Interfaith gave me permission to use their name, although in the end they decided not to join the dialogue programme. There were other people whom I contacted, who did not wish to have their names recorded. I was still in contact with Mehmet Saral of the Muslim Executive, and he did, as he said, give me six voluntary participants who were authorized to speak for the Muslim interfaith community. Two of them did not arrive on the day. One slept in, and the other simply did not arrive. One of the Jewish participants was unable to come, and one of the Christian women had a migraine. That left 15 participants out of a total of 19. The Jewish woman who could not come had a sick child. All the participants gave of themselves generously. All of them were well-informed and well-educated. I was very grateful for all who joined me in my study of interfaith groups, and I thank them sincerely.

The Explanatory Statement (Appendix 4), the Information for focus group Participants (Appendix 5) and the Consent Form (Appendix 6) gave very specific information to both interfaith groups and participants.

Research Process

A strong group that respects individual differences will strengthen autonomy as well as solidarity. "With a more explicit understanding of what we have in common and the goals we seek to attain together, the differences between us that remain would be less threatening." (Bellah 1985, p. 287). Libresco puts it this way: "A group of individuals working tougher to analyse a difficult concept can usually understand that concept more quickly than one individual can"

(Libresco 1983, p. 51). However, group interviews tend to present the views of the group as a whole, or of its strongest spokesman, rather than long-winded views of each group participant (Libresco 1983, p. 52). As moderator, I made every effort to see that each person in the group felt free to speak and to voluntarily write answers to the questionnaire. As it happened, participants were all too busy listening to everyone else to write. Shannon's fundamental theory of communication states that calculated redundancy has its uses by enlarging the probability that the message will get through. Feminist research principles are elucidated by Montell.

There is a consensus that feminist research is characterized by researchers 'striving to adhere to and achieve certain principles in their research'. Cook and Fonow (1986) identify five basic epistemological principles that concern feminist researchers: 1) attention to the significance of gender; 2) the need to challenge the norm of objectivity and the rigid separation between the researcher and the researched; 3) the centrality of consciousness-raising as a methodological tool and 'way of seeing', 4) an emphasis on the transformation of patriarchal institutions and the empowerment of women; and 5) concern for the ethical implications of the research. (Montell 1999)

No specific questions were included on gender, however gender subjects did arise. I would have to agree that there was not a rigid separation between the researcher and the researched. I gave them my whole self as I listened to them, and they in return did the same. They revealed deeply who they were, how they became committed to their religion, and what they were dong to make the world a better place.

Data collection

I collected the data on Monday 6 and Tuesday 7 July, 2009, at the Barristers Dispute Centre, Level 1, 174 Phillip Street, Sydney. Over two days, I gathered together participants, sound recordist, and court reporter for the transcript. The tools for data collection were interviews, observation, audio recording, and field notes. Field notes were valuable to track down arguments presented by the groups. The dialogue was intense as the participants told their stories of faith and practice in their religions.

After investigating many ways of audio recording, including a digital voice recorder with a 16-hour tape, the idea emerged of a professional organisation to do the voice recording and the transcription. Camera Video Hire attended for the two days and used a hooded camera for the audio for the whole group. Bradley Reporting, a court reporting firm, attended for the two days and transcribed every word. There was a separate DVD for each group.

Data analysis

The framework for the data analysis was a compare-and-contrast framework. For the defining dialogue on Jewish identity Scheff's methodology of relating the smallest parts to the largest wholes was used. This method is suitable for an important dialogue. "When part/whole methods are applied to verbatim texts, the intricate filigree of even the simplest human transactions are revealed ... the intricacy of human expressions is not a luxury, but an elementary requirement of human science" (Scheff 1997, p. 1). The phrase "least parts and greatest wholes" is taken by Scheff from the philosopher Spinoza. If you want to understand homo sapiens it is necessary to relate the least parts to the greatest wholes.

To correctly understand ordinary language, humans must have access to part/whole algorithms that allow them to understand the particular meanings of words (and when face to face, of gestures) in context: that is, the meaning of an expression produced by a particular person in a particular dialogue, in a particular relationship, in a particular culture, at a particular time in history (Scheff 1997, p. 2).

The design of most studies of human beings assumes that the words and sentences used by the researchers and their subjects are largely unambiguous, and also assumes that their subjects' intelligence is not extraordinary.

"The problem is that humans are capable of not understanding or misunderstanding standardized research situations, or of using them to their own ends, concealment, getting the researcher's sympathy etc. Similarly, it is all too easy for the researcher to misunderstand or not understand their subjects' responses" (Scheff 1997, p. 3). The aim is to take as our data verbatim records of human expressions. Verbatim records include transcriptions based on mechanical recording of interaction and all written material.

Any text taken out of context becomes ambiguous. Scheff has a theory and method to deal with the relationship between meaning, text, and context. All texts are undecidable when removal from context implies an equal and opposite corollary: in context, the meaning of a text is decidable. Scheff believes that no matter how exhaustive the analysis of a text, the determination of meaning will be incomplete, and therefore partly subjective, without referring to relevant historical and biographical knowledge. The historical and biographical histories were available for this research from the participants themselves.

Open and Axial Coding

In analysis, 'open coding' enables the researcher to locate themes and assign initial codes to begin to form categories. Afterwards, by contrast, with axial coding, the researcher begins with an organized set of initial codes, and then focuses on the initial coded themes more than on the data. These themes will be human needs, ethical communication, forgiveness leading to peace construction. "During axial coding a researcher asks about causes and consequences, conditions and interactions, strategies and processes, and looks for categories or concepts that cluster together" (Neuman 1997, p. 423).

Profile and coding of participants

Group A consisted of an attractive young Jewish woman with children, a middle-aged Christian woman minister of religion, and another Christian minister aged 76. Both ministers had worked in outreach situations. Group B consisted of a middle-aged Jewish woman with grown children, an older Christian woman, and a middle-aged Christian man. The Jewish woman was an educator, the Christian woman had worked in outback Australia opening schools and hospitals, and the Christian man had experienced a long and varied faith journey. Group D consisted of a middle-aged Jewish man, an elderly Christian man, and two young Muslim women. The Jewish man had a vast amount of experience in inter-faith matters. The Christian man had made great strides in welcoming people from others faiths. One of the Muslim women was a student. They were both young, smart, and integrated with Australian society. One was born overseas.

Group F, the largest group, consisted of a very elderly Jewish woman, a middle-aged Christian woman minister of religion, a middle-aged Christian man, and two young Muslim scholars, a male and female. The Jewish woman was very caring of the young Muslim man, who arrived late to the focus group meeting. She was loving to all of the participants, and she made the group her own at one stage when she called a coffee break while the Muslim participant prayed. Many of her family had been killed during the Holocaust. All had interfaith experience.

These participants are coded so that their identities are not revealed. In the code the first letter represents the focus group. The second letter represents the identity i.e. Jew (J), Christian (C) and Muslim (M). The third letter is "A" or "B" standing for first or second participant of the same religious grouping.

The 15 participants are coded as below:
    A-J-A; A-C-A; A-C-B
    B-J-A; B-C-A; B-C-B
    Focus Group C: Cancelled
    D-J-A; D-C-A; D-M-A; D-M-B
    Focus Group E: Cancelled
    F-J-A; F-C-A; F-C-B; F-M-A; F-M-B

In all there were four focus groups with seven hours of group interviewing. Two further focus groups had been scheduled, C and E, but they had to be cancelled as there were not enough participants. In July 2009 the study brought together members of Jewish, Christian, and Muslim communities in Sydney at the Barristers Dispute Centre to engage in dialogue in four focus groups. The dialogue highlighted differences and similarities among the Abrahamic religious organizations as the participants considered the construction of peace. Participants concentrated on four themes: human needs, ethical communication, and the role of forgiveness and the construction of peace. This study reports on the ways these themes developed in the dialogue within the focus groups. A court reporter recorded 80,000 words from the four focus groups for accuracy. From this raw data, it was possible to draw common responses and to make comparisons in the responses between Jews, Christians and Muslims, as well as comparisons of the different groups themselves, two of which had Jews and Christians dialoguing, and two of which had Jews, Christians and Muslims dialoguing. A central comparison in the study is the comparison between the language of individuals belonging to different faiths. Both similarities and differences evident in the focus groups enabled a wider understanding of the processes

Focus Group	Date	Time	Duration in hours	Jew	Christian	Muslim
Group A	6/7/2009	9:30am	1.5	1	2	-
Group B	6/7/2009	3:30pm	1.5	1	2	-
Group C	-					
Group D	7/7/2009	9:30am	2	1	1	2
Group E	-					
Group F	7/7/2009	3:30pm	2	1	2	2
Totals			7	4	7	4

Table 5.1
Focus Group Participants

of cooperation and friendship within Abrahamic communities as well as confirming the significance of communication through personal language, media messages, and religious heritage.

The focus groups became a faith journey of 15 Jews, Christians and Muslims and provided a snapshot of commitment to their faith as they thought through the meanings of images, of dialogue, of values, of forgiveness, of friendship and peacemaking. No one overtly held back. One decided that if this kind of dialogue could be a regular occurrence, then eventually some remediation could occur to enable people to work together to make a better world, a world of different faiths and different dress, with respect for differences, with common ground, with some connections among all the people, so that there would be a possibility of more harmony than exists today among the three Abrahamic religions.

Summary

This chapter has discussed the conceptualization of focus groups through which the views of Jews, Christians and Muslims were given expression. It has also provided an account of the analytical approaches that will be taken. There is the added approach of Neal as to whether there has been any change in values or in interests. The research findings, in Appendix 1, are a reduction to approximately 17,000 words of the 80,000 words of transcribed focus group data. The themes were mainly taken from the issues that the groups discussed. These themes were previously coded, and are to be found in Appendix 7. Chapter 6, which follows, provides a framework with which to listen to the dialogue of the 15 participants in the four focus groups.

Chapter Six
Activity Report: Focus Groups

Introduction

This chapter describes the focus group activity. It details the individual participants in the focus groups and records the dynamics and what transpired during the focus groups in order to provide a framework with which to listen to the voices of participants. The purpose of this chapter is to observe what happens when people from different religions, all with their own individual memories, engage in dialogue in a controlled setting to discuss forgiveness and develop friendship in steps towards the construction of peace.

The Participants

As described earlier there were 15 participants including three Christian women clergy and 12 lay people. Coding of participants and groups have also been provided earlier. The focus groups began with a deep listening session during which time the participants shared their faith journey, revealing more about their religious and cultural backgrounds. Were they born Jewish, Christian, or Muslim? When did they first believe, and what effect did this belief have on their life decisions? The responses fell into three categories: their family circumstances, their commitment to faith, and their concerns about making the world better. With regard to family circumstances, some participants were practicing the religion of their families and some were not. The deep listening sessions produced the following common responses about family and religious background.

With regard to their commitment to faith, the deep listening sessions showed that with or without religion being a high priority in the families of the participants, all had come to a time in their lives when they made a commitment to their particular faith, even though in some cases disruptive relationships had required personal questioning. On the subject of commitment to their particular religion, there was a turning point in the lives of all participants. The four Jews found their commitment in the practice of their religion. One woman had to have help from her school teacher to defend her commitment when she was accused of killing Jesus Christ. Three of the Christians said their commitment to Christ came from a preacher: the evangelist Billy Graham for two of them and Dorothy McRae McMahon for the other. One Christian affirmed her faith in her community in no particularly dramatic way. One Christian was affirmed by the Iona community during her faith journey. For the Muslims, the September 11 terrorist attack had made them think about God and the Muslim religion, but all had come to their commitment through reading the Koran and associated texts and by joining the Muslim interfaith group, Affinity. The following selection of responses illustrate the diversity of faith journeys and the influence of family and inherited religion as well as the influence of individual thought processes.

Focus Group A

AJA(F) "Went through a conversion process at age eight and became Jewish according to Jewish law.

ACA(F) "The most formative thing for me was going to work on the Island of Iona." And it was this community that drew her "along a path of commitment in faith that was expressed in things like going to Greenham Common and … sleeping outside nuclear bases in Scotland."

ACB(F) "I remember as a very, very young child just having a sense of a presence beyond myself." In her teenage years: "I thought I had made a commitment to Jesus Christ, our Saviour and Lord … the sort of person who thought that I was connected to God who asked me to give up everything that I liked most …. That sort of deprivation was supposed to be a sign of my commitment to Christ, (but) I moved past that … partly because of my very special parent … I was restored to what I believe is a much broader and deeper faith."

Group B

BJA(F) "Belief isn't in Judaism often discussed and it wasn't part of growing up … It was all about practice; what did you do that reflected your faith or your Judaism. The rhythms of our life as a family were around Judaism. Every single week the Sabbath, Friday night in particular is a family night, and Saturday to the synagogue."

BCA(F) "I just sort of grew up with the faith and then at significant times I…affirmed rather than a dramatic experience. At university "I became very much involved in the Student Christian Movement."

BCB(M) "By the time I was, I reached about 16, I had a very strong feeling that I should be baptised and I wanted to be baptised … I made the decision and I was very pleased … and then I became very involved in the church … and…in my late teens I became an elder in the church and actually participated in communion." He became an atheist after his church had removed his liberal thinking minister. Then he "went to the (place name)

Uniting church and Dorothy McRae-McMahon gave a talk ... and everything she said sort of connected for me."

Group D

DJB(M) "During the Day of Atonement you really are in a relationship with God. You're not thinking of people, you're thinking about sins that you may have committed ….and at some time and age different people are going to say 'Well, do I believe or don't I?' If I don't believe this doesn't make sense. It only makes sense if you believe that it's – that you have some relationship with the divine."

DCA(M) "When I was in later years at school, high school (I) drifted away a bit from going to church …. And then at university, I went to one of the crusades that existed in that time, Billy Graham Crusade, and was converted into Christianity, back into Christian faith at the age of 18, and since then have been in the church since as a Christian."

DMB(F) "It was September 11 that really I suppose shook my entire world and understanding of what faith really was … I certainly took a defensive stance because, first of all, I didn't know whether what had occurred was in fact a part of Islam or not... I certainly had no theological background or understanding. And it really was the first time that I thought about God. And I thought if faith is this, then what kind of God, you know, are these people following?...(She learnt for herself) ..about the faith from I suppose its original sources, like the Koran, and really reading up on deeds which are traditions of the Prophet. And obtaining those things from people I trusted and I knew had sound, I suppose, foundation in those areas. So it was through that, that I suppose my own faith was or belief was found, I suppose you could say."

Group F

FJA(F) "I'm not sure when I believed ... my parents had the sense or were able to flee Europe ... then I grew up in a household where people were mourning the dead ... 29 members of my family were killed ....and what did my belief do to me? Well, at school .... I was accused of having killed Jesus when I was eight years old .... I packed my bag and left school in the middle of the day. It was only another eight year old that said it to me, but that's what they taught in social studies ....and the teacher came to get me ... and the child that said it to me was told to apologise. And I think that was my first step in realising that you have to confront your situations and you have to deal with them and people have to be quiet about their prejudices."

FCA(F) "I started going to church as an 11-year-old child .... By the time I left school and went to university, started a science degree I had already gone into the Missionary Society and said 'I want to be a missionary.'"

FCB(M) "I trundled down to a Billy Graham crusade at Parramatta Stadium and got converted."

FMA(F) "I started to question a lot – and then (in) my second year of uni I started to get involved with Affinity, which is what we do here, interfaith organisation doing interfaith work. And from thereon I kind of really started to see that I had this missing thing in my heart of what I wanted to do in my life and I always thought there was something missing. And I find that this was it, it was God, you know."

FMB(M) "I felt a bit of a calling to read the Koran or investigate God. I think this also – I like to pretend to be – I like to be someone rational and reasonable. And in science at school evolution, these topics, somehow put an ideological battle; whether I should believe or not believe. And I chose to believe. I chose to believe in God."

Making the World a Better Place

Each participant came from a different faith perspective, but the responses demonstrated that all were working personally or professionally to achieve a better world.

Group A: Making the World a Better Place

AJA(F) Her interfaith work was in her own family. There were Scottish Presbyterian, Irish Catholic, Muslim and Jewish members in her family, with everyone very tolerant of everyone else's beliefs.

ACA(F) "I worked for the Save the Children Fund in a deprived area of Edinburgh setting up a project for parents and under-fives, and I lived in a small community house in that area as well... my faith in that was integral." She immigrated to New Zealand to marry her husband, a minister, and then to Australia, where she trained for the ministry. But she said I "always (had) this call to be with those who are most marginalised ... so I work now as a mental health chaplain in a psychiatric hospital ... and because my commitment was to being in the community, (I) became involved and started off an interfaith group."

ACB(F) After she had brought up her four children she "became responsible for the Christmas Bowl appeal, which is the international aid appeal ....the Churches arranged for me to go to Israel, Palestine and Lebanon..(then)...my friends said to me, you're enjoying power, aren't you? – who are you becoming? ... and ... I put myself under spiritual direction of a very fine nun ... so, I went through two years ... thinking about ordination." When a minister – and acting upon the anti-racism stance of her father she "stood with the Jewish community at that point ....because they also ... were being graphitied and attacked".

Group B: Making the World a Better Place

BJA(F) "Spent a year in Israel, did my first degree at UNSW, where I was very active in Jewish student politics and ... did a Masters in New York .... I have brought up four children.. (and) when I decided to make the switch into adult education I've met amazing people with amazingly diverse stories."

BCA(F) Her husband became a patrol padre in the Australian Inland Mission. "We went out bush where nobody could care less about our qualifications. And then we came back to parish work, and I actually started doing a bit of teaching ... and became very much involved in interfaith activity."

Group D: Making the World a Better Place

DJB(M) "I didn't go to a Jewish school at any stage of my life. (I) was always observing Jewish dietary laws, festivals, the Sabbath et cetera. So, it became an issue where I had to be able to think about these issues and understand where I was in relation to others from quite an early age. And, you know, I come across people through the glories of Facebook that I haven't spoken to in 40 years or whatever – and they remember coming to my home and seeing Jewish things that I wasn't even conscious were anything other than other people's houses, but they would remember on the various occasions what they saw around the house." In his interfaith capacity, DJB(M) still does this kind of work."

DCA(M) "Especially since I've retired, about 10 years ago, I've been involved with a lot of interfaith dialogue .... And I've been rather blessed by being involved in interactions with, with Islam, with Judaism and with other faiths. And very pleased to have broadened my outlook to include them as part of our society, as part of our way of life, and have been helped I think in my understanding of people a lot more, by being involved in that way."

DMB(F) "It was really my own research – and my own investigation – that opened up, I suppose the whole world of faith to me. .. The more I've engaged with different faiths and different people from different backgrounds the more I've learnt more about myself and my faith and God. And my relationship with God has, I suppose, strengthened through my connections with other people."

Group F: Making the World a Better Place

FJA(F) "I don't want to ever see the world as ugly. And the only way you won't is to make friends. And I think that working in interfaith has – two of us do together, in the same group, is – as it just so happens – is – you can see that you can become friends. And it just – as people. And learn to appreciate each other's faith."

FCA(F) She went to Africa to be a missionary. "Fortunately I taught in a government secondary school, which had all faiths in it, including Muslims. By the time I got back to Australia after 16 years I was no longer single. I was married ... and had four children, and had become passionate about theology ... I have continued to read theology to this day." She has been with the same interfaith group for eight years.

FCB(M) "In my 25 years in the bank I had 17 overseas trips. And so I got very quickly an understanding of other cultures and in fact many of my friends became people in those countries ....part of my faith journey in the last 15 years has been my realisation of how connected I am to other faiths. Not just by the application of believing in something but actually their incredible depth of history, of theology and of what in essence we believe God to be ... it only has happened by the choice of taking myself out of the confines of the – theological confines."

FMA(F) "I take interfaith as my formal service to God .... I know that I'm doing service because to serve God you serve through humanity, ... and I find that I always feel so much more spiritual when I'm meeting in gatherings like this. I feel that close to God because of that zone."

FMB(M) "I believe, as a Muslim, God has spoken to Jews before and to Christians. So, when I speak to them sometimes I want to hear what God had spoken to them. Because I know God spoke to us ... so, that's the enjoyable part."

Introduction to Coding of Questions

In this thesis we examine carefully, and in a deep way, the coded information from the four focus groups. Neal (1965) says that it is very important to examine the patterns in these codes. Each code retains the actual words of a trained Abrahamic leader of both the separate Abrahamic religions, and also their interfaith involvement. The codes grew out of the participants' answers to questions on the subjects of enemies, dialogue, values, forgiveness and the construction of peace.

Neal (1965) analyses social change from the viewpoint of values and interests. This examination occurs in chapter 8. But here, let us bask in the positive codes that show, beyond any reasonable doubt, that everyday acts of respect and kindness can construct peace. Forgiveness comes first, and in its fullness, there is reconciliation

(Shriver 1995). Anger has to be overcome, AJA(F) was very angry, but let it go during her focus group. Truth has to be pursued, and as DMB(M) discovered, it can be found, even though it might not be reasonable. We will find out later that it is possible to be an atheistic Jew.

Neal is adamant that the coding of interview material taken from tapes constitute the critical center of the entire research design. (ibid., p. 91). She believes that the content analysis of the responses of high scorers in the four groups should reveal any patterned or characteristic mode of resistance or acceptance of change. We will see that there are some very high scores showing negatives in Group B, and a pattern for the Jewish participants as a whole to report painful experiences. For instance, here is the pattern for negativity:

Group A reported 7 negative experiences:
    5 Jewish, 2 Christian
Group B reported 12 negative experiences:
    7 Jewish, 5 Christian
Group D reported 7 negative experiences:
    6 Jewish,   1 Muslim
Group F reported 6 negative experiences:
    4 Jewish, 2 Christian

Total negative experiences:
    22 Jewish , 9 Christian, 1 Muslim

Maybe this is just the everyday reality of being a Jew in Australia, and not a sign of defensive behaviour. For example, on the other hand, there were very high scores showing forgiveness in Group F. Also, there are high codes for remediations in both Groups D and F. Of these the overall pattern of the four groups was:

	Jewish	Christian	Muslim
Remediations	15	22	7
Forgiveness	8	13	6
	23	35	13

So the remediations and forgiveness in the Jewish participants cover over the negatives, while the Christians, who do not have as much negatively to report, are high in remediations and forgiveness. Many of the reported Jewish negatives were, of course, stories of deceitful Christian evangelization. The Muslims, with only four members, as there are also only four Jews, have low scores on negativity, remediation and forgiveness. We will find out later that they have high scores in God issues and peace. Now, let us continue to examine the answers to the question on enemy images.

ENEMY IMAGES IN RESPONSES TO SET QUESTIONS

After the deep listening session, participants responded to set questions revealing images they held of other groups. Particular themes emerged in their responses. Those themes appear in this chapter under the categories of communication, culture, forgiveness, friendship, God, negativity and remediation. To prompt discussion about the participants' images of others and their experiences of other people's images of them, they considered the question: "What images do you have of your neighbouring Abrahamic communities?"

Group A: Negative Responses

Group A gave seven negative responses. They included distrust, fearful experiences of anti-Semitism following an attack on a child, absence of contact between Jews and Muslims, nervousness about wearing the Star of David, and negative depictions in the media. The media were biased against Israel, reported in a way that did not encourage dialogue, engaged in stereotyping, and sensationalized people of Middle Eastern appearance. The participants also reported remediations, such as a belief that there were many ways to God, contact with Christian/Muslim dialogue groups, sharing pain, and shedding tears.

There are seven codes for negatives in Group A, 5 Jewish, 2 Christian.

Group B: Negative Responses

Group B reported twelve negative experiences. The first was fear. Fear could arise if, for example, a person had not met a Jew but had seen anti-Semitic messages through the media. Another kind of fear was evangelization fear, the belief people would burn in hell if they didn't accept Christ. All agreed that the origin of these kinds of messages came from the Catholic and the Protestant churches. Islamic people were known to participant BCB(M) only by media generated images, thus Australians "would be fed a mixed bag of messages". Muslims had a negative stereotype of Jews, and these images were recycled back through the media to mainstream Australia as well. The difference in Group B was that they talked about friendship. BCB(M) had Jewish friends. BJA(F) said that Jews needed friends to exist, and BCA(F) worked with Women's Interfaith and with the Affinity people (Muslim). There were also seven references to remediation. These included sitting and talking with Muslims, having lots of friends across lots of faiths, and the hope that people who met Jews would have a positive response and know that "we're just normal." BJA(F). The neighbor who is different means that "we have to work a bit harder to open ourselves to the difference of the other." BJA(F). The idea emerging in the dialogue was that people were to act on good images and control negative responses. From a cultural point of view the Hajib sent a message that women were oppressed, according to participant BCB(M).

There are twelve codes for negatives in Group B, 7 Jewish, 5 Christian.

Group D: Negative Responses

Group D reported seven negative statements. Participant DJB(M) said the Muslim image had been used and abused by people for their own reasons. Christianity came under fire from DJB(M) when he said that the methods to try and convert Jews were deceitful. These methods included misrepresenting Jewish texts and befriending people until they became Christian and then leaving them on their own. He referred to a perception that for a Jew to be complete it was necessary to become a Christian. The difference in group D was that the participants referred to identity as a sign of other characteristics. DMB(F) said: "My immediate perception of anybody who identifies themselves as someone of faith is someone who is of peace." In references to God, Christians had a soft spot for Jesus, according to the Muslim participant DMA(F). They had a sense of connection with the Jewish people as well.

There are 7 codes for negatives in focus group D.

Group F: Negative Responses.

Group F revealed only five negatives. A young Muslim scholar instigated a pertinent dialogue about Jewish identity. That exchange is analyzed in detail in chapter 7. It injected a happy atmosphere to the group. The negative references included fundamentalism, the demonization of Jews, and a belief that many people still had an image of Jews as being responsible for the death of Jesus. Christian blood is used to make the Jewish unleavened bread Matzah, one participant stated. Conversely, there were eleven instances of remediation. The Jewish woman FJA did not accept hate messages but accepted positive messages. FCA(F) talked about being friendly with her Muslim neighbours. FCB(M) addressed the issue of why people had to be so different, or why they dressed so differently. He saw that it was really not an issue of faith but "really an issue of personal and social difference". "And yet it's clouded often in religious issues." He said people needed to put themselves in the other's shoes. He had an experience in China when he was the only white person: "2,000 people just suddenly stopped talking and looked at me." Education helped to overcome fear and prejudice, because ignorance was born of misinformation, participants agreed. With education, people would understand Jesus better, and two-way relationships would lessen fear. Home visits also helped to overcome fear, enabling people to move from having no preconception of what was going to happen to having a conception built on personal understanding.

It was dangerous to categorize, the Muslim girl FMA(F) said: "What interfaith does really well is it allows you to realize that religion is just a way of getting to connect with God."

By identifying a common value, that statement highlighted an objective of the thesis: to investigate the possibility that religion could be a source of peace while being also a source of conflict. FMB(M) replied that as he had encountered Jews and Muslims; each encounter had confirmed, enhanced, or changed some of his ideas about them. Again, his recounting of this experience was crucial to the objective of the thesis: to investigate pathways to peace through dialogue. He was searching for the truth by communicating with others. Cultural issues were also discussed, including the black clothing with eye-slits, for a Muslim woman, which could hinder communication. It was wrong to judge on appearances, such as clothes, participants agreed. Appearances were not religious but physical. "They are not the actual issue of faith." FCB(M).

There are six codes for negatives in Group F, 4 Jewish, 2 Christian

The Institutional Context

The responses of these individual participants were occurring within a wider context of institutional engagement. In the past two decades, there have been public institutional instances of remediation, starting with the interfaith dialogue in 1991, which was a Uniting Church-Jewish Dialogue. The Catholic Bishops joined in 1999 and the Anglicans in 2005. There followed the National Dialogue of Christians, Muslims and Jews, formally operating since 2003. Interfaith organized prayers after September 11, 2001. Much of the dialogue in the focus groups reflected remediation. DCA(M) agreed that interfaith did tend to alleviate a considerable amount of hostility and had given him an opening to dialogue with people on a reasonable basis. DMA(F) pointed out the difference between those people who actually knew about Jewish and Christian communities and those who were shaped by socio-historical, socio-political and socio-economic events, who would think that Muslims were extreme, not very spiritual, and not very human. But the discussion in the focus groups showed that there were similarities between the faiths.

The issue of the head scarf came up more than once, from participant DMB, who wore one. This generated a dialogue in microcosm similar to the one that had taken place globally. Some people in the group congratulated her on wearing the scarf. When asked where images associated with the head scarf came from, the answer the participants gave was religious texts and media (as positive). When asked whether they acted on these messages, one man said he didn't have much trouble overcoming xenophobic images now. The Muslim DMA(F) spoke about the importance of bringing a human face to interfaith, and with it followed understanding.

In summary, the responses to the above-mentioned questions established that all participants carried images of the other. When asked where they came from, participants answered media and family. While these groups were different in religious association, the members of the groups addressed both the negative signs within the three Abrahamic faiths and also the positive signs, or remediations, that would heal those conflicts. One-on-one personal relationships were by far the most important of these remediations. In the responses to the question, "How can people of Abrahamic faiths, faiths implicated in a geopolitical confrontation, cooperate within religious organizations," participants established that the media could generate stereotypes and recycle misinformation but that positive personal experiences could change people's attitudes towards one another.

The Impact of Dialogue

To prompt discussion about the impact of the dialogue described above, participants considered the following questions. How did the experience of listening and reacting to the others affect them? Did they have a new understanding after this experience of interaction? If yes, what was that understanding? The responses revealed that all participants had a new understanding of "the other" and of their own religious heritage as a result of the interaction in the focus groups. This suggested a progression from dialogue to forgiveness to peacemaking and finally to friendship.

Group A: Impact of Dialogue

Group A expressed only remediating responses. People can learn to be enriched from every other faith while still practicing their own, participants stated. Hearing people's stories enabled human connection in a way different from any other kind of learning, ACB(F) stated. "I always think when the disciples of Jesus said 'Oh they're not one of us' and Jesus said, 'By their fruits you will know them' ... I think he meant, 'You will find the people of God.' The response was another example of commonality of religion, a starting point for peace. More important, the identification of commonality did not negate the validity of difference. It demonstrated rather, that through difference, there could be remediation without loss of difference; a central tenet of the thesis is a respect for difference. All the three women in this group said that they had a new understanding of this interfaith experience of interaction.

Group B: Impact of Dialogue

Group B revealed two negative responses to the impact of difference and commonality on pathways to peace. Evoking thoughts of globalization and quoting a Columban priest, Patrick McInerney, BCA(F) said that "commonality is a greater threat than difference. If you just keep on the things we've got in common all the time, when say the Muslims or the Christians (say) "Oh, yeah, but our faith is being modified or being compromised." BCA (F) answered: "And that can then lead to anger and so on." All agreed on trust and respect for differences. The pathway to greater peace was not to be at the expense of loss of religious individuality. BCB(M) put forward the notion of "the fear of syncretism", a fear of losing the purity of the faith. BCA(F) concluded that there are many paths and One God. This group believed that dialogue strengthened faith and enhanced trust, that in interfaith "we're all pretty established in open communication", and that, in the words of BCA(F), "in our interfaith group we have established trust".

Group D: Impact of Dialogue

Group D opened the discussion with the startling information that historically "a Jew who supports Jewish-Christian dialogue is a traitor or doesn't know history" (DJB). He countered that by saying his experiences had been enriching and positive, thus setting a harmonious tone for the group. DCA(M) replied that anyone could learn from other faiths. DMA(F) brought up the identity issue again with her understanding that people of faith were naturally associated with peace. DMB(F) replied: "How can you not love the

Creation if you love the Creator? I think you can't love something or someone if you do not know them. So, I think it's vital that we do listen to each other."

Group F: Impact of Dialogue

Group F was different from the other groups. Their responses are reported here under the theme of communication, because they concentrate on how to communicate. They believed in the importance of listening and learning, in being open and adventurous, in being prepared to risk, and in acknowledging vulnerability. A limited and confined world was a safer world, they said. To the question, what was the understanding you received from the dialogue in the focus groups, everyone agreed that their new understandings were openness and learning, and understanding that the other was really not too different. This group also identified cultural tensions. FMB(M): "A lot of the times it's really not interfaith dialogue. It's not about religion, it's about social differences; it's cultural dialogue. FJA(F): "Cultural differences." FMB(M): "Sometimes it's even political dialogue. World political issues. So yeah, sometimes dialogue has to be qualified." FCB(M) referred to children's education as being not open.

In summary, each group presented negative tensions and negative memories, in various ways, but in dialogue there was general agreement on the core issues affecting ways of responding to one another. Remediations outweighed the fears that had been emanating from inside and outside religious faith. Unresolved was whether issues arising among the three religions were indeed religious or cultural.

Forgiveness

To find a dialogue for forgiveness, the groups considered two questions: What experiences, principles, and people did they most value?

And, what forgiveness rituals did they use to take back people into their families and community life after someone had stayed away by shunning family and community values? And to find a dialogue for peace making, they considered three questions: Where they aware of the common belief of the Jews, Christians and Muslims, to love God and neighbour? If so, from where did they obtain that information? And how could a peace process be formed, relying on this common teaching? This section of the focus group discussion on forgiveness and peacemaking brought to the surface memories of a traumatic past for one of the participants.

Group A: Forgiveness

ACA's father, a minister, had left the family. ACA(F) continued to think about this experience during the focus groups. She searched for a forgiveness ritual within Christianity. Another participant, AJA(F), had a traumatic experience when her young son was accosted while going to synagogue. A stranger took his skull cap. ACB(F) had experienced racism and injustice: "The activities of this neo Nazi group were turned on our church and myself …. Finally they lit a fire on my doorstep and burned an effigy of a woman. And at that point they arrested seven people." There were no Muslims and no men in this group.

Group A: Forgiveness Codes

No particular ritual / accept and love, Try not to judge	AJA(F)
Forgiveness core of relationships, broaden into Sorry Day	ACA(F)
Create something which leads into grieving, sharing tears	ACB(F)
In family, equal sharing of humanness	ACB(F)
Day of Atonement, sins against God	AJA(F)
Five codes to do with forgiveness in Group A,	2 Jewish, 3 Christian

Group B: Forgiveness

Group B has BCB(M) bringing up the right to disagree, and the need to "respect individual journeys. But this is not enough, BCA(F) wants us to understand and love when we disagree, and the Jewish understanding given by BJA(F) is that the wicked, wise and unlearned are welcome at the Passover Seder.

Group B: Forgiveness Codes

Right to disagree	BCB(M)
Understand, love when disagree	BCA(F)
Wicked, wise, unlearned welcome at Passover Seder	BJA(F)
Respect individual journeys	BCB(M)

4 codes for forgiveness in Group B, 1 Jewish, 3 Christian

Group D: Forgiveness

Echoing BJA(F) above, DJB(M) says that no Jew is refused a Sabbath meal, God is merciful (DMA(F) and Ramadan lives the principle of connection (DMA)(F).

Group D: Forgiveness Codes

No Jew refused a Sabbath meal	DJB(M)
God is merciful	DMA(F)
Ramadan – live out principle of connection	DMA(F)

Three codes for forgiveness in Group D, 1 Jewish, 2 Muslim

Group F: Forgiveness

There is a large number of codes for forgiveness in Group F. There are 15 of them, and they are wide ranging. There is an insistence on God's love, and of asking God's and people's forgiveness. From family, to church to ritual, it is all there, forgiveness makes us humble, allows us to recognize God's unconditional love.

Group F: Forgiveness Codes

Say what you have to say, then accept	FJA(F)
Unqualified love, forgiveness and acceptance for family	FJA(F)
No ritual for people I have offended	FCA(F)
In church pronounce forgiveness before Confession	FCA(F)
God unconditionally loves us	FCA(F)
We're sorry because we don't deserve God's unconditional love	FCA(F)
Ask people's forgiveness	FJA(F)
Ask God's forgiveness (Yom Kippur)	FJA(F)
Ask people to lay aside bad feelings at funeral	FCA(F)
Forgiveness makes us humble	FCB(M)
Recognize God's unconditional love	FCB(M)
Ask God's forgiveness	FMA(F)
Ask forgiveness community and family	FMA(F)
Islam Hajii, asking for God's forgiveness	FMA(F)
Islam- allows 3 day grudge period	FMB(M)

Group F: 15 forgiveness codes, 4 Jewish, 7 Christian, 4 Muslim

Forgiveness gives us a fusion of God and his people. We are to ask for forgiveness from God and from people. The connection between God and people is very strong. The outcome will be:
1. That we, as a people will be humble.
2. That we will recognize God's unconditional love
3. That we will lay aside hard feelings
4. There will be acceptance for family
5. We will try not to judge
6. We will have a right to disagree
7. And keep on loving when we disagree
8. Which means we will respect individual journeys
9. And experience mercy from God and his people.

Focus Groups and the Journey from Fear to Friendship

It is to be hoped that the energy and creativity engendered by these Abrahamic leaders will spread across the planet. Peace construction is the end-beginning of a long circular journey, always evolving, always deepening, and always going around, being communicated from person to person. In the crisis, the journey is from fear to friendship. We have heard from Galtung about the need for security and peace. The security, in this thesis, does not come from guns, it comes from a friend, or friends, in your neighbourhood, whom you can trust. A friend is someone who could belong to another Abrahamic religion, but whom you have intentionally, and with good purpose, dialogued with, and understand.

Journey from Fear to Friendship

	From fear	To friendship
Group A		
AJA(F)	Distrust how I am perceived as a Jew	Common ground
	Experience of anti-semitism sorrow/fear	Shared Values
	Shame no contact with Muslims	Respect
	Nervous, won't wear Star of David	Point Out where wrong

	From fear	**To friendship**
	Acts on negative images	Although you may argue still there when you don't follow what think
ACA(F)	Shame, Christians not understanding Muslims	Friendship, trust vulnerability, walk alongside
ACB(F)	Sad, confession – Christian colonizing	Friends forgive you They are loyal Not afraid of strength or vulnerability Friends forgive you
Group B		
BJA(F)	Fear/friendship – not met a Jew	Jews need friends to exist
	Jews and Muslims negatively stereotyped	Caring friendship when children at war Evangelization fear
	Catholic said accept Christ or burn in hell	
	Negative images from Catholic Church	
	Anglicans still teaching that	
	Some love by forcing people to be the same	
BCA(F)	Suicide bombers, war not peace	A friend trusts
	Commonality a threat if differences not recognized	A friend respects

	From fear	**To friendship**
		Connections with women's Interfaith
BCB(M)	Fear Syncretism	There is something deeper, deeper than respect
	Negative messages from Baptists	
	Islamophobia	Empathizing with another human
		Has Jewish friends
Group D		
DJB(M)	Image of Islam good but abused by some people	A level of comfort and caring
	Christian conversion of Jews deceitful	
	For a Jew to be complete they have to be a Christian	
	Muslims have to grapple with Koran references to Jews	
	Jews killed Jesus, justifies anti-Semitism	
	Jews traitors if dialogue with Christians	
DMA(F)	People shaped socio-historical, socio-political, socio-economic events – Muslims seen as Extreme, not very spiritual, not very human	Friendship is intimacy at varying levels
		Sharing some aspect of yourself

Focus Groups and the Journey from Fear to Friendship

	From fear	**To friendship**
DMB(F)		Compassion
DCA(M)		Loving and respecting
Group F		
FCA(F)	Negative images for fundamentalists	
FCB(M)		Patience
FMA(F)		Forgive
FJA(F)	Jews demonized	Honest
	Jews stereotyped as responsible for death of Jesus	Sharing
	Matzah made with Christian blood	

This journey from fear to friendship has to be undertaken by all of us in today's world, with its mixture of tribes, religions and nations all of a sudden in close proximity to one another.

And while the codes of friendship show what friends are like it is the actions from these friends that "make" them a friend. Here are some of the loving remediations practiced by these participants.

If we take the 3 highest scores for remediations from Groups D and F and put them into three columns, Thoughts, Words and Actions we find that:

Thoughts	**Words**	**Actions**
Hatred not accepted	Education helps	Accept difference
Positive images for neighbour	Interfaith helps	Home visits
Put yourself in others' shoes	Two-way relationships	Hospitality

Thoughts	Words	Actions
Understand other	One-on-one understanding	Act positively
Be open	Speak to overcome negatives	Affirm people of Book
Don't categorize	Some people have knowledge of Abrahamic communities	Act on positive images
Overcome xenophobic images	Interfaith dialogue	Positive experience with Christians
	Interfaith prayers	Create experiences with other faiths, learn
	Dialogue with Christian church	

Truthful dialogue makes a small way for the creation of peace.

Peace construction was made with the help of the common commandment to love God and neighbour. The "God" codes, among other things, show that the participants knew about this commandment.

The God issue – knowledge of commandment to love God and neighbour came from:

Group A: God issues
From Old Testament – religious text   AJA (F)
From Christian/Muslim dialogue groups   ACA(F)
From The Old Testament – religious text   ACB(F)

Group B: God issues
From formal study   BCA(F)
From explored religions   BCB(M)
Worshipping together in trust   BCA(F)

Group D: God issues
From curiosity	DJB(M)
Slowly	DCA(M)
From dialogue encounters	DMA(F)
From encounters with others	DMB(F)
From the Koran	DMA(F)
Commonality of belief, Single God	DCA(M)
Reconcile dualities from understanding our texts	DMA(F)
Christian spirituality, soft spot for Jesus	DMA(F)
(Jews) connection spirituality but also application of the law	DMA(F)
Images come from religious text	DJB (M)

Group F: God issues
Religious texts versus life experience	FMB(M)
Interfaith way of getting to connect with God	FMA(F)

The pattern shows that Group D, particularly the Muslims, with eight mentions, had God on their minds. Religious text was the most common source of knowledge of the commandment at 5 explicit mentions, but knowledge also came from interfaith and dialogue encounters and worshipping together and explored religions. The most important thing, for those interested in Abrahamic dialogue, is that these participants were not unaware of this important commandment and could position it in their texts.

And so, we come now to the construction of peace. Reconciliation has come from the fullness of forgiveness, and our thoughts and words and remediating actions have paved the way for the actual construction of peace.

The Construction of Peace

The next part of the circular, ever deepening journey is the construction of peace. We are not frightened, we have a circle of friends we can trust, and now with intention we can put into motion those initiatives that will actually build peace in our time. The participants were asked to construct peace with the help of the common commandment to love God and neighbour.

Group A Peace Construction

Mutual respect	AJA(F)
Understanding	AJA(F)
Common ground	AJA(F)
Loving our neighbours together	ACA(F)
Understand difference	ACB(F)
Historical differences/Messiah/dividing land	ACB(F)
Difference expressed in attitudes	ACB(F)

Seven codes for the construction of peace in Group A, 3 Jewish, 4 Christian

Group B Peace Construction

Teach love God and neighbour	BJA(F)
Define neighbour	BJA(F)
Love not sufficient for peacemaking	BJA(F)
Tension loving neighbour/holding true to faith	BCB(M)
Loving neighbour to include everyone	BJA(F)
Parable Good Samaritan	BCB(M)
Recognizing good in people you disagree with	BCB(M)
Don't tolerate evil, unacceptable	BJA(F)
Recognize good and wrong	BCB(M)

Nine codes for the construction of peace in Group B, 5 Jewish, 4 Christian

Group D Peace Construction

Start with common ground	DMA(F)
Compassion	DMB(M)
Respect	DMB(M)
Love	DMB(M)
Tolerance	DMB(M)

Five codes for the construction of peace in Group D, all Muslim

Group F Peace Construction

Peace has to be bilateral	FJA(F)
The other side has to agree to peace	FJA(F)
Justice you shall pursue	FJA(F)
Put money spent on defense into dialogue	FCA(F)
People have to like forgiveness	FMB(M)
Go to negotiating table ready to negotiate	FMB(M)
Go into peace for the sake of peace	FMA(F)

Group F: 7 codes for the construction of peace, 3 Jewish, 1 Christian, 3 Muslim

The Teaching of the Focus Groups

1. They have defined neighbour as everyone, and we are to love them together.
2. They tell us that peace has to be bilateral. The other side has to agree to peace, but we must pursue the justice of peace. We must put the money spent on defense into dialogue, and go to the negotiating table ready to negotiate. We have to learn to like forgiveness, and go into peace for the sake of peace.

3. Our attitude should be one of tolerance, love, mutual respect, understanding and compassion, and we begin the journey with these, and whatever common ground we can discover. (For the Abrahamic communities, the common ground is the common commandment from God to love God and neighbour.)
4. Above all we are to teach these steps in the construction of peace to our children, and everyone on the planet. There are difficulties, and love is not enough for peacemaking. We are not to accept evil, but are to recognize good from wrong, and, most importantly, recognize the good in people we disagree with.
Christians are to remember the parable of the Good Samaritan. The high status priest passed by the man in need of help, the traveler from another tribe stopped to care for him. Our neighbour is everyone.

Summary

This chapter has described the focus groups selecting particular texts to comment on, showing what happens when individuals from the three Abrahamic religions bring their memories to a controlled group setting. The responses to the above-mentioned questions established that all participants carried images of the other. When asked where they came from, participants answered media and family. While these groups were different in religious association, the members of the groups addressed both the negative signs within the three Abrahamic faiths and also the positive signs, or remediations, that would heal those conflicts. One-on-one personal relationships were by far the most important of these remediations.

In the responses to the question, "How can people of Abrahamic faiths, faiths implicated in a geopolitical confrontation, cooperate within religious organizations," participants established that the media could generate stereotypes and recycle misinformation but that positive personal experiences could change people's attitudes towards one another. They engage in dialogue, discuss forgiveness and develop friendship in steps towards the construction of peace.

Conflict> memories of conflict> meeting in controlled setting> dialogue> friendship> peace

The task of remediation, forgiveness and reconciliation is the task of moving from fear, risk and vulnerability to trust, respect and understanding. This is done through friendship which in itself involves patience, honesty, an ability to argue a different point of view.

Chapter Seven
Behaviour and Attitudes of Participants in the Focus Groups

Introduction

In chapter 7 participants were described at length and observations were made based on focus group records that they engaged in dialogue, discussed forgiveness and developed friendship in a series of steps that led towards the construction of peace:

Conflict> Memories of conflict> Meeting in controlled setting> dialogue> friendship> peace

This chapter centres on the coding of the information gathered from the participants' answers to the questionnaire (Appendix 2). This questionnaire asked for responses to key themes, Human Needs, Dialogue, Forgiveness, and Peace construction. Both Open Coding and Coaxial Coding methods were used in the research, and the resulting information was the basis for the analysis on values and interests as interpreted by Neal (1965). This analysis then leads into the connection of the focus group dialogue to theories in the humanities, social science and religion.

Open Coding Analysis

As previously stated in the section on methodology, open coding analysis enables the researcher to locate themes and assign initial codes to form categories. From the 80,000 words recorded during four focus group sessions containing 15 participants, the dialogue was edited down to 17,000 words. Using the tools from deduction of Human Needs, Ethical Dialogue, Forgiveness and Construction of peace, issues were coded and themed into 12 categories: communication, culture, forgiveness, friendship, God, identity, negative themes, media, peacemaking, remediation, similarities in faith traditions, and values. The broad division was between negative and positive outcomes of communicative action.

Code	Human Needs, Ethical Dialogue, Forgiveness and Peace Issues
C.1-19	Communication
CR.1-10	Culture
F.1-27	Forgiveness
FR.1-31	Friendship
G.1-21	God
I.1-7	Identity
M.1-14	Media
N.1-32	Negative experiences
P.1-28	Peacemaking
R.1-44	Remediation
S.1	Similarities in faith traditions
V.1-22	Values

The language revealed 32 instances of negative experiences and 171 instances of positive experiences under the themes of communication, forgiveness, friendship, peacemaking, remediation and values.

Coaxial coding further extended the analysis of these initial codes. In this method, the focus on the initial codes shifts towards coded themes and away from the raw data. These themes then coaxially reflect on the themes in the literature: human needs, ethical communication, and forgiveness leading to peace construction. The result was a little different, and clearer.

Coaxial Coding

During axial coding a researcher asks about causes and consequences, conditions and interactions, strategies and processes (Neuman 1997, p. 423). All the participants in the focus groups were voluntary. Upon reflection the common threads for the Jews were that they were 'practicing' a religion, not a 'faith' and the reporting of anti-Semitic events in Sydney. The common threads, as I saw them, for the Muslims, were that the four participants were young, attractive, well educated, and deeply researching their faith after the destruction of the Twin Towers on 11th September, 2001. Two of the girls, DMB(F) and FMA(F) were sisters, and FMB(M) was their cousin. The Protestants were gained from kind, voluntary people handing out material at various churches. All were willing to talk expertly and with love and compassion about their religion.

Here is the coaxial coding:

Name: "Generating Forgiveness and Constructing Peace through Truthful Dialogue: Abrahamic Communities." Abrahamic communities are fighting each other in various parts of the world. How is it that they can meet together and begin, and continue, with friendships, which lead to co-operation and the construction of peace? Four focus groups were called together from interfaith groups in Sydney to find out how they deal with the issues of truth, reconciliation and forgiveness. They gave information to answer the question "How are people of Abrahamic faiths, faiths that are implicated in a geopolitical confrontation, able to cooperate within religious organizations?"

Events: Human Needs. In the event that the human needs of people are unmet, consequent behaviour can earmark the 'other' as 'enemy'. The media recycle these events as negative stereotyping. The four focus groups gave evidence of ways to deal with the issues of truth, reconciliation and forgiveness. There are also on-going difficulties between Palestine and the Jewish state of Israel.

Context: Ethical Dialogue. The context of the interviews was the NSW Barristers Dispute Centre, where 15 people from Jewish, Christian and Islamic faith groups met to dialogue, to share their faith journey, their commitment to their faith and their subsequent work in interfaith. Their dialogue was open coded into themes of communication, culture, forgiveness, friendship, God, identity, negative issues, issues to do with the media, peacemaking. remediation, and their stated values. For this open coding I asked myself the questions, 'what is this about', and 'what is being referenced here?'

Intervening conditions: **Values and Forgiveness** These 15 participants were able to articulate 22 personal values, and it is from these values that you could see how they would step outside of their 'sanctuary' their 'safe haven' where their communities were, and be willing to be vulnerable, and 'risk taking' to share their faith journey in their religious lives, and their faith commitment, and also the actions that came from these commitments The Torah, Getting to know God, Many paths one God, Integrity, Wisdom, Making the world a better place, Offer the hand of friendship, Appreciate diversity, be Compassionate, Respectful, and willing to Speak from the heart. These values enabled these participants to speak about the experience of forgiveness in 27 different kinds of ways, and friendship in 31 different ways.

Actions/strategies: Peacemaking. Understanding religious text to Love God and neighbour. One of the action strategies came from the dialogue on the common text, to Love God and neighbour, and the peacemaking actions started to flow from this common text. All agreed that they knew about the text, and from whence they had heard it. They articulated a language of peace, which is used in friendship, to discuss, co-operate and continue on to remediation. This kind of language can initiate social change. To discuss what this social change actually is, we turn to Neal (1965).

Neal maintains the main variable found in theories of social change is the value-interest dimension. "Values refer to widely shared conceptions of the good; societal values refer to conceptions of the good society." Both can be seen in this research. The goal, making the world as better place is a societal value. It is done with widely shared conceptions of the good, the good applied to their neighbour.

SOCIAL CHANGE: VALUES AND INTERESTS

An argument is presented for social change being brought about by Abrahamic interfaith groups.

1. Pressure to Change

A Muslim terror attack on the USA was the catalyst for social change in the Abrahamic communities. The fall of the Twin Towers in New York on 11th September, 2001, was cited by Cahill, and participants DJB(M), and the 4 Muslim scholars, as being the beginning of changed behaviour. For DJB(M) it was to call Abrahamic communities together to pray to God for help. For Cahill, it was to research the consequences in all Australian interfaith communities, and for the Muslim scholars, it began their deep research into their own religion.

2. Interfaith, the Beginning of Social Change

Looking carefully at the coding of participants' answers to the questionnaire, we are aware of what Glock and Stark (1965) speak about – the presence of the divine. These Jews, Christians and Muslims are all committed to their religion, and they have been asked to participate in "a study of peace as a human need, ethical communication and peace, forgiveness and peace, and the process of peace construction within interfaith organizations. The purpose of the study is to find out members' views of how peaceful interaction is constructed within their interfaith organizations" (Explanatory Statement Appendix 3). We also get a glimpse of the divine life of forgiveness and reconciliation.

The coding of the interview material constitutes the critical center of the entire research design. The content analysis should reveal any patterned or characteristic mode of resistance or acceptance of change that is typically associated with this typology. The central expectations are two:
1. That the responses will be related to the four functional problems of social system: adaptation, goal attainment, integration, and pattern maintenance
2. That they will indicate that these respondents are making strikingly similar choices of action in response to similar stimuli in social situations and are thus affecting the historical process (Neal 1965, p. 91).

The moment in history is of rising media negative stereotyping of both Jews and Muslims. We are looking for a mind, image and relationship change.

What is the "mind" change?	From closed mind to open mind
What is the image change?	From stereotype to "real"
What is the relationship change?	From enemy to friend

We are also looking at the process. What is the adaptation, the goal attainment and the pattern maintenance?

What is the adaptation?	Hospitality and respect towards other Abrahamic religions
What is the goal attainment?	Co-operation for peace
What do they use for pattern maintenance?	Interfaith Abrahamic groups and conferences, emails and visits
What is their response to stimuli in social situations?	Leaders called together Abrahamic Faiths to pray after September 11, 2001 attack in USA

Neal wants us to find out if this kind of interaction changes values or interests. Neal maintains the main variable found in theories of social change is the value-interest dimension. "Values refer to widely shared conceptions of the good; societal values refer to conceptions of the good society. Interests refer to desires for special advantages for the self or for groups with which one is identified. Interests refer to short term desires to protect or to maximise institutional positions of the individual or the group" (ibid., p. 9).

Into this global framework, I also introduce Neal's understanding that if there is a change in either values or interests, then this could be an historical change, according to the situation.

To begin, let us examine the information that the participants have given as to their own values. In all there are 22 values, we will look at them in different categories.

There are five values to do with God from the four focus groups, and they give us a good overall look at the understanding of the presence of the divine in this group. With the word of God there are many paths to God, where there can be connection and mystical experience, within an attitude of humility.

Values Referring to God

Torah central to my life	AJA(F)
Many paths, One God	BCB(M)
Mystical experience	BCB(M)
My connection (with) God	DMB(M)
Humble about their faith	FMB(M)

Values to do with God, 5; 1 Jewish, 2 Christian, 2 Muslim

People are made in the image of God, the Jews and Christians believe. So what about their values regarding people? There are 6 of those, covering family, friendship, community, involving others to make the world a better place, which would include accepting difference, not stereotyping, with humanness, honesty, love and justice, and getting to find the common intersection. You could also say that this was their goal attainment. Here is a summary;-

Values about People

Family	AJA(F)
Involve others in making world a better place	DJB(M)
Offer the hand of friendship	DJB(M)
Humanness, honesty, love, justice, community	ACB(F)
Value people, do not stereotype	DCA(F)
Get to know, find common intersection	DMA(F)

Values to do with people, 6; 3 Jewish, 2 Christian, 1 Muslim

So now we have a picture of God and a picture of people. Where does the intention and the energy come from to go out and meet diverse Abrahamic people, to make them your interest as well as the people in your own religion? What can we say about those who manage to achieve a change from exclusion to inclusion? They tell you that it is by virtue that they are able to do this. For instance, let us examine humility, the first virtue mentioned.

> *In the Qur'an, Arabic words conveying the meaning of humility are used and the very term "Islam" can be interpreted as meaning 'surrender (to God) humility'. ... In Catholicism, St. Bernard defines humility as 'A virtue by which a man knows himself, as he truly is, abases himself. Jesus Christ is the ultimate definition of humility" (Definition humility Wikipedia). A virtue is "moral goodness or excellence". (Cowie 1994, p. 1422)*

Compassion is mentioned as a value "compassion, pity for the sufferings of others, making them want to help them" (ibid., p. 235). Then there's wisdom, "experience and knowledge shown in making decisions and judgments" (ibid., p. 1466), and add to this integrity, "quality of being honest and morally upright" (ibid., p. 652). Honesty and speaking from the heart help to change a person from exclusion to inclusion. This is especially true if the person is respectful, willing to cross boundaries of difference and also a person who actually appreciates diversity. This inclusion helps with social integration.

So these virtues and human gifts are the power houses of a person who changes a society into integrated communities where cooperation is possible, and hope begins to open new vistas for living together in peace.

The achievement of a change from enemy to friend – the values are:

Humility	BJA(F)
Honesty and straight forward	FJA(F)
Compassionate	FCA(F)
Integrity	ACA(F)
Wait for wisdom	ACA(F)
Cross boundaries of difference	ACB(F)

Respectful	FCB(M)
Appreciate diversity	DMA(F)
Speak from the heart	FMA(F)
Compassion	FMA(F)

Values to do with change, 10; 3 Jewish, 4 Christian, 3 Muslim

All these values, when acted out, make a better world, a world where there is cooperation for the construction of peace, which is the goal.

Making the world better place	AJA(F)
Making world better place	DJB(M)

However, when we make our argument that the change is "in the world" through people accepting people who are different to them, in belief, and dress, but the same in the common humanity, and also having a common commandment (to love God and neighbour), we are also to look for:

Either a change in interests, or a change in values. "Values refer to widely shared conceptions of the good. Interests refer to desires for special advantages for the self or for groups with which one is identified" (ibid., p. 9).

Then, in any given situation facing change, four types of responses can be distinguished among the actors depending on their definitions of the situation:

1. A value-change orientation
2. An interest-change orientation
3. A value non-change
4. An interest non-change orientation (ibid., p. 11)

Abrahamic interfaith, as a whole, using the values that we have coded, has definitely changed the interests of its people from their individual own religion to the broader Abrahamic religions. While defining their differences, they also cooperate around their commonalities – especially for cooperation for peace.

So the change is from an interest in their own faith, which is unchanged, to an added interest in Abrahamic interfaith. This change, energy being directed to interfaith dialogue, has been achieved with their values.

There was mainly no change in their values. There was a definite change in behaviour, and you could say an extension of their values, though, during the four focus groups from two people. They were a Jewish woman, and a Muslim man. Her values were the Torah and her family. She extended her values to the wider Abrahamic family, with her intention to visit Muslims in her area. You could also say, because her attitude to the Muslims had been negative, that she had begun the process of forgiveness, as she began to look at the other's story, as she started to make, as Shriver (1995) tells us, a new story with two strands. On the other hand the values of the Muslim scholar were to be humble about his faith. He extended his humility to cast aside his prejudice of what he thought it was to be a Jew, to what the Jewish woman, FJA(F), said it was to be a Jew. He had thought it was not reasonable that there could be an atheistic Jew. She convinced him that the Jews thought differently. The most important thing about the atheistic Jew was that his mother was a Jew, and he was a Jew, and this superseded everything. He belonged to a community beginning with Abraham.

When speaking about values, it can also be said that most of the Christians had followed their values to the Church that they had chosen. The Uniting Church is liberal, and pledged to uniting and cooperating. One participant, DCA(M), had once been xenophobic, and ACB(F) had also been tempted with fundamentalism, but her father's strong liberal, open behaviour had helped her to retain her openness. So, in one way, you could say that there had been a value change in these participants, but it didn't happen in these particular focus groups, it was part of their journey, as they made their commitment to Jesus Christ.

Neal also talks about defensive behaviour (ibid., p.140). There was also some defensive behaviour from Jews in groups D and F when the subject came to forgiveness, after the question asking for values. There was a hesitancy mainly, more a need for further explanation. It then seemed less threatening when I made it clear that I was talking about forgiveness in family life, not public life. Defensive behaviour was also shown by DJB(M) when discussing friends. Friendship had been used to evangelize and then abandon some young Jewish people, and he was angry about this behaviour. On second thoughts, there was pain exhibited with regard to both forgiveness and friendship. Using Neal's four functional problems of adaptation, goal attainment, integration and latent maintenance as guides, I could say that forgiveness and friendship, which have been used in this thesis to bring about change, led to hesitant behaviour with some Jews.

Values and Leadership

When considering the leadership of Abrahamic interfaith groups, persons concerned with adaptation should perceive the social structure as something that can be changed through new ideas, new division of labour, and new ordering of role relations. "People concerned with goal attainment should perceive the social system as something that can be manipulated by individuals striving to realize specific goals. On the other hand, if the concern is with integration, then a person's interest should focus on social harmony, order, cooperation, and conformity" (Neal 1965, p. 101).

It can be seen that the common values of these participants referred to widely shared conceptions of the good. Generally, we are not prepared to bargain with our values. The value oriented actor is more likely to bring about those programs, behaviors, and artifacts that she/he believes reflect the values to which she/he is committed. "Shared definitions of what is accepted as true or real will immediately make a difference in how stimuli to change are received and interpreted" (ibid., p. 102). It can be said that the shared values of the group definitely prepared a base for the beginnings of friendship and cooperation.

To strengthen Neal's work let us make a distinction between situational short term, and structural long term, phenomena. How aware, was I, a mainly Melbourne person, of the history and issues in Sydney? Only in a vague way, so it was new material for me to find out that the Anglicans did not have an interfaith, and that a book used in Sydney on evangelisation had been very troubling to the Jews. It was reported by DJB(M) that Jewish opinion about the book was that it was deceitful and detrimental to the Jewish people. I begin to think, now, about the long term effect that the cooperation shown in the dialogue in this thesis will have on the Sydney communities.

Interests and values are both vital for understanding social change, and that the social science literature has failed to accomplish this with the focus on structures and not on situations.

So, to begin let us start with the question "What is the situation? The situation, in 2013 is still not good between Muslims, Jews and Christians in Middle Eastern countries, or, in our own country. On our television we see the Jewish population of Israel putting on gasmasks because of the threat of a chemical war coming from Iran, and on 11th December, 2012, Israel and Gaza ceased fighting after 8 days of war (The Guardian). I, myself, sign a petition so that a Christian girl is not killed because she purportedly had in her possession a few burnt pages of the Koran. Refugees from these countries die at sea, drowning, as boats capsize as they attempt to reach Australia.

The Structures

In this thesis we have the scientific structure of citing "the problem" and then attempting to solve it with empirical evidence. While attempting to fulfil human needs, this thesis presents a new kind of peace constructed with the help of God. God cannot be touched or seen, His reasoning is different from human reason, and He has been banished by the academics since the Enlightenment. Could we say that this is a new paradigm? We are of course seeing the effects of God coming through people who are made in the image of God, and who believe him to be loving, compassionate and forgiving. These people are agents of change. They open their minds and hearts to be ready and willing to cooperate with other branches of the Abrahamic religions. This is a history making change. As has been documented in chapter Two, there is also a large group of people who think that God wants them to kill on His behalf. A God who wants you to have the open heart, open mind and open hand of hospitality is most certainly a history making change. We are introduced to this God through the actions of the participants in the four dialogue groups. These actions bring about social cohesion, a social change we need in Australia and the world.

Abrahamic interfaith has been expressed and identified by 15 participants in 7 hours of intense dialogue. What can be said of the future of this dialogue.

COMMUNICATION AND SUSTAINABILITY OF SOCIAL CHANGE

Those seeking strategies for international peace have considered the meaning of oneness, and at the same time trends in international communications are contributing to the oneness of humankind by providing new mechanisms for interaction (from chapter 2, International Communication).

Mattelart, one of the earliest international communication scholars, argues that communication serves first of all to make war. Not many have connected war with communication, but Mattelart points out that this blind spot obstructs the fact that "war and its logics are essential components of the history of international communications and of its doctrines and theories, as well as its uses" (Mattelart 1994, p. xiii). In the context of international communication, propaganda and disinformation are weapons.

Contemporary movements around the world, whether in groups, communities, or nations, are constructing more humane, ethical, traditionalist, antibloc, self-reliance theories of societal development. "It is the quest for dialogue that underlies the current revolutionary movements around the world." (Mowlana 1996, p. 96). The ultimate ethical power of communication institutions within this context is to serve the public, and the zenith of serving that public is reached when a communication entity succeeds in raising a group, a community, a public, or a world to a higher level of understanding and insight. (Mowlana 1996, p. 98). So we are on track, according to Mowlana. But will our communication in private interfaith groups be enough to create actions that will change the society in Sydney? What do the participants say about communication and media?

The way the participants communicated:

JEWS
Images obtained from personal experience	AJA(F)
Jewish, Christian and Muslim groups as plural, they are diverse	DJB(M)
Actions louder than words	DJB(M)
Actions more important than teachings	DJB(M)

CHRISTIANS
Little communication with Catholics	BCA(F)
All pretty established in open communication	BCB(M)
Learn from one another	DCA(M)
Sign of cross, open to misinterpretation	ACA(F)
You respond in some way to images in media	ACB(F)
Listen and learn	FCB(M)

Be open and adventurous	FCB(M)
Interfaith communication entails risk taking	FCA(F)

MUSLIMS

Perceptions confirmed by constant communication	DMA(F)
Listen to each other – can't love without knowing	DMB(M)
Each Encounter with Jews, Christians - enhances or changes preconceived views	FMB(M)
When I interact with Jews/Christians - searching for the truth	FMB(M)
Interfaith communication entails risk	FMA(F)
Interfaith vulnerability	FMA(F)

There were 17 instances given of communication in this thesis. The majority came from:
    Group F   8 instances.
    Group D   6 instances
    Group A   4 instances
    Group B   2 instances

The Christians were pretty happy about their communication. Communicating with Catholics was a bit of a problem, but for the rest you can listen and learn, and their communication is open. It took till Group F and FCA(F) to come up with a negative understanding of communication. Interfaith communicating entails risk taking. She doesn't actually say what the risk is, but in her other conversation she refers to her Muslim neighbours, and how difficult she finds it to communicate with a Muslim woman in full covering, with only slits for the eyes.

When the Jews described their understanding of communication, it was DJB(M) who dominated, and he had a particular point to bring home. It was an interesting point, because it tied it to the Habermas communicative action theory. DJB(M) wanted us to know that actions were more important than words or teachings. Now this is a solid kind of point to make, as so many fights have been fought over religious text and teachings. And words, how many interpretations of religious words have we heard, and how many times do we actually use religious words today? Not many. But actions? We are considering actions in the course of thinking and are actually moving into actions most of the day.

The Muslims were the searchers. They were looking to understand people of interfaith, searching for the truth, but also acknowledging, as did the Christians, that interfaith entails risk and vulnerability. The risk dialogue came from Group F, and it was preceded by this dialogue:

FCB: And learning about the—I certainly feel learning about not just what the other faiths' concepts are, but the very specific things, like going to a synagogue or a, a mosque and understanding what things mean, makes it so much more, ah, easy—

FJA: Are we on now?

FCB: —to understand. I'm constantly bewildered by the, you know, people are so reluctant to want to hear these stories, go and listen and learn. And again it comes— because it's easier to be, it's easier to be negative and confining than it is to be open and adventurous. Because open and adventurous does require a degree of—

FMA: Risk.

FCA: Risk taking.

So they define fear as the feeling that stops the impulse to be open and to listen and learn. Maybe some of this fear could be attached to cultural issues.

Cultural Issues

Cultural issues have something to do with communication. For instance, there are 11 cultural codes. Most of these came from the Muslim FMB(M), so let's start with him first.

Wrong to judge on clothes	FMB(M)
Social dialogue/as against religious dialogue	FMB(M)
It's cultural dialogue	FMB(M)
Sometimes it's political dialogue	FMB(M)

The dialogue from Group F is mostly from FMB(M). He tells us in an aside that his sisters wear Australian clothing, rather than Muslim scarves, but the matter certainly is causing him to think. He and FJA(F) work it out together. While it is wrong to judge on clothes, when you think of social dialogue as against religious dialogue, you come to the conclusion that it is cultural dialogue. No, says FJA(F), it's cultural differences, and he quickly answers, "and sometimes it's political dialogue."

Hijab sends messages women oppressed	BCB(M)
Cultural issues, head scarf	DMB(F)
Cultural clothing as opposed to superb English education	FJA (F)
Black clothing with slits hinders communication	FCA (F)
It's not religion, physical issues not faith issues	FCB (M)

The hijab communicates to BCB(M) that women are oppressed, and he tells us that he feels uncomfortable about this. FCA(F) also feels uncomfortable. She specifically cites communication as the most difficult problem with a Muslim woman who wears black clothing with slits for the eyes[13]. Maybe we should listen to FCB)(M), he is very well travelled, and in his reasoning, it is not a religious question. This kind of clothing is to be seen as a physical issue, not a faith issue. What then do communication and cultural issues have to do with issues and interests in the understanding of Neal? The social change that we are advocating is brought about by communication. And it is plain to see that cultural issues such as clothing can hinder the social change of opening yourself up to another culture if you reason that the woman you are trying to talk to is oppressed, and because of the hijab (nigab) you cannot get the facial clues as to the meaning of her speech. There is another issue. A person, for instance, a Jew, who is wearing some traditional Jewish clothing might look very foreign, but in fact, have a superb English education. Judgement of people by their speech and clothing is hardwired into Western culture. But, by the theory that we have chosen to use, Habermas and his communicative culture, and also from DJB's cited opinion that actions are louder than words or teachings, perhaps in this social change by their fruits we will know them. By what they do, and not do, will we come to the conclusion as to whether we can trust them and move into cooperative action. Another question concerns identity.

Identity

Will you lose your identity if you change your social values and include the Abrahamic religions in your interests. In general, not

---

13   Definition of hijab: a head covering worn by some Muslim women. Definition of nigab: A veil worn by some Muslim women in public covering all the face apart from the eyes <OxfordDictionaries.com>

so, but it is dangerous and unsafe to move out of a limited, confined world:

Once a Jew, always a Jew	BJA(F)
At the core of Christianity is the notion of grace	BCB(M)
Someone of faith is someone who is of peace	DMB(F)
People of faith associated with peace	DMA(F)
People in our societies live in a limited, confined world	FCB(M)
Jews are a people, beginning with Abraham	FJA(F)
It's safe (to live in confined world)	FCA(F)

Clothing, of course can communicate identity, but the participants tell us that by their actions you will know them. For instance, people of faith are associated with peace. At the core of Christianity is the notion of grace. Someone of faith is someone who is of peace. Both the peace entries came from the Muslims, and this was their message to us overall in the focus groups. The message from the Jews on identity was uncompromising. Once a Jew, always a Jew, and they are a people beginning with Abraham. The difficulty with moving into having an interest in another Abrahamic community comes from the clear message that people in our society live in a limited confined world. This from FCB(M) the traveller. He is quickly answered by FCA(F) that it is safe to live in a confined world. So safety is an issue.

What is out there that is unsafe. They all agree it is the media.

Media

Media sensationalize	AJA(F)
Does not respond to media stereotyping images	ACA(F)
Media sensationalize people of Middle Eastern appearance	ACB(F)
Media biased against Israel	AJA(F)

Media does not report in a way that encourages dialogue	ACB(F)
Media stereotype	ACB(F)

Group A 6 media issues – all negative

Knows Muslims only through media generated images	BCB(M)
Not met a Jew, fed media images of Jews	BJA(F)
Negative stereotypes Muslims Jews recycled through media	BJA(F)
Sons have conservative images	BCA(F)

Group B 4 issues to do with media – all negative

Misinformation about Islam	DMA(F)
Media positive	DJB(M)

Group D 2 media issues, one positive, one negative

Ignorance born of misinformation	FCB(M)
Images (Jews Christians Muslims) come from media	FCA(F)

Group F 2 media issues, one negative

When we examine the media themes, we immediately see that if there is to be a social change with regard to the Abrahamic communities as a whole, the media will have to be changed as well. As it is now, according to most of the participants, the images that media communicate to the world are badly stereotyped and negative.

If we begin with images of Jews, Christians and Muslims which come from the media and look through the eyes of the participants we see that:

(1) media sensationalize, especially people of Middle Eastern appearance
(2) media stereotype, and channel misinformation about Islam,
(3) ignorance in the community is born of misinformation from media

(4) community knows Muslims only through media generated images.
(5) media is also biased against Israel, does not report in a way that encourages dialogue.

Therefore, if you have not met a Jew, and there are many people who have not met a Jew, you are left with media stereotyped images of Jews. BCA's sons have conservative images from the media, and only DJB(M) has a positive view of it.

These negatives do not have the remediations to heal them, and therefore, unless something is done to counteract these negative images of Jews and Muslims in particular, it would be difficult to see how a general social change could take place. However, media report on what is going on in the community, and if Abrahamic communities get together and for instance, such as in Sydney, put on a conference to support the Aboriginal community, then the reporting of this in the media can begin to open up people's mind and hearts to their Abrahamic neighbours.

All the interfaith groups also have a presence in the world wide web, and their newsletters regularly report what is happening within their ranks. Google delivers to my computer every day reports from all over the world of interfaith endeavours. During this time a criticism was made that this thesis was just propaganda.[14] It had to be answered by showing that the participants were truthful and not biased or misleading.

---

14 Propaganda: information of a biased or misleading nature used to promote or publicise a particular political cause or point of view, (Oxford dictionaries).

Soft Power or Propaganda

The activity at the centre of this thesis, focus group discussion, was a soft power vehicle. The term soft power rests on the idea that the first and most important attraction to a human being is the common good. Soft power in politics, as Professor Nye tells us, will help the public opinion of countries – enabling, rather than disabling, them to work together (www.youtube.com/watch?v=F8udhM8QKxg). It is our own opinion of ourselves, and our own comprehensive awareness, that will build national soft power. It will enable us to know and share the common good at home first and then in the world at large (Roseman 2009).

The negative side of soft power is that it could verge on propaganda, and there is a risk therefore that the researcher and participants could gild the lily. To determine whether this thesis draws on propaganda or on truthful material about the faith of individuals, and their communicative expression of that faith, it is necessary to re-examine the definition of religion that appears in chapter 2. French sociologist Hervieu-Leger states that religious leadership is important. She also argues that religion exists when the authority of tradition supports the act of believing. "As our fathers believed, and because they believed, we too believe" (Hervieu-Leger 2000, p. 81). From her viewpoint, any form of believing is religious if it adopts a chain of belief.

The chain of belief in the focus groups came from an act of believing. All participants came from either Jewish, Christian or Muslim families. Eight of the participants came from families where belief was important. Six came from families where religious belief was not important. Of those who came from families where religion was not important, one Christian was sent to Sunday school and another had a Christian education. Yet another, AJA(F), had a Jewish father. The participant codenamed FMB(M) also remembered being in the mosque with his father: "He helped me. He got a teacher for us to teach us Arabic." All participants had arrived at their commitment to God through their own personal journeys, some of the young Muslim women being helped by the interfaith movement itself. The participant ACB(F) believed as her father believed. He intervened when she was veering towards a more fundamentalist type of Christianity. The commonality of the 15 participants resided in the commitment to serve the One God, who by their consensus was forgiving. They also agreed that they had in their religious texts the commandment to love God and neighbour. Together, their people make up more than half the world's population. One indication then of the focus groups was that if they could be at peace, the world could be at peace.

Chapter One summarizes the Jews' description of their religion as a community chosen by God to be the light of the world. Yet to non-Jews, the evidence of a light shining from the Jews, a light coming from their fathers, could be unclear, the discussion revealed. In the focus groups, leadership came from participant DJB(M), whose father was a Jew. This participant gave the group an account of the history of interfaith remediation: "The National Dialogue of Christians, Muslims and Jews, which is formal, has been going since 2003 only, although the informal dialogue of those three groups was going back much further." He also wanted the group to know about the impact of the attack on the Twin Towers in New York on September 11, 2001.

I think it's important to know what happened in Australia, which showed how good things were here. Within two days there were thousands of people at the Sydney Domain, in the Domain, where the Jews, Christians and Muslims had organized prayers for our Common Humanity, and other groups, other religious groups, came along as well, and all over Sydney radio and whatever people from the different faiths together were going and saying now is a time for common humanity, a time of distress or whatever, which was almost the opposite of what was happening in virtually every other country in the world, where groups were at loggerheads and defaming and angry. (DJB(M))

These instances of leadership were in a metaphoric sense filled with light. The leadership this participant referred to gave remediation to a wounded community. By their actions you will know them. Faith of the fathers also applies to Christianity. "Christianity developed when a group of Jews two thousand years ago gathered around the Rabbi Jesus of Nazareth " (Crim 1981, p. 69). The three Christian woman ministers in the focus groups worked for the marginalized, the victims of racism, and one, plus another layperson, had been missionaries in Africa and in the Australian outback. They were all still engaged in justice, education, and healing. They told the group that God was forgiving and waiting at the gate.

Another light on the notion of forgiveness is evident in the paper of the 138 Muslim scholars, "A Common Word Between Us and You", in reaction to Pope Benedict's statement: "Show me just what Muhammad brought that was new, and there you will find things only evil and inhuman, such as his command to spread by the sword the faith he preached" (Pope Benedict). The Muslim Scholars' paper appeared one year later. Rather than engage in polemic, the signatories adopted the traditional mainstream Islamic position of respecting the Christian scripture and calling Christians to be more, not less, faithful to it. In this paper:

... [S]ouls are depicted in the Holy Qur'an as having three main faculties: the mind or the intelligence, which is made for comprehending the truth; the will, which is made for freedom of choice; and sentiment, which is made for loving the good and the beautiful. Put another way, we could say that man's soul knows through understanding the truth, through willing the good, and through virtuous emotions and feeling love for God. (138 Muslim Scholars)

The words of the Muslim Scholars were a warning: "We say that our very eternal souls are all also at stake if we fail to sincerely make every effort to make peace and come together in harmony." They were believing as their fathers believed. Islam means "entering into a condition of peace and security with God though allegiance or surrender to Him". The Muslim participants did this. As fully committed Muslims they were fully involved in interfaith, sharing their faith, and working towards peaceful relationships in the Abrahamic communities. They were also researching in the hope of bringing greater peace and understanding to the dualities of their religious texts.

Truthful dialogue is dialogue where words are followed up by comparable actions. It can be ascertained that this was the case in the four dialogue groups. This thesis is not propaganda, it is real life lived in the service of the One God.

Chapter Three refers to a continuation of the political communication, with the following statement from the Jews: "We call to dialogue all of those who affirm that our mandate as leaders is to guide our communities in accordance with values that are beneficial of human society" (Seek Peace and Pursue it: a Jewish Call to Muslim-Jewish Dialogue.) A question central to the thesis was the extent to which participants pursued peace. To pursue peace was to highlight the common repudiation in Judaism and Islam of murder, violence, injustice and indignity.

Interfaith dialogue is a compacted knowledge base for the integrated lifestyle, commitment to religion, and social awareness that are the threads to a new social intelligence. In interfaith work, the necessity to uphold the "difference" is a breakthrough in social living. This became evident when a Jewish woman in the focus group enabled one of the Islamic men to leave the group for a while to pray. The woman took leadership and stopped the group for coffee while he was absent. The political communication in chapters 2 and 3, and the definition of the religions in chapter 1, give witness to the authentication of these participants as role models and leaders who can reveal the way ahead in dialogue and in action from dialogue.

New Learning and the Role of the Moderator

The author of this thesis had studied the Jewish faith for many years but during the course of the research learned more about customs and lifestyle. A Jew could be an atheist and still go to the Sabbath meal. The wicked, the wise, the people who didn't want to learn, and the simple would all be welcome at the Sabbath meal. Dialogue from the Muslims in the focus groups turned up fewer surprises. They spoke easily about asking forgiveness of God and neighbour, and mostly they affirmed that God was compassionate and that all were connected to God. Relevant to the integrity of the research was the fact that the Muslim scholars, three born outside of Australia, were chosen by their faith to be participants and were well integrated into Australian life. Also relevant was that Sharia law was not discussed in the focus groups. The Protestant participants went out of their way to assist the research process. Most had been missionaries. Thus they presented a positive view of evangelism. They had worked in the service of Jesus Christ for many years, but the research revealed in one participant a void in her Christianity: the absence of a forgiveness ritual. This void prompted an examination of people's openness to others.

In facilitating the focus groups, the role of the moderator was to be welcoming, non-judgemental, and open minded. But in one section of dialogue the researcher could feel the difficulty of accepting, rather than arguing and saying that she was 'right'. The researcher also noted a difference between groups A and B, who had no Muslim presence, and groups D and F who did. The Muslim scholars were young and exuberant and "lightened" up their focus groups.

Key Ideas in the Focus Groups

Using six words to categorise the participants' references to aspects of peacemaking, the following frequencies emerged in the dialogue in the focus groups. The results reveal that the Muslims, in their use of language, spoke the words God and forgiveness more than did their Jewish and Christian friends. Both the Christians in groups A and B and the Muslims in groups D and F used the word connect, and the groups A and B used the word friend more than the others.

Table 7.1
Summary of references to aspects of peacemaking in the 4 focus groups

	Jews	Christians	Muslims
God	31	51	64
Connect	2	27	27
Spirit	3	25	14
Love	21	20	5
Friend	33	39	11
Forgiveness	6	4	14

The Muslims spoke about God 64 times and connectedness 27 times. Everyone was "connected" to God, to one another. By comparison, the Christians spoke of connectedness 27 times, but this could be explained by the fact that there were four Muslims and seven Christians. The Jews used the word twice. The word connected brings to mind the theorists Dewey and Hervieu-Leger, who used the word chain to convey the connectedness of thoughts and beliefs. The Muslims used the word compassion four times. This was in relation to compassion in community, in friendship, in witnessing the Christian focus on the love and compassion of God, and in witnessing Christian compassion. Compassion was mentioned once by the Christians and not at all by the Jews. The word respect occurred nine times in group A, 17 times in group B, 10 times in group D, and 9 times in group F.

Discussion of Findings in Terms of Theory

Intercultural Communication and Conflict

In chapter 2, science and religion were presented as complementary to one another. As well, theories of conflict and cooperation were presented at both the international level and the organizational level. As mentioned above, Mattelart (1994, p. xiii) believed that international communication served to make war. War frequently uses communication that is deceitful. This gives birth to actions that are coming from an enemy who manipulates the situation, especially with unfounded fear. In the focus groups for this project, participants actually identified negative stereotyping and misinformation as dangerous.

Alternatively, the theorist Pettman sharpens the idea of language, by identifying how the language of dialogue opens up relationships. Words and their arrangement can provide an account of world affairs, giving the power to put together a particular kind of world from personal knowledge and imagination. "The power of language makes possible both memory and imagination – the capacity to recall the past and to anticipate the future" (Pettman 2000, p. 31). The language of the focus groups was recorded verbatim by the court reporter. At this point, the language revealed a creation of a particular kind of world, an everyday kind of living and speaking. But relevant to any interpretation of that language is that the language of interfaith groups is a special language. It controls negative responses. It is the language that moves into the reality of the open hand and of hospitality, it is the language speaking about positive images of neighbours, accepting difference, and putting oneself in the other's shoes. It produces behaviours that are open and cooperative rather than aggressive or defensive. This language of peace from both religious and secular theorists appears in threads through the thesis. The whole is greater than the sum of its parts, but the parts are connected to the whole, the whole being, for this thesis, the construction of peace by the Abrahamic communities of the One God.

Theories of International Conflict

Huntington's desire that the West acquire "a profound understanding of the religious and philosophical assumptions underlying other civilizations" is manifest in Australia, as in other parts of the world, as Jews, Christians, and Muslims meet to share their faith and their lives. Six of the 15 participants in this project were born outside Australia, hence the difference between faith and culture emerged as a debate in the focus groups. As the participants discussed questions about peace, they also negotiated to respect each other's differences, unconstrained from defending their particular version of faith. The dialogue reflected the remediation that "information about the other groups became interesting and sought after, rather than something to be ignored or interpreted to fit existing conceptions of the out-group (Sherif 1967, p. 93). Sherif's superordinate goal, which, he said, enabled cooperation, was the goal to make the world a better place. In the focus groups, everyone agreed that the authority of the One God was evident in the common belief to "Love God and neighbour", which existed in their religious texts. Bellah states that religion can provide ideals and models for new lines of social development "with the growing symbolic, individual, and social differentiation" (Bellah 1970, p. 17). The focus groups then were theory coming to life, or learning by imitation. People look around for someone who is doing what they themselves want to do, someone admirable or at least acceptable. And then they take that person as an example to follow.

American sociologists were the first to discuss reference groups as groups whose behaviour served as a model for others. Then a breakthrough came about with the emergence of reference individuals, particularly people to imitate. Then a diversion followed to call these people reference idols to match contemporary concentration on heroes. In the 1950s, the sociologist Robert K. Merton distinguished between reference individuals, who served as patterns for living, and role models, whom others might imitate in specific roles such as playing basketball, or parenting. Thus role models can model whole lives as well as particular skills. This research project presents the participants as role models not only in interfaith dialogue in an international framework but also in everyday life.

Theories of Communication

Habermas explains what happens in focus groups with his idea that two people can use language to come to some kind of "action" together. Or in his own words: "There is then a fundamental connection between understanding communicative actions and constructing rational interpretations" (Habermas 1981).

The communication scholar Weaver states that the core issue is often the nature of communication in groups. He has exerted his influence on this research because he suggests using a contrast and comparison approach. It is important to identify the differences. This was particularly easy in the four focus groups, because as reported in the Findings (Appendix 1), a great deal of the time was taken up with explaining who they were as individuals, and who they were as groups of Jews, Christians and Muslims. Comparisons were also evident in looking at the issues people fought about, which included the clothing worn by Muslim women and some Jewish men. It was agreed by all, without any dissent, that these were cultural issues not religious issues. The dialogue demonstrated clear definitions of the different religious issues. The Jews had their religious texts, and when they were written there were no Christians or Muslims. The Christians on the other hand believed that Christ was the Messiah, so long awaited by the Jews. And the Muslims had to engage with their religious texts to understand what they said about both the Jews and the Christians. So the differences were there, and they were discussed. There was no attempt to make one another 'the same'. On the other hand, as Weaver says, similarities were also considered. And there was overwhelming consensus that all the participants in all the groups shared a firm belief that they had to love God and neighbour. They did not deny the existence of different cultures, but they were proceeding to move forward to cooperate to make the world a better place. (Weaver 2003, p. 76–7). Chapter 4 provides case studies of communication and conflict resolution in South Africa, Ireland, and Israel. One of the Jewish participants, BJA(F), mirrored the issue central to these case studies: is it possible to be friends with enemies? Her son was a member of the Israeli army at the time of the Lebanon war, and her Muslim friends always asked her kindly how he was. She saw this as a sign of real friendship.

Construction of Peace

Reconciliation, a consequence of successful conflict resolution, is needed today as the frequency, intensity and deadliness of deep-rooted conflicts continue. Today, this conflict is "not across national borders, but between ethnic or other identity groups within a single political unit." (Kelman 2008, p. 15). It is mutual trust and mutual acceptance that have to be highlighted when we think about interaction between groups who are sensitive about their security, dignity and wellbeing. The need for assurance about personal and group survival is probably the central issue in a conflict and in efforts to resolve it. So, it is not peace as the central issue, as Galtung sees it, but identity and security bringing peace. "This issue is directly linked to what I see as the psychological core of the Israeli-Palestinian conflict" (Kelman 1987, p. 354). For the group identity, "someone of faith is someone who is of peace", the young Muslim girl said. But in a world of the media, "victims and perpetrators and those who thought that they were just innocent bystanders now realize their complicity and have an opportunity to participate in each other's humanity in story form" (de la Rey 2001, p. 260). A society that deals with computerized images of Jews and Muslims, which are biased with misinformation, is living in an unreal world.

Analysis of Negative Dialogue

Scheff (1997) has shown that shame brings spirals of anger. Of the 32 instances of negative references in this research, many concerned shame and humiliation. Fear then begins to grow alongside a reluctance to show signs of religious affiliation. The coding shows 22 instances of negative experience from the Jews, 9 from the Christians and one from the Muslims. The word fear is used four times with regard to syncretism, evangelization, friendship and anti-Semitism. The participant DMA(F) revealed that Muslims were sometimes seen as lacking humanity and Christians were still telling Jews that they would burn in hell if they didn't accept Jesus. However, after these negative responses and observations, expressed through the dialogue, emerged not revenge but remediation. In the dynamics of the focus groups, the diabolic enemy image defined in the work of Ralph White (1984) was diluted and remediated by the participants' creation of positive experiences.

According to Lindner (2006), humiliation is the enforced lowering of a person or group, a process of subjugation that damages or strips away pride, honour, or dignity. To clear the mind of ancient negative narratives requires humility and friendship. Lindner defines the skills of friendship as "warmth, loyalty, solidarity, mutual recognition, dialogue, and humble acknowledgement of equal dignity – this is friendship." (Lindner 2006, pp. 147–8). Without the remediations these people were practising, the response to this humiliation could have been spiralling violence of the kind described by Scheff (1997). There were 15 instances of remediations from Jews, 22 remediations from Christians and 7 remediations from Muslims.

This thesis projects that the remedy, peace as a culture of unity of human beings, is within reach. In the dialogue in the focus groups it was obtained by identifying legitimate goals by mutual inquiry. "In other words, by dialogue and diversity as a source of mutual enrichment" (Galtung 2007, p. 24). Chapter 3 describes the concepts of peace as a human need, forgiveness, and ethical communication. In the social sciences, peace as a human need and the different parts of it - ethical communication, forgiveness, and peace construction - are all-encompassing. This thesis argues that in this way, historical memories of pain and suffering can be overcome at micro levels. People have the capacity to make choices. Enright (2001) states that point without compromise. Forgiveness is a choice, and a process. When people successfully complete the forgiveness process, if for instance they have decided to refrain from disparaging remarks about someone, then they have reduced or eliminated negative feelings, thoughts and behaviours towards the offender (Enright 2001, p. 35).

In every individual's day and time is a change in society to suit the human needs of the individual (Burton 1990). Needs are related to value. The need for self-esteem "is perhaps the most pervasive of any of the needs in humans" (Sites 1990, p. 19). This principle emerged in many ways in the focus groups. The whole concept of loving the neighbour is to "work harder to open ourselves to the neighbour who is different", participant BJA(F) and BCA(F) stated. The really dark negative to this loving, participant BJA(F) stated, was the way that "some loved by forcing (people) to be the same". Throughout the seven hours of interviewing, the same theme was evident again and again: to respect and understand difference. Loving a neighbour meant loving everyone, and this meant recognizing the good in people despite disagreements, participant BCB(M) stated. To participants BCB(M) and BJA(F) it also meant to recognize good and wrong. "Don't tolerate evil, which is unacceptable," BJA(F) stated.

In the broad social science paradigm, developing the skills needed for understanding the role of social meaning in sane societies brings forth a sacred social vision and includes the bonding of the creative individual with the social enterprise. This will fulfil "the deepest, most human of all our needs: those for social attachment and psychological purpose" (Clarke 1990, p. 36). The sacred social vision was evident in the dialogue in the focus groups. Participants reiterated many pathways to God. Participants presented this as a value and also twice as a remediation.

SEQUENCE OF FRAMEWORKS FOR COMMUNICATION IN THE FOCUS GROUPS

The focus groups in this research project demonstrated a theoretical pathway to greater peace. That is to say, changes occurred in their expressions of values and in their interpretations of experiences during the course of the group interaction. Belief in One God, and in the principle of 'love God and love thy neighbour' were the constants, common to all participants. This process of movement toward peace in a controlled setting can be summarised as a series of steps towards friendship (Fig. 7.1), friendship being the new framework that replaces the old one. Along the way is dialogue, through which people express and interpret their own inherited values, religious and secular, vis- à-vis the values of others.

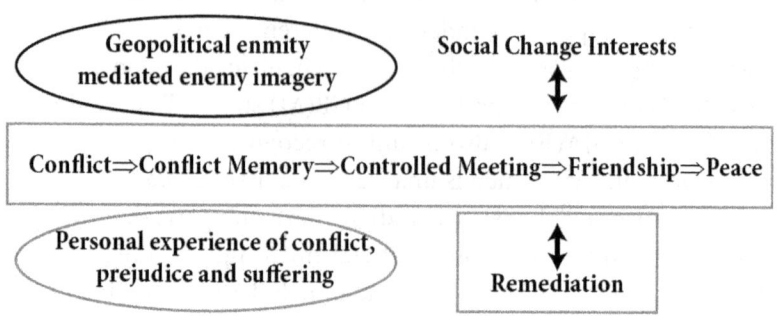

Figure 7.1
Steps towards peace: A framework

There have been countless generations of families, tribes and clans who have told stories about who is acceptable, and who is not acceptable to their particular religious culture. There are still some remnants of these stories, a few retold in the focus groups in this thesis. But the wider group is giving immediate remediation, immediate remedy to cover over and replace the prejudice of generations with respect and kindness. This is very real and hopeful! I watched it happen, and recorded it with a court reporter.

From conflict, which many times comes from prejudice, individuals and by implication societies, can move to a state of coexistence. Coexistence can lead to dialogue, which can lead to a social change of the old conflict model, which results in friendship, the new framework for meeting human needs. The South African and Irish experiences described in chapter 4 provide examples of secular models. Contemporary interfaith dialogue is providing an example of a religious model. The focus groups in this study provided a snapshot in microcosm of the same principle.

Coexistence is when a person accepts the other's right to exist. Dialogue follows, and social change is the final stage, where people in dialogue construct a new frame to meet their needs and transcend the conflict (Nudler 1990, p. 197). The new frame is the frame of friendship. There is doubt among researchers that this is happening on a large enough scale to influence world peace. Beyond the focus groups in this study though are encouraging signs in Australia that dialogue is leading to friendship. The necessary condition, according to Scimecca, is freedom. Scimecca's position is that self-consciousness, the ability to think back and reflect upon one's actions, needs freedom and that only freedom of thought enables self-reflexivity to fully develop (Scimecca 1990, p. 208). Freedom in the context of the four focus groups was defined as "being yourself", being able to wear the clothes you want, if you want to.

This thesis is a remediation for the negative effects of both shame and humiliation. The remediation is friendship and forgiveness, which come from open dialogue and trust.

The Letting Go of Prejudice

Bearing in mind Sheff's theory, the following analyses a central, critical dialogue on identity, between an old Jewish woman and a young Muslim man, a scholar. Scheff uses a verbatim text approach. The researcher has access to features of the text which were often ignored by the participants, and to instant replay, which is also seldom available to the participants (Scheff 1997, p. 10). Scheff says people need the living present in the human sciences to breathe life into our enterprise. Using transcripts or verbatim texts as data, one interprets the meaning of the smallest parts (words and gestures) of expressions within the context of the ever great wholes within which they occur: sentences, paragraphs, the whole dialogue, the whole relationship, the whole culture and social structure (Scheff 1997, p. 16). The meaning of human expressions and behaviour can be determined, but objective interpretation requires disciplined investigation of the complex three-way relationships between meaning, text and context. If something is taken out of context, any text becomes ambiguous. No matter how exhaustive the analysis of a text, the determination of meaning will be incomplete and therefore partly subjective and missing relevant historical and biographical knowledge.

In the instance of the dialogue that is set out below it was known that both the old Jewish woman and the young Muslim scholar had committed themselves to their respective faiths. Also known was that the Jewish woman lost 29 of her close relatives in the holocaust and that the young Muslim scholar came to Australia from another country and was questioning what was true and what was false after 9/11 and the loss of life inflicted by the Muslim suicide bombers. Understanding ordinary language requires the mind to be a general problem solver. It relates the smallest parts (words) and wholes (not only systems of grammar and syntax, but a vast array of cultural practices).

Scheff looks for meaning in the text and rephrases it in part/whole language. The researcher had understood this ancient teaching that the whole was greater than the sum of its parts and applied it in analysis of the focus group transcripts. The method of prospective and retrospective understanding that Scheff works on implies that understanding ordinary language requires searching of the local and extended context. "Although the local context is strictly finite, the particular text of which an expression is a part, the extended context is not. The prospective context is all that happened after the expression, the retrospective context all that happened before it" (Scheff 1997, p. 37).

Those in the focus group knew what had happened before this dialogue. They knew that the Jewish woman was very kind and caring when the young Muslim scholar came late to the group, and she enquired whether he was hungry. He then asked permission to leave the group to pray. Permission was given, but the Jewish woman extended the permission and said the group would all wait for him and have a cup of coffee while he was away. In the researcher's opinion, he felt loved enough to begin to ask questions. The following is a selection from the transcript.

FMB: You know how you said about one of the stereotypes they see Jewish people as a race?

FJA: Yeah.

FMB: I think I'm guilty of having that, a bit of that stereotype. Because when I read many of our people who are prominent atheists, you know, they still identify themselves as being a Jew.

FJA: Yes. It's no problem with that, because we are a people. And you can be a cultural Jew, you can be a Jew—you are born of a Jewish mother, you are a Jew.

FMB: So it is a race?

FJA: No, it's not a race. It's a—we belong to a cultural group, we belong to a people. And it's like belonging to a tribe. You know?

FMB: Okay. But it's an ethnic thing?

FJA: Even the most atheist of Jews come the Passover will share the tradition of the Passover meal.

FMB: Okay.

FJA: It's, it's not just a religion. It's a culture as well. Judaism is also a culture.

FMB: Okay. What makes it not a race? I don't understand.

FJA: If you've got black Jews and you've got Chinese Jews and—

FMB: Okay, so—

FCB: Race is biological.

FJA: We're not biological.

FMB: So, it's a multiracial people?

FJA: No, just a people.

FMB: A people. Yeah. I get it. All right. I get it.

FJA: Beginning with Abraham, a people, born of—so you can be an atheist and still observe certain of the traditions and still call yourself a Jew. Just you can. You can do that.

FMB: So, there's more than just the faith element to being a Jew?

FJA: Yes. Much more, yes.

FMB: There's a cultural and there's—

FJA: There's much more, yes. Yes.

FMB: Thank you.

This dialogue showed how people could have different ideas in their minds about others and their communities, as to how they could identify themselves. As the dialogue showed, the young Muslim scholar had reached the point where he could see that he was maybe guilty of stereotyping. But it was so hard for him to give up his ideas about the Jewish people. The kindness and patience of the Jewish woman evidently allowed him to pursue his thoughts and to keep on going until they had reached a conclusion. Eventually, he knew, absolutely, that the Jews were a people beginning with Abraham.

This revelation is seen as the pinnacle of the research. The living out of truthfulness about whom we are, the ability to ask questions about the images we hold about others, and the decision to ask, listen, and then accept somebody else's definition of whom they are. Scheff asks what comes after that. Friendship was the vehicle in the focus groups to carry attitudes and behaviours to enable dialogue and cooperation, which would in turn lead to looking for, and finding, a better way to live together.

Summary

The unique situation in the world, and the remediations offered by interfaith dialogue groups have been analysed as to change or no change in values and interests. The change in interests, the opening up of the mind and the heart to their Abrahamic brothers and sisters is a milestone in the history of the world. The energy to make the world a better place is now three-fold in cooperation and hospitality in interfaith. A change for the "good".

This chapter has given a deeper insight into the workings of an interfaith group, and we can say confidently that:

(1) There has been a change in interests in the four focus groups that participated in this research. They have moved from an interest only in their own religion, to an interest in the three Abrahamic religions together.

(2) The men and women in the focus groups were authentic messengers of their different Abrahamic religions, communicating truthfully in word and action.

Religion exists when the authority of tradition supports the act of believing. New interfaith spaces are constructed slowly, with risk and vulnerability, and are cemented with trust and respect, and something deeper than respect, the ability to empathize with another person in an Abrahamic faith. This vehicle of friendship reminded the members of their historical ties to Abraham and of their connections with spirituality and the One God. They imagined the possibility of loving God and neighbour in a cooperative way. Their attitudes were open and their behaviour was hospitable. The conclusion to this project, which follows in chapter 8, looks forward to Abrahamic communities making new memories and acting on them.

Chapter Eight
Conclusion

Introduction

This chapter is a final evaluation of this project that has extracted the views of participants drawn from Abrahamic interfaith groups in Sydney on issues drawn from social, scientific, humanities and religious theory and analysed the data in three steps in chapter 6, 7 and 8. The research question that the thesis project sought to answer was as follows: 'how are people of the three Abrahamic faiths that are implicated in a geopolitical confrontation able to cooperate within interfaith organizations at the local level?' We found it was answered by fulfilling the needs of people for respect and recognition, with dialogue going from fear to friendship. This chapter will first evaluate whether there was any change in values or interests in the focus groups, and whether or not this change can be seen as an historical change. After this, there will be the evaluation of the research question, and how this question has been answered by the thesis, a critical self-reflective and then a discussion of future prospects for peace construction based on the insights drawn from the thesis before discussing possible future areas of research and ending with a conclusion.

Social Change

To make the results of this thesis clear, Neal (1965) has been used to precisely inform, with coded information, if there has been a value change, or an interest change in the behaviour of the participants. The results are:
1. No overall change in values
   (although the history of the Christians would show a liberal value change in their journey to their commitment to Christ, their values remained the same during the focus groups.)
2. A definite change in interests encompassing all participants from interest in their own religion to an added interest in the three Abrahamic religions
3. This interest change helps the social integration of the Abrahamic religions in society, and could be called an historical social change from enemy to friend

The overwhelming result is that yes, there has been an interest change in the 15 participants in the four focus groups in this thesis. They are all committed to either the Jewish, Christian or Muslim faith, but they have expanded their interest in their own religion to take on added interests in the whole 3 of the Abrahamic religions. They have travelled a journey from seeing the other Abrahamic religions as 'enemy' to being friends, and this has been done mainly with a language of peace giving birth to good deeds. These good deeds begin with an attitude of respect, and can be described as emanating from the open mind, open heart and open hand of hospitality. They also comply with the theory of Habermas when he says that truthful dialogue is communicative action.

As the participants in this research are agents of change, we also have looked deeper into their religious commitment, a glimpse into the presence of divinity, and of course Neal's understanding of values, and the change in either interests or values where there are agents for change. Most importantly, it has been shown that negative issues can be healed by remediations, good deeds, that we are all able to do in our everyday life. And values such as the virtues of humility and compassion are powerful agents for social integration.

Our concept of the world, since the Enlightenment in Europe, has been that anything science can think of, can be done, without reference to a higher power, God, creator and sustainer. But according to Jurengensmeyer we have to come to the end of this kind of thinking. The Muslim populations of the world are growing, 2.2 billion in 2011, and still rising. And we have to reincorporate some kind of space to God thinking again. Asking people how and why they are committed to their understanding of God is a beginning. Looking at the effects of this commitment is the next step. And evaluating those effects is the third and most crucial step. This is what this thesis has done. Racism is a curse upon the human beings on planet earth. The kind of peace language taught in interfaith, and spoken in a communication action that includes, rather than excludes, is a mighty step forward for the world. When the astronauts went to the moon they said, "one small step for a man, one giant leap for mankind" (the late astronaut Neal Armstrong).

Has the Research Question Been Answered and How?

Unlike in a thesis based on a hypothesis and positivist data that is shown to prove or not prove the hypothesis, this thesis was grounded in a hybrid approach that identified a research question at the outset, explored the areas of the research question through a review of relevant literature, selected concepts that were used to organize the field research and data and then reported on it (Appendix 2), analysed and discussed the data in two chapters (chapters 6 and 7). The question, 'how are people of the three Abrahamic faiths that are implicated in a geopolitical confrontation able to cooperate within interfaith organizations at the local level?' has been answered in an elaborated manner in these two chapters. The answer has been reduced to a framework, "Steps towards Peace" (Fig. 7.1) page 260, which has been unpacked at the end of this section. The sequence goes from conflict and memories of conflict, through a controlled meeting, with dialogue bringing friendship and peace. The social change is in the interests of the participants, which brings remediation.

But first, it is also possible now to answer the question asked in chapter 5, "Will a Jewish, Christian, Muslim approach to the human needs of respect and recognition, ethical communication (dialogue), values and the role of forgiveness, be the same as one another, or different?" The answer is that in the main, the approach was the same. And within focus groups, of Jews, Christians and Muslims together, will they come to the same or different conclusions as to the pursuit of peace construction? The answer is the same, as they must submit to the common sacred command to love God and neighbour. "As in any argumentative paper, your thesis statement will convey the gist of your argument, which necessarily follows from your frame of reference. In a compare-and-contrast, the thesis depends on how the things you've chosen to compare actually relate to one another (Walk 1998).

The answer to other questions that one might pose may help flesh out the frameworks as well. How did the Abrahamic communities relate to one another? Did representatives from these three religious groupings not only dialogue with each other during the focus groups, but also want to continue this dialogue into cooperation, and then into friendship? From the actual research it can be said that most of the people in the focus groups had already formed friendships with some of the participants, as all were members of interfaith Abrahamic groups in Sydney. They were able to cooperate with one another because they were using their energies to listen and to learn from one another, to be patient and kind and open minded and forgiving and respectful of difference. They are beginning to empathize with one another. There were more common conclusions, discovered in dialogue, than unbridgeable disagreements. Their values and concepts of friendship and religious teaching on loving God and neighbour, which came from religious texts, were all very similar. Nobody seemed to like fundamentalists. The differences they discussed were in the main cultural, clothing, specially Jewish and Muslim clothing, differences in interpreting some religious texts and some very negative aspects of evangelisation by Christian churches in Sydney. This was apart from their basic religious understandings such as the Messiah has not come, the Messiah has come, which are accepted and not debated.

While they dialogued together freely, it soon became apparent that the differences came from the inner workings of their "faiths" – or as the Jewish participants said, we do not have a 'faith' – we are a people who practice. DJB(M) pinpointed a few of these differences. "Well, there's—you say—in Jewish teaching in what Christians call the Old Testament, we call the Bible, there are 613 times where God says to do something, and we say those are the 613 Commandments. People talk about the 10 Commandments. These are the 613. These are positive and negative."

The Muslims saw the Jews as legalistic. The differences in the Protestant participants was their ability to move from one Protestant Denomination to another, even in one situation, using the services of a Catholic nun for spiritual help along the journey of their faith This is opposed to the very closed shop of being a practicing Jew – once a Jew always a Jew – but they are able to come back at anytime to celebrate the Passover Seder Meal whether they were "wicked, wise, did not want to learn, or were atheistic." There were two groups without a Muslim presence, in the first instance because a Muslim woman slept in, and for unknown reasons for the other participant. When a compare and contrast was carried out, it was seen that the youthfulness of the Muslim group stood out – they were pre or just post graduates and spoke about God and connectedness. Everyone was "connected" – to God, to one another. It was a happy message to reflect upon. We have a relationship with God and neighbour.

That wars could be stopped by education for peace, as shown in Ireland and South Africa – that men and women could be taught to respect those who dress differently or who have different belief systems from theirs, is an almost magical thought. But when thinking this thought through, one remembers that it has been education, or interpretation of religious texts that has caused a great deal of trouble for the Jews, the Christians and the Muslims. The regular occurrence of Jews being told they are going to 'burn' in hell because they do not recognize the Messiah as Jesus, the historical difficulties of the Muslims, and also their difficulty with the dress code of secular people (immoral), and the difficulty of secular people to accept the Muslim women's dress code, (repressive), masks the much wider division in the world, the inability to accept difference, and resist the impulse to make everyone the same as we are.

The geopolitical enmity and mediated enemy imagery surrounding the clash of civilizations under the Abrahamic aegis and personal experience of conflict, prejudice and related suffering at the local level may be reduced to the notion of 'conflict' on the left side of a progression from conflict to peace. These experiences are to be found in memories of conflict that may surface productively in what I call a 'Controlled Meeting' for individuals belonging to the three faiths - controlled in that it is structured in such a way that dialogue is possible and friendship is the likely result. Interfaith groups provide such spaces. The Dialogue to Friendship stage in the Conflict to Peace pathway is as important as the Controlled Meeting or Controlled Space stage. It provides opportunities for reconstruction, which has been shown as social change, an expansion of interests, and remediation. The remediation results in reframing of the other faiths in the minds of participants and could cumulatively lead to a remediation of media images.

The final result is peace, which in this interpretation includes the idea of a holistic development.

Critical Self-Reflection

One of the strengths of the thesis is that it responds to international communication scholars such as Mowlana (2003, p. 19), who argues that the "border between philosophy and religion must be rethought". This thesis is such a rethinking and from that point of view it is ambitious; it has not gone so far as to wipe out the borders. It has drawn on insights from social sciences, humanities' and religious texts but retained a hybrid social scientific methodological approach that is partly deductive and partly inductive.

From a philosophical point of view, at the present moment we have, according to Kaplan, on one side science and technology, on the other side, religion, morals, politics, and art. The tradition of realism and empiricism has been largely scientific and human values only given a subjective emotional involvement. The idealist tradition may do justice to human aspirations but are not able to add to the science and scientific method consistent with its own presuppositions. Other philosophies - like those of Descartes and Immanuel Kant, take the easy way out and "settle the conflict between science and religion, between rational good sense and emotional sensibility, by assigning to each its own domain within which its sovereignty is to be undisputed" (Kaplan 1961, pp. 16–17). This separation, this lack of relationship, will not be helpful in the foreseeable future. There is work to be done to present a complementary knowledge of science and religion that is compatible with human needs for us to approach a fuller understanding of ourselves. Maybe we might be entering into that vision of Spinoza where "full freedom of thought and religious practice, subject to behavioral conformity with the laws of the land" is practiced, from "Tractatus Theologico Politicus" in Honderich (1995, p. 845).

The thesis includes a critical understanding of Western culture by Charles Taylor, and the striving for individual achievement that takes the whole culture into shallow and narrow water. This thesis is not shallow, it is deep. These participants are fully conscious. That is, according to McGilchrist (2009 p. 222), they are action ready in their full conscious state of comprehensive awareness. We know a great deal about their personal, social and religious life, and that by their actions they are trying to make the world a better place. Glock and Start talk about the presence of the divine, and here, in the pages of their dialogue, they make a God space, small enough as there are only 15 participants, but deep enough to convey an understanding of the One God of the ancient religions, a transcendent experience.

Many opinions of the mind have been presented in this research. Spinoza says we can advance from the passive to the active state, and this is what freedom means for us. And it is precisely by possessing adequate ideas that we become active. "Adequacy of ideas is tantamount to power; the more my ideas are adequate, the more I am independent" (Grayling 1995, p. 459).

The thesis has attempted to quarantine the religious views and reflect on them using social scientific instruments, but I am aware that my humanities side has resulted in my own persuasion being revealed in my opinion from time to time – outside the Personal Statement which of course contains my personal views. I do not personally see this slight seepage of personal views as being detrimental to the project, and hope that others might see the value of this humanising of content in a similar light.

Future Prospects

In looking forward to the future, we take with us, in memory, the knowledge that has been gained from both theory and practice of peaceful dialogue. There is no dramatic conclusion, just a whole emerging from ancient knowledge which has been linked together with new knowledge. It can be said now that science and religion are complementary to one another. They give rise to new issues, as presented by the participants in the four focus groups. Both individual and group identities are strengthened and expanded as they interact. The participants are leaders and role models who have been educated in the language of peace. Education in this language is crucial – teaching from both religious and secular sources. Peaceful language in communicative action is able to affect the whole world, making it into a better place.

The heart of this thesis, beating through this analysis, is the reality that we are human. Both the Jews and the Christians believe that human beings are made in the image of God. So we are sacred. The focus groups, in their turn, articulate what our human needs are today. We have to face the task delineated by Derrida, the task of each one of us to move into the knowledge and communication action of forgiveness. There is also the attendant necessity for each Abrahamic religion to examine their sacred scriptures, threading out the authoritative command from God from its cultural and political background. This is the way forward in the 21st century.

Universal Themes

The subject matter in this thesis is universal. On 20th October, 2010, a resolution launched by H.M. King Abdullah II bin Al-Hussein, was passed by the United Nations. It proclaims the first week of February of every year to be the World Interfaith Harmony Week between all religions, faiths and beliefs. It encourages all States to support on a voluntary basis, the spread of the message of interfaith harmony and good will in the world's Churches, Mosques, Synagogues, Temples and other places of Worship based on love of God and love of neighbour. HRH Prince Ghazi introduced the resolution and spoke about the misuse of religion. Religions must be part of the solution, he said, but warned that the forces inciting inter-religious tensions (notably fundamentalisms of various kinds) are better organized, more experienced, better coordinated, more motivated and more ruthless. "They have more stratagems, more institutes, more money, more power and garner more publicity such that they by far outweigh all the positive work done by the various interfaith initiatives" (UN Resolution A/65/L5). These words would remind us that here in Australia, in Sydney and Melbourne, there has been evidence of terrorist activities with a Muslim base. The new resolution would co-ordinate and unite the efforts of all the interfaith groups doing positive work, harnessing education, and permanently and regularly encouraging the silent majority of preachers to declare themselves for peace and harmony (UN Resolution A/65/L5).

The Family as the First Beginning

Loving God and neighbour has to include some form of forgiveness, and as I have spent the best part of 40 years studying and dealing with family life, I centred the core theme of forgiveness in the family, where the human being first experiences the sense of belonging. Negative actions damage this sense of belonging. When the cultural environment surrounding the family is negative, abusive actions can accelerate, justified by enemy images, so that the victim is seen to be not human. It is then that the great void of hatred and revenge, shame and humiliation begins to spiral. Society only works when the members are able to work in security with the assumption that they are able to live without fear. This thesis unfortunately shows how much fear is experienced by members of the Sydney community if they are Jewish or Muslim, or indeed, even a Christian when they are fighting racism. When society begins to unravel at a group level, it also unravels at a personal level. And in human society, our humanness begins at a thinking level. What we think will become words, and our words will become actions. It was my wish to analyse this thesis as a whole, including the 50 thousand words of theory, to show conclusively that my participants were 'living theory' in action. It was not possible for me to do this. So the future for me, after this thesis, will be to show to the world that their social sciences and humanities reflect the one God – because they reflect the human being, and human beings are made in the image of God.

So, while you have human beings on planet Earth, and while you have academics studying their behaviour, some knowledge will appear of God. Particularly important is the idea that living is a thinking exercise, and that there are limitations as to definitions of some major occurrences in our world. Consciousness has not been defined, neither has religion, maybe because both consciousness and religion are of the spirit – and it is the effect, not the substance, that you can measure.

In this thesis I have measured the outcome of role models in Abrahamic interfaith communities who responded with the spirit of God to remediate a negative action. They are successful in the main in doing this, even though they may be small successes. It is hoped that many more people will read this material that I have researched, and put the outcomes concerning peace and forgiveness into practice for themselves. For we all are, in some way, wounded. We are all in some way separated from our community. The idea of forgiveness truth and reconciliation bringing remediation and a new start is tantalizing. But you need others to do it with you. You need partners of the same mind.

While the issues of human needs have been discussed within the theories of philosophy, psychology, sociology, international communication theory and religious knowledge from the three Abrahamic religions, there is still a human acknowledgement of their wisdom when they are facing the reader as a whole. Some of the links between these religious people are being repaired – they are giving us role models of a new kind of world where difference is accepted, and where self-reflection on difference opens up new visions to light the way forward. These insights and remediations will empower human beings to live peacefully today and tomorrow. They are a gift from the Jews, Christians and Muslims working together, living out the command of sacred scripture to love God and neighbour.

Identity, Personal and Collective

The stories of Jews, Christians and Muslims, of how they have found God in their respective religions, and made their life commitment, have been presented. This is their personal reality. "Reality construction is done primarily by communication, real or imaginary, with other people; and hence people hold the keys to each other's identities (Collins 1974, pp. 56–61), As a conscious person, we learn to self-reflect – to match new information with the knowledge stored in memory. From the 80,000 words of dialogue in the four focus groups there is much new information for self-reflection. Self-reflection will "strengthen the capacity for empathy … awaken the creative potential for imagining a new reality through dialogue" (Galtung 2007).

Memory develops through our intercourse with other people. It comes into us from outside. This "outside" communication has been called communicative action by Habermas. With another person we establish a relationship, and then seek to reach an understanding of a situation and our plans of action "in order to coordinate (our) actions by way of agreement" (Habermas: Vol. 1, p. 86). Talk can have the result of binding us to one another in a mutually-shared pursuit of understanding where sincerity and factual correctness enables mediation. There was much factual correctness in the four focus groups. Not many things were swept under the carpet, from remembering that Christians told the Jews that they would burn in hell, to a discussion on suicide bombers. These negatives were overcome by remediations. Our cultural memory will be changed from these dialogues. This is the beginning of another research initiative. How are we culturally changed when we are still ourselves, with our differences, but are able to talk over those differences to find a way forward? Or perhaps put it another way, to use those cultural differences to dig us out of some kind of self-righteous hole that we have dug for ourselves.

How Are We to Live?

The focus group sessions lived out Plato's question "how are we to live?", especially the vision of Derrida that we would live with an "urgency of memory" of self-indictment, and justice carried beyond the level of country and national state. Two Christian ministers both shared their sorrow at the effects of colonization which came from Europe; ACB(F) "They took the land with one hand and offered the Bible out with the other." Cultural co-operation is beginning to flower over the dire forecasts of Huntington and the seeds of this new flowering come from those leaders that Sherif and Sherif ask to give their followers a superordinate goal in times of conflict (Sherif and Sherif 1964 in Sherif 1967, p. 53).

It is in intercultural friendships we find out the values and interests of the other and disclose ourselves (Van der Horst 2007). This we have experienced and, in précis pass on to you, the reader. The faith journey from birth, the personal commitment to an Abrahamic faith, and the various areas where friendship is exercised to collaborate and remediate and 'make better" is an inspiring story, Groups not only can be "interacting spheres" (Schaeffer 2004) but are now, networking with each other in Australia and in many other places in the world. Human beings are linked, especially the three Abrahamic religions – or should we say in the word of the participants, there is a connection – a connectedness, to do with God and spirituality.

The Power of Language

Speech acts are applied reasoning. The mind finds or makes order in the world (Onuf). The imagination is affected when taking into mind the idea that the thoughts and reasoning expressed by Jews, Christians and Muslims are actually re-making our world. The consciousness of a person is actually changed. The power of language makes possible both memory and imagination – the capacity to recall the past - in this case a "sorry" past, to experience a different present, and from this present to anticipate a future where friendships forged by truth, brave speaking from the heart, can make a new way for co-operation. As a whole world, we are moving from tribal communities to open communities where difference is accepted and affirmed, and work on the issues of the day (especially racism) can be imagined and put into practice (Pettman 2000). The focus on peace (Galtung 2007), is a way to overcome enemy images that we have remembered from our tribal lives that have, in this thesis, been traced to personal experience, religious texts and the media, (White 1984). Hidden shame may triggers anger spirals, (Scheff 2002), but it was reported in Group A that outspoken shame can be used as a deep commitment to remediate and make better. With DMA(F) indeed telling us that forgiveness releases the load, or in theory "bondage of denial, shame, hurt and anger." (Thompson 2005)

FUTURE RESEARCH

What has been applied in an Abrahamic religious context may be tested in relation to other families of religions or even ideological communities that may be in conflict. Could the basic model of encouraging dialogue in a controlled model be examined to advantage in relation to communities that are strongly committed to the same apex values, such as the Reds and the Yellows in Thailand, many of whom revere the Thai monarch or right-wing Republicans and left-wing Democrats in the United States who all belong to a broad liberal tradition – even if the right has problematised the term liberal? This would mean setting up controlled spaces where people with these extreme ideological positions will be comfortable to enter for purposes of the research. Asking this question immediately raises the question of whether people of extreme positions among Abrahamic communities join interfaith groups? If they can see and in some way experience the outcome of these interfaith groups, there may be some chance of an historical change and a new open mind attitude. There are opportunities for further research on psychological and ideological profiles of interfaith group members to see whether they belong to the type of people who are probably more likely to enter into dialogue, forgive and make friends.

Most importantly of all, there is an educational challenge facing the three Abrahamic communities. It concerns:

(1) Standing up to behaviour that is unacceptable.
(2) Making a choice to forgive.
(3) Looking for the good in the other person, even if they disagree with you.
(4) Building on that which is good, instead of honing in on that which you think is not good.
(5) As a sign in our times, a way out, a new educational challenge.
(6) Speak out the peace texts in Abrahamic religions.
(7) Let them come alive in communicative action. By their fruits you will know them.

We now know our 15 participants' movements through life. Their journey from birth to conversion has been documented in this thesis, the journey, for some, from prejudice to praying for one another. We understand that, living in the Western culture, there is a tendency for science to take over from God, with a self-centred life style taking precedence over the common good (Taylor 1991). The movement in "interest" goes from fear to friendship, from exclusion to inclusion, and then from interest to full cooperation. Travelling alongside the interfaith dialogue there is a loyalty to personal traditional values, highlighting a common sense, commitment to the good, communication, mutual understanding, mutual deep knowledge, acceptance and respect for difference. These participants are constructing peace at the local level in Sydney, NSW It is hoped that this peace will permeate our minds and hearts in Australia.

Abrahamic groups making friends in Australia are absolutely essential for social survival, and the process, from needs (healing bad memories) – to dialogue – to forgiveness – to peace-making, with all participating, is necessary in any constructive organization. Every last person has some wisdom and grace to offer interfaith organizations. They relate the least parts to the greatest whole.

Conclusion

This chapter has shown that the research question has been answered and that a flow chart has been developed to show the path from conflict to peace in interfaith group settings, - despite the ideological turbulence at geopolitical level as reported in the media. This thesis has also presented the findings according to Neal's coding analysis and found that yes, there has been an interest change in the participants from interest in their own religion, to an interest in the three Abrahamic religions as a family group. It has been claimed that this is a historical change for the good of social integration. It has provided a critical self-reflection, discussed future prospects for peace construction based on the framework developed in the thesis and discussed possible future questions of research.

Appendices

Appendix 1: Findings

Introduction

Through selective reduction of the 80,000 words of focus group transcripts to 17,000 words, this chapter presents examples under the inductively derived themes, viz. (1) personal histories and views on (2) needs, (3) dialogue, (4) forgiveness and (5) peacemaking, under sub headings of 'common' and 'different'. These deductively derived categories are presented in succession after this introduction. Following this, prior to the summary, inductively derived data from the focus groups is presented under the heading of 'remediations'.

Personal Histories

Identification of broadly common themes with examples

The beginning of life

Theme 1: Family of Birth

A striking common theme of difficulty arose from separated parents, leaving the country of birth, mourning relatives killed in the Holocaust, and coping with blaming attitudes.

ACA(F) "Things fell apart completely when my father left."

ACB(F) "I was rejecting the sort of conservative stuff that, believe it or not, was coming from my own church saying things like, 'What could you have done that your son has been brain damaged?'"

AJA(F) "Basically what happened was my parents divorced and my mother married a Christian who had five daughters."

BCB(M) "My parents had a very strange and unusual relationship at the time. My mother was married and separated and she met my father. They fell in love, and they had a baby illegitimately and my mother had to get a divorce from her separated husband and there was quite a big family scandal"

DMB (F) "We moved out from (place name) obviously a very volatile situation there. Moved into (place name) and we lived in (place name) for about four and a half years or so. And there I really had my childhood."

FCA(F) "My family was fairly unhappy and when I was about 10 or 11, I was in bed and there was a big fight going on in the kitchen between my older brother and my mother. And I remember trying to pray, saying, 'God, if you're there would you please stop that fight?', if there is a God. And the fight didn't stop, but I did become aware of a presence— something in the room which made me think, well, there's something in this religious stuff."

FJA(F) "My parents had the sense or were able to flee Europe and able to come here,—then I grew up in a household where people were mourning the dead. We had lost—29 members of my family who were killed."

DMB(F) and FMA(F) were sisters. FMA(F) said "my parents divorced when I started year 7. And for me my mum moved to (place name) because she wanted to get away from my dad as far away as possible. And for me growing up on the (place name) and doing high school in that area—I think for my whole school year I had a huge identity issue. "

FMB(M) sums up: "I think I was born a human. And that's what—when I look back at who I was, I wasn't a Muslim as such. I don't think anyone is born with a religion. I think everyone is born a natural universal baby, a human baby. Hence I think life experience maybe changes us or our parents, our families."

The Process of Commitment

Theme 2: Conversion, Commitment to Religion, a Journey

The word "journey" was used 16 times by the Christians. For all, there was a discernible time when they committed to their religion.

Jewish Conversion

AJA(F) "I was born to a Jewish father and a Christian mother, so according to Christianity that made me a Jew, and according to Judaism that made me a Christian. But the faith that was practised in my home was Judaism. I didn't grow up in a particularly religious home in any way, but that was our core 'beliefs and values' system. I was sent to a Jewish day school and I actually went through a conversion process at age eight and became Jewish according to Jewish law. I guess I always believed in Judaism, but it didn't play a hugely important role in my day-to-day life until I was 17, where I decided I believed very deeply in Judaism and started learning a lot about my faith and practising my faith and making it the overwhelming influence in my life."

Christian Journeys

ACA(F), a Christian Minister, when thinking about a recommitment of baptism said "I decided that I didn't want to do that just as part of the process." She continues, "The Abbey, (in Iona) was another kind of watershed experience on my faith journey." And "My journey then brought me to this side of the world. I immigrated to New Zealand." "Then we came here (Australia). And I had to candidate again here. And I then trained in ministry here."

BCB(M) "As part of that journey I moved away from a sense of God out there and, um, I started developing what I would understand as the God within. As an inner kind of connecting with God. Rather than an outer worshipping of a kind of cosmic figure it became a much more personal inner experience which was part of the bigger, the higher self-connecting with the higher being, I guess."

DCA(M) "My journey was initially as a fairly evangelical Christian in that I saw Christianity as the only way of living and felt that the only way a person could be a Christian is, ah, through Jesus... now I'm—as I've continued on in my Christian life, I've, I've increasingly taken a more social justice inclusive stance in, in Christian life."

FCB(M) "For me the journey has been that as I've released myself from the confines of my faith and realise that I can actually find something wider to express my faith in my own faith context, I've actually found that I've crossed over into others."

Muslim Journey

FMB(M) "And I chose to believe in the Prophet Mohammed as a messenger. And in a, you know, in a hereafter, in angels, in revelation. And I found, I found a lot of comfort in that belief. But more importantly, I found that that belief made sense to me. It explained unexplainable things. So, that's my religious journey."

Commitment Recognized by Community

Theme 3: Actions Stemming from this Conversion/ Commitment

There are many and diverse actions stemming from commitment.

Jewish

AJA(F) "I think my family is like a little microcosm of how peace could be in the world between the religions. And certainly everyone is very tolerant of everyone else's beliefs and we all just do our thing and accept the other's. But probably within that family group I'm the most practising of my faith in there, which makes me stand out a little bit there." She added "my faith is—impacts on every single decision I make—who I marry, the reasons I marry for, how I bring up my children, the work I do. There is probably nothing in my life that isn't impacted by what I believe. So I'd say it's definitely my whole life guidance system."

Christian

ACB(F) "I said, well, I won't go through to ordination. By this stage I'd already started training for it, so I thought, 'I'll get my degree in theology, but I won't be ordained.' And then I was, I was still working for Ecumenical Council. I was doing this part time. And I went into the Eucharist at King Street Anglican Church here in Sydney, and sat there fairly forlornly because I just still had this sense of longing and loss, the thought of not going through to ordination. And I went up to the communion rail to receive the Elements and—and as the priest placed the chalice on my hand there was a light around it and I—this is going to sound weird, but I have this in my family, these sorts of things. Light around it. And as he took the chalice from me the light stayed in my hand. I just had this inner sense of a God who said, 'You may now proceed.'"

BCA(F) "And we were—in various places, Birdsville, up in the gulf country and Cape York Peninsula. And then went to—the John Flynn Church in Alice Springs had been built. And we went there for five years. So, in a sense the emphasis in the working out of our faith changed from a traditional sort of role to a very practical one where the bush people were not interested in anything but, you know, the practicalities. So, we established hospitals and so on. "

Muslim

FMA(F) "And then my second year of uni I started to get involved with Affinity, which is what we do here, interfaith organisation doing interfaith work. And from thereon I, I kind of really started to see that I had this missing thing in my, in my heart of what I wanted to do in my life and I always thought there was something missing. And I find that this was it, it was God, you know." She added "I started actually practicing being a Muslim. I would pray five times a day and would fast and I got to know God through that."

Identification of Broadly Different Themes with Examples

What is Fundamentalism?

Theme 1: Fundamentalism

Fundamentalism is present in all religions, but was seen by some Christians as a narrow faith which needed to be deepened.

ACB(F) "I was restored to what I believe is a much broader and deeper faith than that sort of narrow conservative fundamentalist almost view of the Christian faith."

ACA(F) asked "does wearing a hijab make people think you're a fundamentalist; does wearing a cross make people think that I'm going to be a fundamentalist sort of Christian? So, it's open to misinterpretation."

ACB(F) "I find myself making a distinction between fundamentalists in each faith and the rest of us. I think fundamentalists are people—I would describe them as those with an absence of doubt. And I think they are the most dangerous people in the world. Whether it's political, economic or religious, an absence of doubt is very dangerous. So, I tend, I must say, to distinguish in all three faiths between that lot who I find it's almost impossible to have a dialogue with really because they're simply not open; they think they know, that's it."

BCA(F) At university. "There were really only three Christian student groups. There was the Newman Society, which was the Roman Catholic one, the Evangelical Union, which was sort of the fundamentalist one, and the Student Christian Movement."

BCB(M) "But then, you see, from another point of view, today—I mean, I don't feel that I know what needs to be known in a spiritual sense. I know that I need to know. But—or I need to explore—I need to search. But I don't have a sense of I know the truth or I know the whole story, which I think a lot of fundamentalists do."

BCB(M) Recognize "the good even in people that you disagree with or that—you know, often, often from our perspective or my perspective it's actually recognizing the good in those people who I regard as fundamentalists… No matter what their position, or what their religion is."

BJA(F) "Some people would believe that the best way they can love someone is to make them believe the way they do, to win them over to their viewpoint. That might be their definition of 'love.'"

BCB(M) "Mm."

BJA(F) "If they feel very comfortable in who they are or they feel very confident that their beliefs are the correct beliefs—then they think they're loving someone by forcing them to be like them."

BCB(M) "Yes, that's right."

BCA(F) I'm thinking about suicide bombers. And the fact that these young people—if they're young—really believe that blowing people up is a sacrifice that they have to do and that becoming martyrs will be the way to wherever. And that's —we've got to somehow understand that. But, see, that's — they're making war, not peace, because of their own faith, aren't they?"

BCB(M) "Yes."

FCA(F) "With Muslims, um—like Christians, there are some very, very fundamentalist ones."

History of Religion

Theme 2: Thinking Things Through – Especially Group B Asking Questions of One Another

ACB(F) "I once knew a theologian, a Taiwanese theologian, called Dr CS Song, and he started to explore the ancient, ancient stories, you know, the oldest stories he could find about the way people understood reality and relationships into the cosmos, if you like, and the, and the common ground between them all was just astonishing. Underlying everything is something which is always beautiful flowerings and blossomings of life and faith."

Group B Dialogue

BCB(M) "Temple Emanuel is a—"

BJA(F) "Non-Orthodox."

BCB(M) "Non-Orthodox."

BJA(F) "Yes. It actually houses two communities, one called Reform and one called Conservative. They are housed in the same—"

BCB(M) "Ah, yes. I have friends who go there."

BJA(F) "They no longer call themselves Temple Emanuel. They call themselves the Emanuel Synagogue now. And that's been an ideological shift in an un-Orthodox world."

BCB(M) "Is that right? Yes. What's the significance of that change in name?"

BJA(F) "In the end of the nineteenth century—or, sorry, end of the eighteenth century/early nineteenth century when the Reform movement started its ideology was: 'We have found the Messianic age here at home where we live. We want to be citizens of all the countries that we're in.' And it was 'a Jew in your home'—German, it was actually in Germany where it started—'and German in the street'. So, your religion was a private matter and your nationality was a public matter. And that meant that you gave up ideas of a rebuilt Temple in Jerusalem. And Zionism was not part of the non-Orthodox movement. But there's been a complete 180 degree turnaround. Nobody could be more passionately pro-Israel and pro-Zionist than the non-Orthodox religious movement. And therefore dropping the name 'Temple' And taking up 'Synagogue' is part of a process of carrying on with that nineteenth century idea that the Temple could be anywhere—the Temple can only be in Jerusalem."

BCB(M) "Yes. In Jerusalem."

BJA(F) "But in America they still have lots of temples and so that will be next generation. You see, I would probably say we're a generation behind America, but in some things they're a generation behind us."

BCB(M) "That's interesting. Many years ago I actually went to what was the Temple Emanuel for a meeting with the Dalai Lama. There was a sort of interfaith meeting there. And I think there were representatives of all religions or a lot of religions there. And it was very impressive. But I also had very good friends—I was born and brought up in [place name]. And I used to babysit for a family who were very involved with Masada College".

BJA(F) "Oh, yeah. I think I possibly know which family. I think I do know which family."

BCB(M) "And I went to the Bar Mitzvah of one of the boys."

BJA(F) "At (place name) Synagogue."

BCB(M) "Yes."

BJA(F) "I was probably there."

BCB(M) "Yeah. That's why you look familiar!"

Respecting Difference

Theme 3 Difference – What Were the Differences?

ACB(F) "Oh, sometimes they were very precious things, either rituals or beliefs that had arisen from their own history, you know, like walking through a history in their faith origins, just like, you know, you can see the people of Israel walking through there."

Group B Dialogue on Differences

BCB(M) "Respect for differences. There is this fear, and it has been raised because we do these interfaith services, there is this fear of syncretism and that somehow you will lose the purity of the faith. But with this, the sort of interfaith gathering it's actually a respecting of each of the faiths. It's not a merging of them. It's actually— what happens is that there are readings around the theme from different traditions. And how different traditions approach it."

BCA(F) "There was a book written years and years ago before you people were even born that I can remember. It was called something like Many Paths, One God."

BCB(M) "Yes."

BJA(F) "I think it was a children's book."

BCA(F) "Now, it was really probably back in the denominational days. You know, it's, it's a very significant phrase, because that's what we're—what we are discovering."

BJA(F) "You know—and like the Abrahamic faiths, because we are worshipping the one God. I'm extremely cautious when it comes to other faiths who might not be. And Buddhists who are not worshipping a God at all. We have to be cautious about that."

BCA(F): You're quite right. And we've discovered that from our other discussions.

FCB(M) "I live in the [suburbs], so they're a very strong presence, and with the Orthodox Jewish communities. And often the, the difficulty I see with people when I talk to them in relating to the, to those communities is their sense of difference. You know, 'Why do they have to be so different to us?' Or, 'Why do they dress so differently?' Of course, you say, 'Well, maybe you're dressing differently in their view the same.' And often it's that question of difference that drives people's attention when really it's not an issue of faith, especially in a, in a—with sort of white Anglo-Saxons you really push them and they know nothing about the counterparty's faith but it's really an issue of personal and social difference. And, and yet it's clouded often in religious tones. You know, 'The Australian way is the Christian way and so forth'; ... being overseas so much with the bank and being in countries that were so dramatically socially different, the best piece of advice I was given by my mentor at the time on my first transfer overseas was: remember commonsense is a cultural thing. And what you think is commonsensical someone else won't. And what they think is commonsense you won't. And be respectful of that difference. And that will bridge an immense amount of, of the acceptance that you have difficulty going through."

Needs

Identification of broadly common themes with examples

Two Fundamental Needs

Theme 1 Security and Peace - Issues in Sydney

AJA(F) "I suppose there's a bit of a distrust of how I am viewed as a Jew. So, the suspicion is not that I have a problem with the other but perhaps they have a problem with me." She continues "Australia is very multicultural but I have experienced anti-Semitism. So, there's that little bit of distrust." She continues "sometimes on a Saturday morning when it's our Sabbath and I'm getting my children ready to go to synagogue we'll get a knock on the door and there's, you know, somone there wanting to give us Christian pamphlets. I find that offensive."

AJA(F) "I've had things like when walking to synagogue people, you know, yelling out a car window, 'Dirty stinking Jews.' Or one time—I mean, it was very frightening. I was with my children, who were four and two at the time, and someone grabbed my son's skull cap off and said, 'Oh, look at the funny little Jewish boy.' It was very frightening. We felt very, like, physically frightened because it was just me and the two children out on the street. My husband wasn't with us. And then also so terribly sad that at age two my son wanted to know, 'Why did he do that to me?' Like, it actually broke my heart for my son at that age to have to confront a world where people are not always tolerant for what we believe in."

BJA(F) "Christians are benevolent and we live in a society where we are given a great deal of freedom and respect. Although you're aware that there are the nutty few out there who expect you to convert and think you'll go to hell if you don't. But that's always the fringe element."

BCB(M) "I have met some Muslims. But I haven't—I don't really have any relationship with them. And I don't have a very strong feeling about their community, what their community is like. I don't have particular images of that. Except media-generated type ones."

BJA(F) "The majority of Australians have never met a Jew and therefore those who are fed by media images or the picture, whatever, are very likely to have a mixed bag of messages as to what Jews are and what they do. You know, there are some that would have very, what we would consider, anti-Semitic and hostile."

DJB(M) "The methods to try and convert Jews were quite deceitful. And misrepresenting Jewish texts, befriending people until they became Christian, and then they were on their own—in their own devices while they went for the next person, this sort of thing."

FJA(F) "When the people are not positive and when there are outbursts of hatred against Jews, well, it's not positive and it comes, it comes from, can come from anyone. Can come from Christian, can come from Muslims. Where there is that, well, I don't accept it."

Interfaith Relationships

Theme 2: Good Personal Relationships Grow from Friendship

A friend is loyal, brave and enriches lives.

ACA(F) on interfaith relationships. "If we are going to have honesty in these relationships then we need to sit with each other in the pain....when it comes to hearing the Jewish—the Jewish people and the Israel-Palestine situation and hearing all of that and trying to understand and respect, and I suppose hold it before God's guidance and wisdom, because it's a much bigger thing."

The Neighbour

BCA(F) "Plus the fact that one of the big problems, the neighbour who is different."

BJA(F): "You have to fight that together. That's not a terrible thing to admit. It's not a terrible thing to admit that we're, we're so oriented towards the like. And we have to work a bit harder to open ourselves to the different or the other."

BCB(M) "I agree with [BJA(F)] that I, I feel sometimes I've really got to control negative impressions or negative responses or—and I think that—and it's not just to do with the veil and so on. I think it's, it's much deeper and it's much broader; that there is a kind of response to the different. But you don't necessarily let that shape your thinking. You know, you can sort of have these reactions. But I would—I mean, I just definitely know that I kind of trained myself through certain years—you know, not to be racist." He adds "you just sort of say, 'Well, no, I'm not going to take—I'm not going with that point of view. I'm not allowing that to control my consciousness.'"

DJB(M) "Jews, Christians and Muslims had organized Prayers for our Common Humanity, and other groups, other religious groups, came along as well and all over Sydney radio and whatever people from the different faiths together were going and saying now is a time for common humanity, a time of distress or whatever, which was almost the opposite of what was happening in virtually every other country in the world, where groups were at loggerheads and defaming and angry. This is the, the peak, the umbrella organizations trying to say, you know, 'This is Australia. We can set the pattern for other countries.' That happened because of pre-existing personal relationships and so many pre-existing institutional relationships."

Friends

DMA(F) "Because you surface all your thoughts or emotions or whatever, to have a friend, you know, particularly to share that aspect of you at that whatever level it is, it's to share a part of you with someone, I think it's very intimate. So, friendship is intimacy at varying levels."

FCA(F) "So I've had a Jewish friend … her friendship is the one that goes back the longest."

FJA(F) and fear of the unknown. "I deal with that with inviting people into my home. And inviting them for a Shabbat dinner and sitting down and sitting at our table and seeing what our ceremony is like."

Communities

Theme 3: Communities as essential

They form Jews Christians and Muslims.

Christian Communities

Christian communities were often Christian Sunday schools for ACA(F), BCA(F), BCB(M), DCA(M), FCA(F) and a Christian military school for FCB(M), from whence they began their faith journey.

Jewish Communities

AJA(F) "I went to a Jewish school, a boarding school in England for high school."

BJA(F) also went to the Cheder, the Jewish Sunday school. "Jews always see themselves in relation to others and that's what we're talking about. We're a tiny minority."

FJA(F) "In the history of the Jewish people being the first of the Abrahamic faiths we ended up being demonized. And this is what religions do, they demonize the faith before them in order to establish themselves." She continues "Beginning with Abraham, (we are) a people."

Muslim Communities

AJA(F) "They asked me will I write an article called 'My life as an Australian Muslim woman'. I said, 'One little problem, because I'm a South African Jewish woman.'" She continues" I went to meet one of the women who's involved with Affinity, and we got on so well. 'And it was a really wonderful experience for me.' And I remember saying to her at the end,

I said, 'Are you typical of an Australian Muslim woman?', and she thought for a moment and she said, 'I'm typical of an Australian born Muslim woman.'"

DMA(F) "We have, you know, arguably a little bit of the spiritual side of Islam and then the application side of Islam." She continues "The image is very much taken/shaped by the socio-historical, socio-political, socio-economic constructions built on the Muslims...where would spirituality fit with this image that I can see of these Muslims out there; very, you know, extreme, and not very spiritual, not very humane even."

Interfaith Communities

ACA(F) "My contact with particularly the Muslim community grew very quickly through the Affinity Intercultural Foundation." She continues "I worked with them on setting home encounters groups, Christian-Muslim dialogue groups, on planning those. So, I got to know a core group of people there. And then became increasingly involved with that community." Then "I was the first chairperson of the Uniting Church's committee for New South Wales on building relations with other faiths. And I carry a sort of shame almost for the Christian community that there is often so little interest in growing this understanding, because too often things become politicised."

ACB(F) "At that point with (place name) we had a service called The Unity of Humankind. And we put a huge banner up in front of the church and invited the community to celebrate the unity of humankind. And we had speakers from the great faiths and others just telling a little story about—unity across these lines."

BCA(F) "There are actually quite a lot of interfaith activities—you know, meetings going on, a lot more than you think."

DJB(M) "I often talk about the Jewish communities plural."

What Is It to Be an Abrahamic Person?

Identification of Broadly Different Themes with Examples

Theme 1 Identity

Christian Identity

AJA(F) "I wear a cross, I wear it to work because it identifies me as a chaplain when I go around the wards."

BCB(M) "At the core of Christianity is the notion of grace."

Jewish Identity

AJA(F) "I have a beautiful Star of David. I will wear it on the Sabbath. I do not feel comfortable to wear it out. I feel nervous."

BJA(F) "Once a Jew, always a Jew."

FJA "We are a people. And you can be a cultural Jew, you can be a Jew—you are born of a Jewish mother, you are a Jew." She continues "Jews are a people beginning with Abraham …. Underneath my white veneer I'm very much a Semite."

Muslim Identity

DMB(F) "Being one of the first families to come out here it was a bit difficult because you tend to be a guinea pig and everybody else follows after you've tested the waters and stuff. ... I knew that my faith or my, I suppose, lifestyle was somewhat different to that of the majority around me."

DMB(F) "Someone of faith is someone who is of Peace."

DMA(F) "People of faith are associated with peace."

DMA(F) "We are very much an Abrahamic faith, especially People of the Book, Christians, Muslims and Jews, the commonalities that we share."

DMA(F) "Misinformation is one thing about Islam that comes strongly."

FMB(M) "Muslims are a minority. But I know when people see me and they know I'm a Muslim they're sometimes thinking about Islam when they look at me."

FMB(M) "I always look back to Prophet Mohammed's life and the Koran."

Statements of How One Religion Sees Another

BCB(M) on Muslim identity I have an "emotional instinctive kind of reaction when I see the hajib – I think, oh, you know, women being oppressed."

BJA)(F) "Within the Muslim community there is certainly a negative stereotype of Jews – these images, unfortunately, are recycled back through the media."

DJB(M) "There's definitely an underlying belief across different Christian denominations that Judaism was there until Jesus came with the next revelation and therefore, if you want to be complete you had to become Christian." He continues "When it comes to Islam also, if you read the Koran, you see references to Jews, which means a Muslim person is familiar with the concept of Jews and has to grapple with the issue."

DMA(F) "If I were to sum up an image that I have to associate directly with a Christian it would be of that spirituality, with a very soft spot for Jesus."

DMA(F) "For many Jews and Christians, sometimes it's overwhelming to know the similarities that we share in our faith traditions." She continues, "when I came to faith and other faith traditions … I saw the Jew for the first time, apart from religious references made to Jewish people. Bringing a human fact to that just reaffirmed – and I was understanding "Wow what a stamp of affirmation it must have been, the People of the Book." She achieved this understanding "with Affinity we had this project called Home Encounters where four Christians and four Muslims would come over the course of six months and have six common topics to discuss on commonalities in a dialogue way."

Theme 2: Understanding of God

To Love God

All are aware of the common belief to love God and neighbour.
Coming from

AJA(F) "Old Testament – religious text"

ACA(F) "Christian/Muslim dialogue groups"

ACB(F) "Formal study"

BCB(M) "Explored religions"

DJB(M) "Curiosity"

DCA(M) "Slowly"

DMA(F) "Dialogue encounters"

DMB(F) "Encounters with others"

DMA(F) "The Koran"

FJA(F) "From religious text"

FMA)(F) "Through interfaith"

Knowing God

FMA(F) "Interfaith (is a) way of getting to connect with God"

DCA(M) says Abrahamic communities have a "commonality of belief, Single God."

DMA(F) says Interfaith has to "reconcile dualities from understanding our texts."

ACA(F) "I could say the Jewish God—the God of the Psalms and the Prophets and those struggles through The Exodus and things like that—that addresses that sort of human cry in a way that is then taken on for me in Jesus and the cross and so on."

ACB(F) "The Book of Habakkuk is just about my favourite book. Because, precisely as we were talking before, I like, you know, Habakkuk shouting, 'What are you doing, God? All of the good people are suffering and the bad people are prospering.'"

DJB(M) "The idea of tikkun olam, or repairing the world; that what a human being can contribute to what God wants is working towards perfecting the world in which we live."

DJB(M) "Historically Christians seem to believe Jews were very legalistic; that if you were Jewish there were a set of laws and you follow those laws and that's what you do, and quite inflexible in that regard. We see these as Mitzvahs or privileges to be able to follow God's instructions."

DJB(M) "Most people before their bat or bar mitzvah are confronted with the issue of Yom Kippur, the Day of Atonement. This is a fast, complete fast, no water, you don't wash. It's just basically prayer for 25 hours or so. And during that time you really are in a relationship with God."

DMB(F) "I always felt—I mean, I know that there was always a seed of belief in my heart. I always knew that there was a God. And even throughout high school I had, I had little bits of—moments of spirituality." She concluded "So, yeah, it was really my own research that I suppose—and my own investigation—that opened up, I suppose, the whole world of faith to me."

FJA(F) "We've got a prayer, our main prayer is the N'shamah, which just says that. Jesus used the N'shamah, he said it. Love God with all your heart and all your soul and all your mind. That's part of the prayer."

FMA(F) "For me the most important thing is that relationship you get with God. ... Religion is just a way of you getting to connect with God. You know, and when you get to learn people and learn how they practise their faith and how they get to, get to know God you realise that that religion doesn't matter at the end of the day; it's how they connect with God. And that's where the connection lies for me personally when I do interfaith, is seeing how people relate to God."

Going Outside of Yourself

Theme 3: Descriptions of Searching for Truth

ACA(F) "I think all that ritual is something the Christian community has lost." ACB(F): "Not sort of in anger but wrestling for the truth. I liked that."

ACB(F) "My understanding that, if you walk towards the things that oppress the people, whether it's you personally or the people in general, you feel as though you're going to die and you just keep going one more step, walk to the edge of the light. And then if you step one more step you find that.... either the rock comes under your feet or you learn to fly. In other words, there's a richer life that lies beyond that moment when you feel you might die—paradoxically—and I think Jesus lived out that paradox—paradigm and paradox that enacts that. So that you know that it's not actually about rewards and punishments, it's, there's something else entirely that—a God who set the creation free, make all these mistakes and it's very complex, but in the end if we work that way towards the darker powers, then, then life flows from that somehow."

ACB(F) "My experience of working across cultures makes me really sad and full of confession that I think the Anglo-Celtic—well, not Anglo-Celtic, the Christian European countries in their colonizing activities in Asia and Africa and Latin America or South America—oh—and all through the Ottoman Empire. Oh, it just breaks your heart. I think that that heritage we are reaping what we sowed sometimes. Especially in missionary activities, you know, where—took the land with one hand and offered the Bible with the other."

BCB(M) "But I don't have a sense of I know the truth or I know the whole story."

FCA(F) "But in those days I thought—and it was confirmed in Anglican theological college, you know, if I don't tell other people what the truth is they're all going to hell. Or something like that. And, ah, so I went to Africa as a missionary."

Group F Dialogue

FMB(M) "There are certain views within the Muslim community of Christians and Jews. I think recently the politics have influenced those. I don't think it's been the typical views of Muslims of the past 1400 years. But I'm aware of certain views that Muslims have, Muslim community has. And when I interact with the Christians and Jews I know I'm sort of representing my community. I think of what they're thinking, what they're saying and I'm trying to see, well, where is the truth in these views?"

FJA(F) "Were you born here?"

FMB(M) "No, I was born in (place name). I learned that practically when 9/11 happened. I mean, I remember 9/11 happened the night before. The next day we had a Mufti there at school. I was in Year 9. And I was asked straightaway, 'What do you think of this?'"

Dialogue
Identification of Broadly Common Themes with Examples

Theme 1: Communication coming from encounters, or no encounters

ACB(F) "I grew up at a time when Protestants did not speak to Catholics."

ACB(F) "The last thing he did before he went was to stand his three daughters in front of him and say, 'Now, I'm going away to the war. I mightn't even come back. If there's one message I want to leave with you it is that you must respect people who are different from you' and 'I will be so sad if I ever knew that you had shouted those terrible things to Catholics or to anybody else, but to Catholics.' And he said, 'If there's one thing I want to leave you with it is that, to be open to a God that is bigger than you might imagine this God to be.'"

ACB(F) "The activities of this group, this neo-Nazi group, were turned on our church and myself. And within weeks of that they marched in, believe it or not, wearing jackboots and swastikas and everything, marched in and placed a message on our pulpit and marched out again. That was the beginning of two years of quite dangerous attacks."

BCA(F) "I go to [place name] Uniting Church. I don't think we have—we don't have, um—I mean, there's a Catholic Church there and so on, but our particular community doesn't have a great deal to do with it."

DMA(F) "What perception I had of the Jews and the Christians, it got confirmed and reiterated with my constant communications"

FMB(M) "When I did meet people I did have all these questions in the back of my mind, 'Is this really how a typical Christian is? What do they normally believe in? Or is this a role model Jew I'm talking to?' I did have those questions. And each encounter of mine challenges those views. It either confirms some of them or it enhances or changes some of them."

BCB(M) We are "All pretty established in open communication."

FCB(M) "Be open and adventurous."

FMA(F) "Interfaith communication entails risk taking."

DJB(M) "Actions speak louder than words."

DJB(M) "Again my image was of diversity. But positive lifestyles for people who wanted to take positive messages. But also potential to take negative messages. I came across many people and it's not because they were Anglican other than the fact that it was an Anglican environment, who would use deceitful messages, you could argue, to try and convert people to follow their lifestyle."

DMB(F) "And my relationship with God has, I suppose, strengthened through my connections with other people. More so with my Christian and Jewish friends than I suppose my Muslim friends. Because I guess with my Muslim friends I talk about similarities and, you know, common practices, whereas with my Christian friends and my Jewish friends there's a challenge in communication. And obviously there's a comfort level and, and a place of respect and tolerance and compassion where we can talk about differences, which is fantastic."

Open your ears

Theme 2: Listen

Listening to People Helps to Understand Them

AJA(F) "I think in all conflict situations, if you can under—and listen, respect and understand where the other person is coming from you can find common ground."

ACB(F) "I expanded my activities. I chaired the dialogue between the Jewish community and the Uniting Church. And I enjoyed that. It was so funny. We would sit there anxiously, you know, listening, us Uniting Church people, while the rabbis fought with each other. I remember saying once, 'Oh, that was a very strong discussion.' The rabbi said, 'Oh, that's nothing. We do it far more rigorously when we're by ourselves.'"

DMB(F) "I think you can't love something or someone if you do not know them. And if you do not know Creation you cannot know the Creator. So, I think it's vital that we do listen to each other."

DMB(F) "And listening, obviously we react. We are humans, we, you know, stimulating when we listen to something or someone."

Group B Dialogue

BJA(F) "Because I would say every time we meet you learn something, but whether that's understanding I'm not sure."

BCB(M) "You might see something new there. But the thing is we're pretty committed interfaith people."

BCA(F) "The first thing that I was aware of is the commonality, the things that—say, the Muslim people or Jewish things or something, you suddenly think, 'Oh, yes, that's from what I call the Old Testament.' And, you know, something is mentioned about the Psalms and so on. 'Oh, we've got those things in common' and so on. So—but that's only the first stage. I sort of personally feel that in our group, our interfaith group we have established a trust—."

Group F Dialogue

FCB(M) "I'm constantly bewildered by the, you know, people are so reluctant to want to hear these stories, go and listen and learn. And again it comes—because it's easier to be, it's easier to be negative and confining than it is to be open and adventurous. Because open and adventurous does require a degree of—"

FMA(F) "Risk."

FCA(F) "Risk taking."

FCB(M) "You know, we've got to remember that most people in our societies have a very limited and a very confined world. You know, you know, it's—"

FCA(F) "It's safe that way."

FCB(M) "It's safer. And plus they have bigger issues that they have to worry about. You know, paying the car loan or having a husband that, you know, is a drunk. Or having a child that is a drug addict or having a wife that is a gambler. To them they are the issues of life, not a desire about—and, look, the trouble is we, exactly as you were saying, we, we, we don't offer the opportunity when a child is, is like a sponge to absorb; we leave it to the family's influence. And that's where the, the trouble starts."

Apply the Information

Theme 3: Learn

An Important Action Which Opens Up the Person to Understanding the Other.

- AJA(F) "I decided I believed very deeply in Judaism and started learning a lot about my faith and practising my faith."

- AJA(F) "I was attending a Jewish day school so that I was getting Jewish learning."

- ACB(F) "I learnt it when we were preparing this common service together and we, we realized that that is a foundational belief for all three."

- BJA(F) "It was just a community that didn't have high levels of Jewish literacy. And I was immediately at age seven in the top class because of what I had learnt already."

- BJA(F) "I think that what I value and the people I can best relate to is an element of humility; that we don't know it all, that we're open to, to learning more and to discovering more. And that sense of humility that there might be another way of doing things."

- BJA(F) "So, love is not the same as respect, the words that we've used before. So, I would suggest that this belief that you're told to love your neighbour is not sufficient in itself for peacemaking. Because people will define it—first of all, they don't learn it."

- BJA(F) "Because I would say every time we meet you learn something."

- DJB(M) "You learn more about yourself by learning about others."

DJB(M) "I think as much of it was probably about learning about Jewish history, tradition; the cycle of the Bible is read over the full year within the synagogue. So, you're just—you're acculturated in the tradition. You know the festivals, you learn about your place as part of a people as much as an issue of belief."

DMA(F) "The more I've engaged with different faiths and different people from different backgrounds the more I've learnt more about myself and my faith and God."

DMB(F) "It was interesting to be at school and to be known as 'the Muslim'. And September 11 occurred. It was quite a, a difficult period, both internally and externally. I certainly took a defensive stance because, first of all, I didn't know whether what had occurred was in fact a part of Islam or not. I did—I certainly had no theological background or understanding. And it really was the first time that I thought about God. And I thought about—if, if faith is this then what kind of God, you know, are these people following? And so it really forced me to do a lot of research on my own."

FJA(F) "All his siblings were killed. And I heard far too much as a child, because she talked to me. I was a little girl but she talked to me because I was in the room with her, so I learnt a lot from her."

FJA(F) "You can see that you can become friends. And it just—as people. And learn to appreciate each other's faith."

FMB(M) "I really liked learning something together from different perspectives."

Identification of Broadly Different Themes

Identification of Dialogue

Theme 1 Social Dialogue/Religious Dialogue

The Participants Put the Spotlight onto Our Everyday Dialogue

AJA(F) "I've had a few of those kinds of spiritual experiences. But even within the religious Jewish community there are few people that you can express that to for fear of sounding like, you know, a lunatic or whatever."

BJA(F) "My Jewish identity was terribly important. And what was interesting there is I found that my closest friends were all religious but all different religions. So, we tended—people who had a faith tended to sort of cluster together. "

DJB(M) "General Sir John Monash, probably Australia's most famous military figure, dated two of my great grandfather's sisters but decided they were too religious for him. But, but he was a typical example of somebody who was not—who didn't find obstacles being a practicing—not only Jewish but a practicing Jew in Australian society to be able to achieve top rank."

DMA(F) "Not so much from religious background and coming to my own faith and the faith of others and sharing that—experience is so holistic. It's not just the eyes and the mind interpreting from the text. It is so all encompassing. And when I engaged in this dialogue of experiencing with the human touch, which I think is magical—fascinated me. As DJB said about my own faith tradition, it was like—I mentioned earlier, it was a bit of an affirmation that truly

I am from the Abrahamic descent, because of the deep fundamental similarities."

DMB(F) Her parents "Would typically practise Islam through the lens of an (place name) I suppose, and interpret things the way they thought was culturally acceptable as opposed to what the faith itself may have said itself. And prayer was one of those things and fasting, for example. So, they might pray—they might have prayed every now and then, but it wouldn't have been something that they did frequently."

Dialogue from Group F

FJA(F) "Yes. Education is important."

FCA(F) "And it's the understanding that the other is not really so different."

FCB(M) "Yes."

FMA(F) "Mm."

FMB(M) "One thing with dialogue is sometimes you've got to qualify what type of dialogue takes place. Because, like—sorry, I forgot your name."

FCB(M) "FCB"

FMB(M) "A lot of the times it's really not interfaith dialogue. It's not about religion, it's about the social differences, like the clothing that people—you know, why the Jews have this Kippur thing. And that dominates the discussion. 'Why do ladies wear this?' Sometimes it's more of a social dialogue."

FJA(F) "It's cultural."

FMB(M) "It's cultural dialogue."

FJA(F) "Cultural differences."

FMB(M) "Yeah. Sometimes it is religious dialogue. And personally I really have a high interest for that, because I think it's more—"

FJA(F) "You can come and join our Women's Interface Network. That's what we do."

FMB(M) "It's more universal religion. Sometimes it's even political dialogue. There's politics. Or I don't know. World political issues. So, yeah, sometimes dialogue has to be qualified."

What Does Clothing Communicate?

Theme 2: Cultural Dialogue/Clothing, on Issue, the Hijab

ACA(F) relates: "My son was there, who was then 15. And it's just such a wonderful experience for him to have, to see—he was a very keen cricketer. Playing cricket in the backyard with Muslim women wearing the hijab."

FMA(F) "If I was wearing that full covering, I think I'd still engage in dialogue. Or even if I'm like this I would still do it. But, you know, there are some who are happy to dress like this, wear the normal kind of hijab because most people are used to it. But they would still not want to talk to people, not be that engaging. So, I don't think it's that ultimately you wear this and that's it, you've caused yourself a barrier. I think it comes down to the individual person at the end of the day, why they choose to wear it and their circumstances.... When I personally wear it I don't look at other people who are less than covered and go or, you know, 'Look at that.' You know, 'Why is she—she's not covered?' You don't think that way. You know, it's—it just doesn't naturally come to you. You are wearing this for yourself, it's something that's between you and God at the end of the day."

FMB: "I think it's how, how would you feel—I mean, it's a pity we live in a world where still a lot of people are judged by clothing. Like, probably some Muslims, many Muslims, might think of Western people as a bit—because of the lack of clothing maybe they might put an image of—I don't want to use the word 'immoral'. But they don't understand that that's a cultural reason most people are doing that."

FMB(M) "So, it's wrong for them to judge on clothes. But also many people living in the West should also maybe not judge Muslims if they're wearing that, to say that that's oppression or they must have certain views about people. I think most religious people that do tend to wear Middle Ages clothing, is they do this because they feel that their religion asks them or it's a higher spiritual calling. I personally don't think Muslim women need to wear the face cover. It does look a bit—quite distancing."

FCB(M) "I think often, often they—that's very much again the issue, is, is the physical things that people focus on."

FMB(M) "Not the religious."

FCB(M) "It's not the religion, and yet they couch it in religion. The old expression, in a very Christian society, 'They should do it our way …. When often other communities see us I think they do perceive us as—again the same expression as soulless, too laissez-faire irresponsible, no deep understanding. And yet when you push either side again it always comes down to very physical issues that they're in conflict with, not the actual spiritual issue of faith."

What Do Media Communicate?

Theme 3 Media Sensationalize

The comments, save for one, were negative with regard to the media.

Group A Dialogue

ACB(F) "Mm. Yes. Media do not report in a way which encourages dialogue. And I don't think our politicians engage in that way, either. You know, they put spins out there, sensational—you know, they just put the extremes out there."

AJA(F) "I just know also when we have had things in the media, like, there's a massacre—Israeli soldiers committed a massacre in Gaza. It's front page of all the papers, big headline, so you're walking around feeling uncomfortable about that view. And then by three weeks later there'll be a little thing on page 5 that says the UN has investigated and there was no massacre in Gaza. But that big headline, I feel, must stay in people's minds and that must affect how they see Jewish people."

ACB(F): "But they use stereotype labels, too—there is a certain labeling of people."

BJA(F) "I think that, that there are some negative stereotypes. So, my general feeling is those who have met Jews tend to—I think Australians generally are open minded, warm hearted and respond on a very, you know, it's very positive. But it's of concern to all Jews the large numbers have never met Jews and are reliant on all sorts of media for their images."

DJB(M) In "reference to the media, there was some reference, but also media role models. I mean, without putting too much on it, Hazim El Masri as a positive— somebody who otherwise people who might not come across Muslims or know they have or not knows that's somebody who has a reputation as an outstanding human being, forget everything else, is a Muslim, is something which I think might challenge the negative, ah, preconceptions."

Group F Dialogue

FMB(M) "I think the media but also certain voices in the community. Ah, I remember I, I went and spoke at a church. And a few weeks before that Fred Nile had spoken in that church. And the people said, 'Look, we had no idea you guys are like this. We were just told something totally different.' So certain people with certain views do preach—I know with my faith community—I feel that—many Muslims do feel like the media have a very anti-Islamic agenda. I don't think that's really the case. I think the media have got a 'making money' agenda. But if anti-Islam helps, they will be anti-Islam."

FJA(F) "I think that goes without—I mean, you've got a cleric that said some pretty horrible things about Jews and—but I don't think too many people take too much notice of him anymore, because—but, you know, it's—people just, ah— probably not bang their own religion when they do things like that; it happens in all religions."

FMB(M) "Yeah, I know but, ah, yeah, the media really like to make a big fuss."

FJA(F) "They do it for money to stir up."

Forgiveness

Identification of broadly common themes with examples

An Approach to Negativity

Theme 1 Sorry for negative issues (32 in all in Appendix 7)

ACA(F) "I made contact again with my father who had walked out after 19 years …quite a bit of contact—and then he died and he was never, ever able to acknowledge that he had caused any hurt. And for me that—it sort of throws open this thing about forgiveness is a very core thing in relationships. And I can say that I understand him and that I got on with him, but there was something that was left unfinished because hurt was not recognised. I could hug him, I could love him, but it's left me with a lingering thing that now I have to process for myself."

DJB(M) "When I spoke about diversity before of perception there's diversity of views, but amongst the, amongst the views—or sorry, something I think needs to be said at the beginning is when the holy books and religious book of Judaism were being written there were no Christians and there were no Muslims. So, there's no reference to Christians or Muslims."

FCA(F) "In the parable that Jesus told of the lost son, the son does all sorts of dreadful things and he plans to go back to the father and say, 'I'm sorry, I've done this.'"

Appendix 1: Findings

Sorry dialogue Group B (Presbyterians joining the Uniting Church)

BCA(F) "We were very much involved. Because the church—we were—when the vote came the—we were at (place name). And the Presbyterians had this funny vote, which was a twofold one, which said: are you in favour of the churches uniting? First question. The second question: are you in favour of this church joining the new Uniting Church? So stupid old (place name)—I don't think they were stupid really— they said yes to the first but no to the second. And my husband was actually always very sorry that he had deliberately refrained from telling people what they—"

BCB(M) "Should do."

BCA(F) "How they should vote"

Sorry Dialogue in Group F

FJA(F) "My neighbour next door is horrible. He's not kind to me. He's very—I often think of that when I'm saying the neighbour. He's just dreadful. I often think of that when you say 'love your neighbour', but it doesn't mean that. I don't think it means the person next door necessarily."

FMB(M) "Why not? It does mean that."

FJA(F) "Well, I don't know how—well, I've, I've tried to say hello. But, you know, but, anyway. I'm joking with that, I'm sorry. Sorry, sorry."

Forgiveness, Heart of Relationships

Theme 2: Forgiveness Is the Core of Relationships

Values were used to enter into the forgiveness questions.

- ACA(F) Her values are integrity, and to wait for wisdom. She said "Forgiveness is a very core thing in relationships."

- BJA(F) Her value is humility. She said "Once a Jew always a Jew. You can't escape." She continues "So nobody is ever shunned. There's always—there's a belief which is a spark and you hope that that spark would be reignited. So, you just—the doors are always open." … "We have the Passover Seder, and you have the paradigm of the four sons. You've got the wise one and you've got the wicked one, and you've got the one who doesn't know how to ask any questions, and you've got the simple one. And notice you include the wicked one and you include the one who doesn't know how to ask any questions; you don't just have the wise around the table."

- DJB(M) His values are to involve others in making the world a better place. "In Jewish families every Friday night we have a Sabbath meal. And depending on the family, they may have a special meal after the synagogue service Saturday lunchtime as well, but Friday night is virtually universal. I've never come across a situation where somebody who wants to come to a Friday night meal has been refused."

- DCA(M) He values people, does not stereotype, "Well, I'm certainly open to anyone. I think that if you shun people you deprive yourself of that opportunity with—to learn from them, to share in the, the love that we, we can share together."

FCB(M) His value is to be respectful. "If I recognize that God has an unconditional love for me and therefore forgives me, then if I'm wanting to express his wholeness and his Son's wholeness, then I have to do that."

FMA(F) Her values are to speak from the heart, and compassion. She said "In the next life we say that God will hold you accountable for what you did to that person's right. And unless that person doesn't forgive you, it will be on you. We, we have the same concept in Islam, where, you know, you have to ask for your rights to be halal—is that how it goes, yeah—on the other person. So that you, whatever you have done to them, that it's lawful for you. You know, so they forgive you.... I guess with the forgiveness of the family, it's a bit difficult. I guess, with family because you live so close to one another and you know each other for who you truly are."

FMB(M) His values are to be humble about faith. He says "with the family thing, she is right. I really like seeing good examples of where some families that united because of that problem—Prophet Mohammed clearly told us—you're not allowed to not speak to someone for more than three days."

Pursuit of Peace

Theme 3 Ask People for God's Forgiveness

We begin with two experiences of being accepted, firstly, by asking.

BCB(M) "Dorothy McRae-McMahon gave a talk and she had very recently become the minister of [church name]. And I was quite—oh, everything she said sort of connected for me. And there was a kind of approach there that just made absolute sense. And I, and I sort of asked her about, about her church and so on. And then very tentatively I went along and it was quite—it felt quite strange to actually go into a church again."

DJB(M) "I suppose you're saying what experience, principles or people do you most value? And where, where I sit, it is often those experiences where you have seen some positive change. So, I was at the base of the advisory group faith communities, the [name]. Originally I was the only non-Christian. And then I had a role in bringing in all the other non-Christian groups. And the work we were able to achieve through the work of prayer, the reconciliation, the education—in an ongoing way, I think—that's the experience that I, I can't match with anything."

FJA(F) Her values are to be honest and straight forward. "We do ask for that forgiveness. I make sure I pay all my bills before Yom Kippur because that's also something that I have to do. Anything that's unresolved I, I fix, we fix up. Some people in our community who even more Orthodox than some other people—I get very long letters saying, 'Dear [FJA], if I have done this, this and this, would you forgive me?' And I think, 'No, you haven't done any of those things to me, but anyway, yes, I forgive you.'"

FJA(F) "On Yom Kippur we fast, on the Day of Atonement. And as a community we ask for God's forgiveness."

FMA(F) "I think forgiveness for me personally I think it takes stages, and depending on where you see it as. For me the most important thing is that relationship you get with God through forgiveness. For me I see it as a way of getting yourself closer to God. You know, the more sins you do the more you distance yourself from God, but every time you ask forgiveness, it's like you're wiping away the sin and getting closer to him, you know.... There's no hiding from people. You know, like it is within a community. But I think that, I think that's where the greatest forgiveness lies, apart from the relationship with God, is with the family. Because with family when they do something it will truly hurt you, but when they forgive or when they—or when you ask forgiveness you truly also mean it. ... Whether you ask forgiveness from God or you ask forgiveness from the community or you ask forgiveness from your own family, you get rid of that burden that builds up in yourself."

Identification of Broadly Different Themes with Examples

Different Rituals for Peace

Theme 1: Some Have Ritual for Forgiveness, Others Do Not

Here some of the issues concerning forgiveness are thought through.

ACA(F) "I can't think of a particular—the word ritual is quite a formalised sort of thing and the question seems to address me more personally on an individual level."

ACB(F) "In terms of family, it depends what the situation is in many ways. But I wouldn't use a ritual there. But, um, it's more a matter of saying—of getting someone to sit with the other person and—or with me—or something and say, 'Well, I'm just aware things are not quite right between us. Can you, can you tell me what, what you're feeling?' In other words, move into a time of honesty as best as one can in, in a context which says, 'Let me start by saying I've made so many mistakes as your mother ... so that you create an environment where you're not the special one and they are the ... in other words, it's an equal sharing of humanness somehow, and a sadness. And usually you can cross the lines there, in my experience."

FJA(F) "Between Rosh Hashanah and Yom Kippur, which is the New Year and the Day of Atonement, there, there's the week, or the eight days. And that's a time that we have, we have that ritual where we go to people that we've—sometimes we write to them, sometimes we ring them up if we've done something wrong, and we ask for forgiveness."

FJA(F) "Well, with family I have a short memory. I just totally—I, I just accept and if—and deal with it. Deal with it. Have—say what we have to say. And then .... Just, as I said, short memory; I just accept and get on with it."

FCA(F) "In my friendship group I do have people who I've offended and who no longer speak to me. I have no ritual, I have no way to force them to come back to friendship. In the church."

FMA(F) "In Islam when we go to Hajj, when we do that, we've got the Day of Arafat where everyone, millions of people all collect at this mount, Mount Arafat, and they ask forgiveness from God."

FMB(M) "I think people have to like, forgiveness, want to do it first themselves. Go to the negotiating table ready to negotiate."

FMA(F) "It starts with yourself. If you don't do it, if you don't take that step, it won't happen. You know, it's the, it's that ultimate saying, if you want to change the world you have to change yourself first."

Some More Differences

Theme 2: Different Understandings of Forgiveness

It is not until we begin to dialogue that we begin to be open to different interpretations of forgiveness.

The Anglican minister shares an answer to forgiveness something different. You are forgiven before you even say "sorry".

Dialogue in Group F

FCA(F) "In my church we actually pronounce forgiveness before people have confessed their sins."

FCA(F) "Because we believe that's what, that's what God does. There were covenants—"

FMB(M) "What church is that?"

FCA(F) "For example, in the parable that Jesus told of the lost son, the son does all sorts of dreadful things and he plans to go back to the father and say, 'I'm sorry, I've done this', but in fact the father rushes out and greets him and throws his arms around him before the son has even says his confession. And if you look at the stories that Jesus told about, which I think are about, meant to be about God, God unconditionally loves us. And if that's the case, I think that confession comes after we're become aware of this unconditional love. So that God accepts us and forgives us. And then we say, 'I'm sorry because I don't deserve that love.'"

FCA(F) "So, that's the, that's the ritual for me. That's a very powerful ritual."

There is another idea from ACB(F). Why does it mean so much? The point of difference.

ACB(F) "Trying to chair a worship committee to prepare worship for the World Council of Churches Assembly … I'd think as the chairperson, 'What will I do?' And I just had this moment—gift from God, I think—where I said, 'Why don't we stop, have morning tea and share why this matters so much to us.' In other words, the point of difference. So—and, and that's where I found that you can make progress, not in agreeing with each other but in understanding why it means so much, why you hold on to something so tightly. So that—and what I found was that that freed up, then, the capacity to move into something that you could do together. Because on the boundaries of that were these deeper understandings. Even if you didn't agree it didn't matter, as to why that religion would hold on to that and say, you know, 'I'm not going to move from here. This is so important to me.' What underlies it? Why does it matter? And that really brought us forward. So we started doing that—every time we went 'grrr' we'd stop and say, 'Okay. Now you tell us why that matters so much, and we'll tell you why, why it matters so much that we oppose that.' In other words, we went deeper into the differences as well as finding the common ground, and that made a huge difference to our relationships. And I've tried that, too, in interfaith dialogue and found the same."

New Creations Appear

Theme 3 Creation of New Forms of Ritual Forgiveness

From Uniting and Anglican woman ministers, plus a new Jewish initiative.

- ACA(F) "I could write liturgies about drawing people back." She goes on to speak about her father not saying sorry and then she said "I have to process for myself in a way that I think you could broaden that out into, into a, a community, a, situation, people who have—like Sorry Day, if you like. There needs to be that."

- ACB(F) "Yes. If, if, if I really think of ritual, and a group of people say in the church or something or some group, I would in fact create something which leads them into a grieving, a touching of the waters of our tears, so to speak, and a sharing of grieving. I, I think if you ask people to say what they did wrong or something you, you end up somewhere else. But if you ask people to grieve, often that brings people together."

- DJB(M) "The Chabad movement or the Lubavitch, they very strongly believe that if somebody happens to be Jewish, by having a Jewish mother or having—sometimes converted to Judaism, then they will one day really want to have everything back, and they work very hard to find people who might not have any interest and find something that interests them and bringing them back within the fold. But that's unusual, because mostly it's that you come—we're open to you whenever you choose. No matter what you've done in your life—"

FCA(F) "I have something else that I've found to be very powerful. As a minister I conduct funerals. And I often say to the people who are present at the funeral, 'Now is the time to lay aside all the regrets of things that you didn't do or wish you had done for this person who has died, because that person wouldn't want you to go on feeling that you have this burden.' And, 'Similarly, if the person did things to you that you found difficult at the time, now is the time for you to forgive that person so that this person's death and their life will not be something that is a burden to you in the time to come.' And people have said how liberating that is to be able to lay aside the bad feelings that there might have been between them and the person who's died so that they can go on from here."

FCB(M) "It's very similar, that sense of forgiveness which allows you to then engage, recognizing that you're probably going to have to be a little humbler and move to the center to find them to move to you. And then falling on the old father's advice, never go to bed with an unresolved problem because it takes on a new life the next morning."

Peacemaking

Identification of Broadly Common Themes with Examples

Theme 1: Find Common Ground, Interfaith Strengthens Trust

Begin to Look Around

All groups were aware of the common belief to love God and neighbour.

Be open

Theme 2 Difference Expressed in Attitudes

Not all is common.

ACB(F) "We had people come and just say, 'I offer my Jewishness' or, or, or their particular race as well as their religion 'into this country'… 61 different groups of people came forward spontaneously and said, 'I offer my … into the life of this society', and you could see the dream, the richness of what could happen if we actually were open to receive from the great faiths and the different ethnicities."

BJA(F) "I think that what I value and the people I can best relate to is an element of humility; that we don't know it all, that we're open to, to learning more and to discovering more. And that sense of humility that there might be another way of doing things. I think if you look for a characteristic I would put humility there."

DCA(F) "A Catholic priest called Patrick McInerney, who was a Columban … (had) written to the organizers of the parliament in Melbourne to say he'd like to offer a paper. And the general theme—and the people have said, 'What's it about?' He couldn't really say. But in effect what he was saying is that commonality is a greater threat than difference. And what, what he was really saying is if you, if you just keep on the common, the things we've got in common all the time, then if you're not careful, say the Muslims or the Christians will put it, 'Oh, yeah, but our faith is being modified or being compromised.'"

DMA(F) "So, dialogue in general you get to know the other from the other's perspective, which is the context and background, which is where those things come from … I think that credibility is very important and actions do speak louder than words. And that's why you have to have a unity between what is said and what is done. However, to me that's where probably the major issue or challenge may be, is that when they're not unified—no matter if they're Muslims. You know, for example, if they say, 'This is what it says in the Koran' but you see a complete contrasting behaviour. That's when I think genuine education is lacking on both sides."

FCB(M) "The best piece of advice I was given by my mentor at the time on my first transfer overseas was: remember commonsense is a cultural thing. And what you think is commonsensical someone else won't. And what they think is commonsense you won't. And be respectful of that difference. And that will bridge an immense amount of, of the acceptance that you have difficulty going through."

FMB(M) "The Koran speaks of Jews and Christians, sometimes positively, sometimes critically. I can't adopt the Koran's attitude always, because that's I believe speaking to his servants." He continues: "the attitude (when) they told him, 'Why are you getting up? He's not a Muslim.' He said, 'He's still a human being.'"

Hand It On

Theme 3: Teach Peacemaking

There is a great need for the common commandment to love God and neighbour to be taught.

BJA(F) "First it has to be taught. That is, we know it's a fundamental tenet of each belief, but the question is are people who belong to those faiths taught that fundamental tenet? My suspicion is not always. And the other question is defining 'neighbour'. I know that in some places they might say that your neighbour is someone who's like you, but might not broaden the definition to include everybody. So, you've got to do two things. You've got to teach the tenet of belief and make sure the way it's taught. And the other thing is love, to go back to my friend when I was 14, there are definitely some people who would believe that the best way they can love someone is to turn them around to their way of thinking."

DJB(M) "With "teaching, the place I would see it is—in any process that's designed to improving a situation you hope people would want to understand with whom they are talking and know where they're coming from. "

DJB(M): "Relying on this common teaching, I would say actions speak much louder than words. And there can be lots of teachings from all sorts of things, but if somebody sees their interlocutor behaving in a different way, the teaching becomes irrelevant. So, you have to have people behaving in a certain way if you want to achieve something in terms of peace process. Even when it comes to credibility. I mean, if somebody comes to you and says, 'This is what we believe, and you see them behaving in a different way'; they believe in a particular sort of ethical behaviour and they're demonstrating a different sort of behaviour, you've got a problem. If they say they love their neighbour and you find they're publishing hate material about you or anybody else you can't say that because they've got a teaching that says something that, that's going to override this."

DMA(F) "When I came to faith and other faith traditions and people from other faith traditions it was as a first-hand education that I got through that experience." She reflects: "that has really, like, deeply moved me to really engage and to really reflect on inner meanings of things beyond the historical, the negative historical or sociopolitical stuff. There's far more, far more, in a sense, in these experiences."

DMB(F) "The inherent teaching of all the faiths, it is peace. And it's what faith does, it's what belief does, it gives you that sense of peace and serenity."

FMA(F) "When dialogue itself is the core objective and you can comfortably feel that in your heart, then you learn a lot. And I think peace is the exact same thing."

FJA: "There's no way that a small child that has, takes notice of any person that's a different colour or anything. They're just accepting. I think a lot of it is taught from the home."

Identification of Broadly Different Themes

Know the Past

Theme 1: Historical Differences

DJB)M) has a lot to say on this subject, as also has ACB(F).

ACB(F) "Muslims I haven't got far enough into the dialogue really. But, again, it was very much—often it was connected with, quite frankly, colonialism and things. It wasn't so much faith. It was the actual history, particularly in the Ottoman Empire, the way that the European powers just divided up things at will and, quite frankly, set up the state of Israel, whether that was right or wrong. But they saw it as sort of an external right."

DJB(M) "I remember that in the very first time there was formal Jewish-Christian dialogue on a serious level in Australia was in 1984 at Shalom College at Sydney—at New South Wales University, which was Jewish-Christian dialogue towards the year 2000. It was Catholic, Anglican, Orthodox and Uniting Christians together with the Jewish community, a full-day seminar. And the idea was to—the idea was how do you overcome the lack of dialogue basically in Australia? There'd already—there'd been groups like Council of Christians and Jews which basically—Christians who liked Jews and Jews who liked Christians. It wasn't quite the same as representatives of the group saying, 'Let's, you know, let's talk about how we live in Australia.' First formal dialogue on a national level—1991 the Uniting Church-Jewish dialogue began with the leadership of D'Arcy Wood from the Uniting Church. The Catholic Bishops have only been doing it since '99, the Anglicans only since 2005. The National Dialogue of Christians, Muslims and Jews, which is formal, has been going since 2003 only, although the informal dialogue of those three groups was going back much further."

DJB(M) "Christians were powerful, Jews were weak. Christians were going to force you to do something by dialogue that you didn't want. That took people, you know, took individuals to say, 'Well, we're going to try it, anyway, you know.' We're not going to—but that was, that was a very important theme. Not about dialogue with other groups but dialogue with Christians, because of history of Christians towards Jews."

DMA(F) speaking of a divided world "But from the Muslim perspective, speaking from our perspective, the unity and knowledge is so, so important. That we shouldn't look at the world so divided to begin with. And to unite so much that when a Muslim is truly educated—in my personal opinion, if a Muslim is truly educated, if a Jew and Christian are truly educated and grounded in their faith traditions, you would not see this dichotomy of what's said and what's acted on. I genuinely wholeheartedly believe that."

DJB(M) "Christian historiography "justifies anti-Semitism, which says Jews killed Jesus ... It's tied up with a history of minority, of being a scapegoat over many years."

FJA(F) "Australia was just so insular. It wasn't out of any meanness... My children didn't have any of those experiences because...Had multiculturalism. They were accepted into homes. My youngest daughter was bridesmaid at her Catholic college wedding."

Know the Good

Theme 2 Recognize Good in People You Disagree With

This advice is at the heart of interfaith. The basis of the language of peace.

Group A Dialogue

AJA(F) "I think if you understand—you know, if you look at what does loving your neighbour mean, I would throw in there, you know, mutual respect, tolerance, trying to understand the other person's needs, feelings, et cetera. And I think in all conflict situations, if you can under—and listen, respect and understand where the other person is coming from you can find common ground."

ACA(F) "I would like to say how enriched my life has been by having—grow—developing friendships with people whose faith journey has been different."

Group B Dialogue

BJA(F) "Yeah, and, and the second point I made about who is your neighbour, anyway, that you have to love, you need to make sure that the neighbour includes everyone. And that the love includes respect for their diverse beliefs."

BCB(M) "Yes, and—well, you know, I think that comes through very strongly in the parable of the Good Samaritan. The most despised people are still your neighbour. You know, and you have to actually overcome those kinds of—"

BCA(F) "The reason that the earlier ones went straight past."

BCB(M) "Yeah, yeah. And actually recognizing the good even in people that you disagree with or that—you know, often, often from our perspective or my perspective it's actually recognizing the good in those people who I regard as fundamentalists …. No matter what their position, or what their religion is."

Group D Dialogue

DJB(M) "I receive probably four or five emails a day from Muslims or Christians, sometimes Hindus and Sikhs and Buddhists, but mainly Muslims and Christians, who I am the Jewish person they feel comfortable asking what they think might be difficult questions about Judaism."

DCA(M) "I think that as a Christian there's been a lot of antagonism between the Christian church and Jewish people and Muslim people, and—but establishing myself as part of the [church name], I think, does tend to alleviate any—well, a considerable amount of hostility and gives me an opening to, to dialogue with people on, on a reasonable basis."

Group F Dialogue

FCA(F) "Don't you think if we could put all the money that's spent on defense and weapons into helping people to have dialogue."

FJA: "No; it's about greed, it's about land, it's about thinking—everybody thinks that they're right. Lots of other things. But 'justice shall ye pursue'; is that the one that you are talking about?" She continues "that's being unilateral. But I think peace has to be bilateral. I think you have to have, you have to have the other side agreeing to, to peace as well. Because you can't make peace just by yourself. You have to have another, you have to have the other side agree to the peace. And that's how—that's what has to happen. Both, both sides have to agree that they want to live in harmony and peace together."

Recognize the Wrong

Theme 3: Recognize good from wrong

ACB(F) "If you ever think you're more loving than God you're on the wrong track."

Group B Dialogue

BJA(F) "But now, I mean, we can, you know, be so open minded that your brain falls out. Like, I don't believe in absolute open-mindedness and I don't believe in absolute tolerance of evil. But I think there are some things that you can say, 'This is intolerable or unacceptable.' Just because there is a person who holds that belief doesn't mean you have to think it's acceptable because it's a human being that holds it. There are some things that I consider beyond the pale. And I recognise that the human being who holds that belief may not be an irredeemable human being, but the belief is unacceptable."

BCB(M) "I'm saying that you recognize the good in the other person but that also means you've got to recognize the wrong—"

BJA(F) "Yes"

BCB(M) "—too."

DMA(F) "Where in your own perspectives and your own respective traditions you can come together, like you were mentioning with your experiences of dialogue since the eighties, you know, you can come with your own particular identities and yet engage with people very comfortably and work on projects promoting and trying to role model good examples of faith and goodwill." She continues "peace … comes with reconciling the dualities which comes with our understanding of knowledge and understanding of our texts. Once that's unified, then you have grounded yourself, then you just get to know the other. And it's a very mature and I think enduring way of forming informed opinion about the other. And loving each other for that reason. And history has had those episodes before. I wouldn't be surprised if it could come again. I'm very optimistic. I think there will be times when we'll cooperate all of us together."

DMA(F) Teachers have a "profound way of, you know, getting students understanding is when they've actually internalized that knowledge. Otherwise, if the knowledge is not internalized, it's just a parroting of the data off your own sacred textbooks. And it goes true with all traditions. And I'm speaking for my traditions."

FMB: "Whenever I hear 'peace process' I think of the Palestinian issue in Israel, so besides the politics—"

FJA(F) "There's Darfur, there's Sudan, there's Sri Lanka, there's Afghanistan. Everywhere."

FMA(F) "It starts with yourself. If you don't do it, if you don't take that step, it won't happen. You know, it's the, it's that ultimate saying, if you want to change the world you have to change yourself first."

FMA(F) "I'm very cynical of world politics because I think many people have—at tables—or even whenever something gets a bit too popular I start getting cynical because I think it's attracting all the non-sincere people. If people go into peace for the sake of peace, that's only when peace can be achieved, not 'what I can get the most from it.'"

Remediations

Identification of Broadly Common Themes with Examples

Open heart, open hand

Theme 1: Hospitality - Opening Doors

The open hand of friendship is the tool of peace.

The overall outcome from the four focus groups was the greater understanding of how much remediation each person contributed to making the world a better place. Opening their hearts and minds to one another, opening their synagogues, their churches and their mosques opened a way to interfaith, each with their own difference, each with their common text that motivates their service, to love God and neighbor.

BCA(F) "Last week you and I were at our interfaith meeting. I suppose I'm—like I said before, I mean, there are actually quite a lot of interfaith activities—you know, meetings going on, a lot more than you think. And this is what, as far as I'm concerned, substituting for the lack of it in my own local area, the fact that we're having so much—so frequently, just conversation. And this meeting we had last week was in the [mosque name], sitting in the mosque talking about things and so on. And this is how some of us who perhaps are deprived, if I can use the word, naturally seeing—where is the nearest synagogue?"

BJA(F) "There is one in [place name], but it's only got a handful of members."

DCA(M) "And we organize educational and, and visits to other faiths and educational dialogues and that type of thing, conferences to do with interfaith, and I've had the opportunity of being involved with visits to mosques, to synagogues. And recently I went to the Great Synagogue and the—and the Jewish Museum …. And the people—these people have been largely involved with the [synagogue name] at [place name]. And I've been to a lot of their social action seminars that they've had on Sunday nights there over at [place name], which has been good for me. I've been able to take people there. In my local church at [suburb] in the [church name] we have a social responsibility committee that I'm the chairperson on."

DMA(F) "All these six common topics we did, and a book came out of that as well, mind you, Home Encounters, Christian-Muslim kind. And then it was also taken to the Jews and Muslims, between Muslims and Jews. So, I obtained this information from direct authentic experience of the other."

DMB(F) "My information was from actually the other, through my encounters with the other, whether it was in my own home or an activity that—like Home Encounters, which I myself participated in also."

DMB(F) "I give a lot of mosque tours. And during the tours, you know, you start out with people who are very, just very apprehensive and they might not know anything about Islam and have very unique or—or not unique, but very interesting views of who you are as a Muslim. Particularly being a female who has a scarf."

DJB(M) "One of the interesting things when I take people through the Sydney Jewish Museum, which I do quite a lot, they want to know—and that is a statement of what Jews believe."

FJA(F) "At a big interfaith Passover at the Sydney Town Hall, we invited everyone—FCA was there. And the two Mennites were there …. One thing we did on the outside was we had matzah making to show what matzah making really is. You know, they had the whole group of these Hasidian—you know, these people with different—making matzah."

Talking Things Out

Theme 2 Control Negative Responses

ACB(F) "I was buying a little mat in a mat shop and it was obviously run by Muslims, because the woman at the counter was wearing a hijab. I just sort of went up to her spontaneously and said, 'I'm really glad you're wearing your hijab. I'm a Christian but I really believe that if you feel that that is important to you that you should be wearing it.' She burst into tears and I just felt—oh, I felt so terrible, you know, that this is what we do to people just because they are wearing a head scarf."

BJA(F) "I made very good friends with a girl from the local Catholic school and we became best buddies. And then we went up. And you know how teenage girls are at the end of a, of a camp; everybody is writing and you used to have autographs. You know, love messages and, you know, throw your arms around each other. And right at the end of this camp this girl that I had become very friendly with threw her arms around me and with great passion and tears in her eyes said, '[BJA(F)], please accept Christ or you'll burn in hell …. She was saying it out of love."

BCB(M) "That's right ... that would have been my position in my adolescent years. Although I never really took that on. I must say I think because my parents weren't involved I kind of didn't—I wasn't absolute—I never bought the whole sort of theology. I never kind of took that on."

DMA(F) "I'm not going to reiterate, 'Oh, they all think we are terrorists and ...' You know, that's a bit overdone, to be honest with you. Yeah, the media do project that. But not many people—they've got a genuine question mark because they don't know where to situate Islam because they don't really know about Islam. But there's this openness also about people that I've found that wants to genuinely know: 'Who are you guys?' And then they get overwhelmed by, 'Oh, okay, it's not that weird after all.' There's chores of similarities."

DMB(F) "It's been highlighted even more so through these mosque tours that I do, because the questions start out with who put the scarf on, and 'Why do you have it?' and very, you know, I suppose, questions where—and as [DMA] said, oftentimes they are very genuine. Simply people are intrigued and just want to know. And, you know, it's important to, I suppose, create an environment where people can ask questions like that...But you'll find that at the end of the tour or toward the end of the tour they just kind of got their eyes wide and they're shocked that you chose to wear the scarf or that, you know, there is that similarity of tradition, whether it's the fasting that's, you know, similar or whether it's the scarf or whatever that, that strikes a chord with them."

Ask for God's Help

Theme 3: God Remediations

AJA(F) "I never remember God not being a part of my life. I mean, from the youngest age I can remember—I didn't know all the prayers, but when I'd get into bed at night I'd say, you know, 'I had a good day today. Thank you, God.'"

ACB(F) "I always think when the disciples of Jesus said, 'Oh, they're not one of us' and Jesus said, 'By their fruits you will know them', I don't think he meant 'which are the true Christians', I think he meant, 'You will find the people of God.' And you see what flows from them somehow in the way their attitudes."

Group B Dialogue

BJA(F) "I didn't know anything about people who know and people who don't know. Have we got time to—I just want to say that in the Orthodox Jewish perspective every Jew has to be a person who doesn't know, because everyone is supposed to be constantly questioning and constantly doubting and constantly—and the sense that you know sounds—I don't know—inappropriate. Only God knows and the rest of us don't know. So, I don't know what you mean by 'they don't know.'"

BCB(M) "Well, I think what he's talking about there is the people who know or experience the spirit."

BJA(F) "That's Christian? 'Spirit' being Jesus?"

BCB(M) "No. Krishnamurti came from a Hindu background."

BJA(F) "Yes, I thought from the name he did, but you mean people who have experience of the divine; is that what you might say?"

BCB(M) "Yes, yes, exactly—a sense of the divine. But of course the whole book is about the journey of development, of, of growth and so on."

BJA(F) "See, you can be a very good Jew and question whether you've ever had experience of the divine. Constantly you, you might hope to. Hope might remain a hope."

BCA(F) "When you say 'a very good Jew', practicing all of the whatnots?"

BJA(F) "It's not about knowing."

BCB(M) "That's really interesting. That's just a very different point of view."

BJA(F) "Very different launching pad, isn't it?"

DMB(F) "I suppose for me the important thing is my relationship with God, and all else, I suppose, falls under the umbrella of that. And so my connection with God—it's not always strong and it's not always there, but it's always the strive. And so everything else, I suppose, falls under that. I guess that's the best way to explain it. And so my connection and my relationship with God, in turn, I suppose, navigates my outlook and value and, I suppose—yeah, value of others around me."

FJA(F) "I used to take my children when they were going to synagogue they were saying. 'Why do I have to say I'm sorry if I've done it?' And I said, 'You're not saying sorry for yourself, you're saying sorry for our whole community. We're asking God for forgiveness for the whole community because we pray in a community.'"

Appendix 1: Findings 347

Identification of Broadly Different Themes with Examples

Both Together

Theme 1: Two-Way Relationship

Doing things together, beginning, and then strengthening the bonds of friendship.

ACB(F) "Some of us couldn't bear all the male language running through our worship. And others found that very, very important to them. And it was important to them because it had always been there and it was sort of part of the grand tradition. And for us it was important that it changed because we were women and we didn't want our— we wanted our, our female part to be in there explicitly or neutralised."

DMB(F) "So, for six months Muslims would go to a Christian house; Christians would come to a Muslim house, and we'd engage in dialogue. The topics were set. And, yeah, so that occurred for six months. And after that we had barbecues and, you know, dinners. So, the relationships continued. And as I say, through the relationships the fruits are that we've had visits to mosques, we've had visits to churches, visits to each other's homes during our sacred times and sharing those sacred times together, which is such a wonderful thing, too. It's your personal space and your personal time, and to be sharing it with somebody who may not necessarily believe in what you do, but to share that with somebody else and for them to be there and to share it with you, it's a very, it's a very humbling experience. It's very nice."

Group F Dialogue

FJA(F) "When I was growing up one side were the Catholics, one side were the Protestants and they were shouting abuse at each other. So, I wasn't the only one to feel—one of the other things that my belief had was that I was never invited into any of the homes .... Friendly at school but not into the homes, because that's how it was for me. And as I said, when my children were growing up it wasn't the case anymore at all. I just—that's how it was. Children, children just take things in and just deal with them. So, my belief was my sanctuary and my culture. My culture and my traditions were my sanctuary; that's where I belonged."

FMA(F) "I guess in a way the story kind of emphasized to me that faith makes you strong. So long as you have that belief, you know, no matter what life throws at you you always have the strength to persevere ... that's what I got from the story."

FCA(F) "I know FJA well and I'm, I'm always amazed at the lack of, the lack of aggression or resentment they have."

FJA(F) "I don't want to ever see the world as ugly. And the only way you won't is to, to make friends. And I think that working in in interfaith has—two of us do together, in the same group, is—as it just so happens—is—you can see that you can become friends. And it just—as people. And learn to appreciate each other's faith."

Telling Our Stories

Theme 2: Speak to Overcome Negatives

We are to speak out to one another, telling our stories, seeking knowledge and understanding.

ACB(F) "We had speakers from the great faiths and others just telling a little story about—unity across these lines."

ACB(F) "The other part of all of the three great faiths, I, I have found deeply enriching to connect with them. Always enlightening for me in opening up new understandings of me, and why, and God as I speak with them."

DJB(M) "It's only really since the Holocaust where most Christian groups have had to say, 'Hang on. Is this really what Christianity should be about?' And you look at Second Vatican Council... But since, only since the Second Vatican Council. The Lutheran Church only changed its attitude in the eighties. The Uniting Church was involved in thinking about the issue, and still is, but didn't come from the same negative position because it was thinking about these in the light of the seventies and eighties, not in the light of the 1920s and thirties, so it was already post Holocaust. But other churches have real difficulties in trying to understand how there can be Jews who are living their religion, believing they believe in God when there has been a subsequent revelation. And in a sense it's less respectful than the Islamic—well, going back to the Covenant of Omar. So, pretty early in Islam, of having Jews and Christians as people of the Book of Protected People. It was not necessarily saying you could control your own life or you could live your destiny, but on a religious level recognising a religious—I don't know what the right word would be, but basically saying there is some religious authenticity to Jews and Christians which can co-exist with Islam. So, I would think that that's already, that's already a change. But when it comes to the images, so many of the images are shaped by contemporary politics as well. And when people have fierce different attitudes to a political question that is going to sometimes shape how people respond to a community. Because if a community believes that the representatives or the figure of a particular religion is acting in a certain way and then you find somebody supporting that, you say this person is automatically—or this person's religion automatically is justifying evil things. It works in all directions, the trilateral, it's not just one on one."

FMB(M) "So I—and I, I remember visiting a church for the first time and I remember visiting a synagogue late at night-time for the first time. It was an important night. And, ah, I liked those experiences and I think I—I believe as a Muslim God has spoken to Jews before and to Christians. So, when I speak to them sometimes I want to hear what God had spoken to them. Because I know God spoke to us. And I believe that. And I read the Koran, but I want to see what God spoke to them and hear God through them sometimes."

Hope Leads the Way

Theme 3: Hope for Positive Response

Human beings need communication for survival.

ACA(F) "We are all humans. And we all—we share the same basic desires, hopes and fears."

Group B Dialogue

BJA(F) "We have to remember that the majority of Australians have never met a Jew."

BCB(M) "Have never?"

BJA(F) "Have never met a Jew. Jews only live in the major cities and only in certain areas of the major cities. The majority of Australians have never met a Jew and therefore those who are fed by media images or the picture, whatever, are very likely to have a mixed bag of messages as to what Jews are and what they do. You know, there are some that would have very, what we would consider, anti-Semitic and hostile. There are those who would have benevolent images and they're not real, they're not based on the personal contact. And, um, I hope—I like to think that once people meet a Jew they don't think terribly much of it, and—normal human beings. But I'm very conscious that the majority of Australians have never met a Jew."

BCB(M) "Very true. I had not thought of that."

BJA(F) "You need to, you need to think about where you are and where the Jews are and, you know, the chances. They may have seen on television, unfortunately— fortunately, you know—these are high-profile Jews, some that are very good and some that are not so good at all ... not meeting Jews can be dangerous in terms of the Jewish image. And I know that the—within the Muslim community there is certainly a negative stereotype of Jews which come from culture outside Australia. .. there are some negative stereotypes. So, my general feeling is those who have met Jews tend to—I think Australians generally are open minded, warm hearted and respond on a very, you know, it's very positive. But it's of concern to all Jews the large numbers have never met Jews and are reliant on all sorts of media for their images."

Thoughts from Group D

DMA(F) "Ramadan is the period that we try to strike that, which is beyond the family and community, with everyone and anyone, to have that relationship and have some kind of an interaction together …. So, hopefully I would like to live out that principle of connection with everyone and anyone indiscriminately, because he doesn't; why should we?"

DCA(M) "Everyone has a, a contribution, has abilities, has their own, their own part to play that I can learn from. And I've learnt that—it's taken me, it's taken me all my life to recognise that, because I have had this idea of stereotyping people, which is very negative and only leads to problems and ignorance and loss of opportunities. I feel that everyone can be valued and has a value."

A Final Thought from Group F

FMB(M) "There was a bit of hopelessness in watching the news and politics. And, and I think I felt a bit of a calling to read the Koran or investigate God."

Summary

These findings have selected and presented a little over 20% of the focus group transcribed data under deductively derived themes viz. (1) personal histories and views on (2) needs, (3) dialogue, (4) forgiveness and (5) peace-making - grouped under 'common' and 'different' views. Also presented are inductively derived data from the focus groups under the heading of 'remediations'. All of this has been provided with a minimum of commentary.

Appendix 2: Interview Themes

The focus group discussion was conducted around key themes. The themes and questions are outlined below.

Needs Questions

What images do you have of your neighbouring Abrahamic communities (for a Jew, the Christian and Muslim communities; for a Christian, the Jewish and Muslim communities; for a Muslim, the Jewish and Christian communities?)

What images do you think these other communities have of you? Where do these images come from?

Do you act upon them?

Dialogue Questions

How does the experience of listening and reacting to others affect you?

Do you have a new understanding after this experience of interaction? Yes/No.

If yes, what is this understanding?

Forgiveness Questions

What experience, principles or people do you most value?

What forgiveness ritual do you use to take back people into your family and community life if they stay away by shunning family or community values?

Peace Construction Questions

Are you aware of the common belief of the Jews, Christians and Muslims, to love God and neighbour. Yes/No.

If Yes, from where did you obtain this information?

How, in your opinion, can a peace process be formed, relying on this common teaching?

What do you mean by friendship?

Appendix 3: Gaining Access to Respondents *

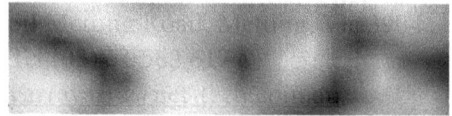

Friday, 28th November, 2008

Mehmet Saral, President,
Affinity Intercultural Foundation, PO Box 496,
Auburn NSW 1835

Dear Mehmet,

Roseman PhD Macquarie University: Research Interfaith Encounter Groups

This is a follow up letter in confirmation that I gave you a draft copy of my Methodology chapter for my PhD in International Communication at Macquarie University during the International Inter-religious Abraham Conference "Walking Together, our Faiths and Reconciliation, in Sydney on Sunday 19th October, 2008. My supervisor, Professor Naren Chitty has given me your Conference material from the outset of my research, and is desirous of working

*Telephone numbers and email addresses in all letters have been made illegible.

with you to complete my thesis: *Intercultural Remediations: Truth, Reconciliation and Forgiveness in Multi-ethnic Abrahamic Organizations.*

When I have completed the four chapters of literature research, it was decided that there will be six focus groups, with six people in each, (both men and women), comprising two Jewish, two Christian and two Muslim participants. They would be given coded names for security reasons, and each group will last exactly 1 ½ hours. I negotiated for an inner Sydney facility, close to transport and with parking, to hold these focus groups, three a day for two days. That is, there will be one at 9.30 – 11 a.m, one from 12.30 – 2 p.m. one from 3.30 – 5p.m. They were to be audio recorded as well as manually recorded and transcribed. The material will include narratives of the faith journey of the Jewish, Christian and Muslim participants, and themed questions, which will be used for a themed analysis, around the human need for friendship, dialogue, forgiveness and peace making.

I do hope that your organization will be able to help me in this endeavour. I am writing my proposal for the Ethics Committee at Macquarie University, and I need you to confirm in writing that you would be able to help me to source Jews, Christians and Muslims for the focus research groups. I would be most grateful if you could answer by proposal by writing as soon as possible.

HILARIE ROSEMAN

Appendix 4: Explanatory Statement

MACQUARIE UNIVERSITY LETTER HEAD

Intercultural Remediations: Truth, Reconciliation, and Forgiveness in Multi-Ethnic Abrahamic Religious Organizations[15]

You are invited to participate in a study of peace as a human need, ethical communication and peace, forgiveness and peace and process of peace construction within interfaith organizations. The purpose of the study is to find out members' views of how peaceful interaction is constructed within their interfaith organizations.

The study is being conducted by Hilarie Roseman, PhD Candidate (mobile xxxx xxx xxx, email xxx@net-tech.com.au)[16] and Professor Naren Chitty, Foundation Chair in International Communication, Macquarie University (Telephone 02-xxx xxxx) email xxx@mq.edu.au) and also Professor Harry Ballis of Monash University, Gippsland Campus. (Telephone 03 xx xxx xxxx, email xxx@adm.monash.edu.au)

If you decide to participate, you will be asked to join a focus group that will comprise of members of different religious faiths which will run for one and a half hours. It will be sound recorded.

---

15 The name of the thesis has been changed to "Generating forgiveness and constructing peace through
truthful dialogue: Abrahamic perspectives

16 Personal contact data have been made illegible for the book publication of the thesis.

Appendix 4: Explanatory Statement

Any information or personal details gathered in the course of the study are confidential. No individual will be identified in any publication of the results.

Only Hilarie Roseman, Professor Naren Chitty of Macquarie University and Professor Harry Ballis of Monash University (Gippsland Campus) will have access to raw data.

If you decide to participate, (English comprehension needed for discussion), you are free to withdraw from further participation in the research at any time without having to give a reason and without consequence.

Appendix 5: Information for Focus Group Participants

Making Friends in Abrahamic Religions

Hilarie Roseman, chief investigator, International Communication Department of Macquarie University NSW, Mobile ▓▓▓▓. Email address: ▓▓▓▓@net-tech.com.au This project, six focus groups of one and a half hour's duration, is a research student's project. It is being conducted to meet the requirements for the degree of PhD International Communication, under the supervision of Professor Naren Chitty Telephone 61▓▓▓▓ Foundation Chair of International Communication of the Arts Faculty at Macquarie University, and also of Professor Harry Ballis, Deputy Pro Vice-Chancellor, Arts Faculty, Humanities, Communication and Social Sciences, Research Unit in Work and Communication Futures, Monash University Gippsland campus, Telephone 61▓▓▓▓

Hilarie Roseman has examined the humanities, social sciences, NGO and religious literature in this thesis because 'communication as survival need' can be met by the practice of peaceful dialogue. The literature search has featured the conflict/resolution processes in Israel, South Africa and Ireland. The thesis aims to show how we can be taught (in interfaith groups) to be ourselves, and dialogue together, which leads to cooperation, and indeed friendship. To finish her thesis Hilarie Roseman would like to lead six focus groups, of different religious faiths comprising of 2 Jews, 2 Christians and 2 Muslims. These participants will volunteer from interfaith groups as an educational model of peaceful dialogue and discuss what it is to be a Jew, a Christian, a Muslim, their images of one another, their values, and the construction of peace. She would be grateful if interfaith groups would distribute this description of her thesis, and let her know if any of their members, with the ability to comprehend English, would feel like volunteering for one and a half hours to discuss their history as a Christian, Jew, or Muslim and be part of this venture of sharing the life of Abrahamic communities. For those interested, there would be consent forms, which would be signed by the volunteer, and also by Hilarie Roseman.

Description of task. Attend one focus group

Information to be obtained. An educational model of interfaith dialogue

Amount of time required. One and a half hours

Acknowledgement of recording. Participants will be given coded names and focus groups audio recorded.

Objective statement of any risks. There could be some sensitive material in a person's biography. I have asked for a counselor to be present from an interfaith community.

Privacy. Information gathered in the course of the research is confidential.

Access. Only by myself and my supervisors. Recordings kept for 5 years in locked safe.

Publication. As themed analysis of human needs, ethical communication, values and forgiveness and construction of peace, with coded names, will be on the International Communication website www.mucic.mq.edu.au

The ethical aspects of this study have been approved by the Macquarie University Ethics Review Committee (Human Subjects).

If you have any complaints or reservations about any ethical aspect of your participation in the research you may contact the Committee through its Secretary (telephone (02) ; email @). Any complaint you make will be treated in confidence and investigated, and you will be informed of the outcome.

Appendix 6: Consent Form

I, (participant's name) have read (or, where appropriate, have had read to me) and understand the information above and any questions I have asked have been answered to my satisfaction. I agree to participate in this research, knowing that I can withdraw from further participation in the research at any time without consequence. I have been given a copy of this form to keep.

Participant's Name:

(block letters) _____

Participant's Faith World, please tick. I belong to the Jewish ( ), Muslim ( )   Christian ( )   Faith

Participant's Signature:

Date:

Investigator's Name:

(block letters) _____

Investigator's Signature: _____

Date:

The ethical aspects of this study have been approved by the Macquarie University Ethics Review Committee (Human Research).

If you have any complaints or reservations about any ethical aspect of your participation in this research, you may contact the Ethics Review Committee through its Secretary (telephone 9850 7854; email ethics@mq.edu.au). Any complaint you make will be treated in confidence and investigated, and you will be informed of the outcome. The results of the research, will be published as themed analysis of human needs, ethical communication and the construction of peace (with coded names) on the International communication website, www.mucic.mq.ewdu.au

Appendix 7: Codification of Themes

COMMUNICATION

C.1	Can't dialogue with fundamentalists	ACB(F)
C.2	Sign of cross, open to misinterpretation	ACA(F)
C.3	Images obtained from personal experience	AJA(F)
C.4.	You respond in some way to images in media	ACB(F)
C.5	Little communication with local Catholics	BCA(F)
C.6	Talks about Jewish, Christian, Muslims groups as 'plural'- they are diverse	DJB(M)
C.7	Perceptions confirmed by constant communication	DMA(F)
C.8	Each Encounter with Jews, Christians enhances or changes preconceived views	FMB(M)
C.9	When I interact with Jews/Christians searching for the truth	FMB(M)
C.10	Images/Teachings of the family	FJA(F)
C.11	All pretty established in open communication	BCB(M)
C.11	Listen to each other – can't love without knowing	DMB(M)
C.12	Listen and learn	FCB(M)
C.13	Be open and adventurous	FCB(M)

C.14	Interfaith communication entails Risk	FMA(F)
C.15	Interfaith communication entails risk taking	FCA(F)
C.16	Interfaith vulnerability	FMA(F)
C.17	Learn from one another	DCA(M)
C.18	Actions speak louder than words	DJB(M)
C.19	Actions more important than teachings	DJB(M)

ISSUES TO DO WITH CULTURE

CR.1	Cultural issues, head scarf	DMB(F)
CR.2	Cultural clothing as opposed to superb English education	FJA(F)
CR.3	Black clothing with slits hinders communication	FCA(F)
CR.4	Wrong to judge on clothes	FMB(M)
CR.5	Its not religion, physical issues not faith issues	FCB(M)
CR6	Social dialogue/as against religious dialogue	FMB(M)
CR.7	Its cultural dialogue	FMB(M)
CR.8	its cultural differences	FJA(F)
CR.9	Sometimes it political dialogue	FMB(M)
CR.10	Hajib sends messages women oppressed	BCB(M)

ISSUES TO DO WITH FORGIVENESS

F.1	No particular ritual / accept and love / try not to judge	AJA(F)
F.2	Forgiveness core of relationships broaden into Sorry Day	ACA(F)
F.3	Create something which leads into grieving, sharing tears	ACB(F)
F.4	In family, equal sharing of humanness	ACB(F)
F.5	Day of Atonement, sins against God	AJA(F)
F.6	Say what you have to say, then accept	FJA(F)
F.7	Unqualified love, forgiveness and acceptance for family	FJA(F)
F.8	Right to disagree	BCB(M)
F.9	Understand, love when disagree	BCA(F)
F.10	Wicked, Wise, unlearned welcome at Passover Seder	FJA(F)
F.11	Respect individual journeys.	BCB(M)
F/12	No Jew refused a Sabbath meal	DJB(M)
F.13	God is merciful	DMA(F)
F.14	Ramadan – live out principle of connection	DMA(F)
F.15	No ritual for people I have offended	FCA(F)
F.16	In church pronounce forgiveness before confession	FCA(F)
F.17	God unconditionally loves us –	FCA(F)
F.18	We're sorry because we don't deserve God's unconditional love	FCA(F)

F.19	Ask people' forgiveness	FJA(F)
F.20	Ask God's forgiveness (Yom Kippur)	FJA(F)
F.21	Ask people to lay aside bad feelings at funeral	FCA(F)
F.22	Forgiveness makes us humble	FCB(M)
F.23	Recognize God's unconditional love	FCB(M)
F.24	Ask God's forgiveness	FMA(F)
F.25	Ask forgiveness community and family	FMA(F)
F.26	Islam Hajii, asking for God's forgiveness	FMA(F)
F.27	Islam- allows 3 day grudge period	FMB(M)

ISSUES TO DO WITH FRIENDSHIP

FR.1	Jews need friends to exist	BJA(F)
FR.2	Connections with Women's Interfaith Network and Affinity (Muslim)	BCA(F)
FR.3	Has Jewish friends	BCB(M)
FR.4	Common ground	AJA(F)
FR.5	Shared values	AJA(F)
FR..6	Respect	AJA(F)
FR.7	Trust	ACA(F)
FR,8	Vulnerability	ACA(F)
Fr.9	Walk alongside	ACA(F)
FR.10	Honest	ACB(F)
FR.11	Point out where wrong	AJA(F)
FR.12	Although you may argue	AJA(F)

FR.13	Still there when you don't follow what they think	AJA(F)
FR.14	Not afraid of strength or vulnerability	ACB(F)
FR.15	They forgive you	ACB(F)
FR.16	They are loyal	ACB(F)
FR.17	They trust	BCA(F)
FR.18	They respect	BCA(F)
FR.19	Something deeper	BCB(M)
Fr.20	Caring friendship when children at war	BJA(F)
FR.21	Deeper than respect	BCB(M)
Fr.22	Empathize with another human	BCB(M)
FR.23	Patience	FCB(M)
Fr.24	Forgive	FMA(F)
Fr.25	Honest	FJA(F)
Fr.26	Sharing	FJA(F)
Fr.27	A level of comfort and sharing	DJB(M)
Fr.28	Loving and respecting	DCA(M)
Fr.29	Friendship is intimacy at varying levels	DMA(F)
Fr.30	Friendship is compassion	DMB(F)
Fr.31	Sharing of yourself with someone (some aspect)	DMA(F)

ISSUES TO DO WTTH GOD

G.1	Christian spirituality, soft spot for Jesus	DMA(F)

G.2	(Jews) connection spirituality but also application of the law	DMA(F)
G.3	Religious texts versus life experience	FMB(M)
G.4	Worshipping together in trust	BCA(F)
G.5	Images come from religious text	DJB(M)
G.6	Interfaith way of getting to connect with God	FMA(F)
G.7	All aware common belief to love God and neighbour	All groups
G.8	From Old Testament – religious text	AJA(F)
G.9	From Christian/Muslim dialogue groups	ACA(F)
G.10	From The Old Testament – religious text	ACB(F)
G.11	From Formal study	BCA(F)
G.12	From Explored religions	BCB(M)
G.13	From Curiosity	DJB(M)
G.14	Slowly	DCA(M)
G.15	From dialogue encounters	DMA(F)
G.16	From/in encounters with others	DMB(F)
G.17	The Koran	DMA(F)
G.18	From religious text	FJA(F)
G.19	Through interfaith	FMA(F)
G.20	Commonality of belief, Single God	DCA(M)
G.21	Reconcile dualities from understanding our texts	DMA(F)

ISSUES TO DO WITH IDENTITY

I.1	Jews are a people, beginning with Abraham	FJA(F)
I.2	Someone of faith is someone who is of peace	DMB(F)
I.3	People of faith associated with peace	DMA(F)
I.4	People in our societies live in a limited confined world	FCB(M)
I.5	Its safe (to live in confined world)	FCA(F)
I.6	Once a Jew, always a Jew	BJA(F)
I.7	At the core of Christianity is the notion of grace	BCB(M)

ISSUES TO DO WITH THE MEDIA

M.1	Media sensationalize	AJA(F)
M,2	Media sensationalize people of Middle Eastern appearance	ACB(F)
M.3	Media biased against Israel	AJA(F)
M.4	Media do not report in a way that encourages Dialogue	ACB(F)
M.5.	Media stereotype	ACB(F)
M.6	Misinformation about Islam	DMA(F)
M.7	Media positive	DJB(M)
M.8	Ignorance born of misinformation	FCB(M)
M.9	Images (Jews Christians Muslims) come from media	FCA(F)

M.10	Knows Muslims only through media generated Images	BCB(M)
M.11	Not met a Jew, fed media images of Jews	BJA(F)
M.12	Negative stereotypes Muslims Jews recycled through media	BJA(F)
M.13	Sons have conservative images	BCA(F)
M.14	Does not respond to media stereotyping images ACA(F)	

NEGATIVE THEMES.

N.1	Distrust how I am perceived as a Jew	AJA(F)
N.2	Experience of anti Semitism – sorrow/fear	AJA(F)
N.3	Shame, Christians not understanding Muslims	ACA(F)
N.4	Shame no (Jewish) contact with Muslims	AJA(F)
N.5	Sad, confession – Christian colonising	ACB(F)
N.6	Nervous – won't wear Star of David	AJA(F)
N.7	Fear/friendship- not met a Jew	BJA(F)
N.8	Jews and Muslims negatively stereotyped	BJA(F)
N.9	Evangelisation fear	BJA(F)
N.10	Catholic said accept Christ or burn in hell	BJA(F)
N.11	Negative message from Catholic Church	BJA(F)
N.12	Same message from Baptists	CB(M)
N.13	Anglicans still teaching that	BJA(F)
N.14	Islamophobia	BCB(M)

Appendix 7: Codification of Themes

N.15	Image of Islam, good but abused by some people	DJB(M)
N.16	Christian conversion of Jews deceitful	DJB(M)
N.17	For a Jew to be complete has to be Christian	DJB(M)
N.18	Muslims have to grapple with Koran references to Jews	DJB(M)
N.19	Jews killed Jesus justifies anti Semitism	DJB(M)
N.20	Negative images for fundamentalists	FCA(F)
N.21	Jews demonized	FJA(F)
N.22	Jews stereotyped as responsible for death of Jesus	FJA(F)
N.23	Jews traitors if dialogue with Christians	DJB(M)
N.24	Suicide bombers war not peace	BCA(F)
N.25	Commonality a threat if differences are not recognized	BCA(F)
N.26	Fear syncretism	BCB(M)
N.27	People shaped socio-historical, socio-political, socio-economic events – Muslims seen as extreme, not very spiritual, not very human	DMA(F)
N.28	Jews stereotyped	FJA(F)
N.29	Matzah made with Christian blood	FJA(F)
N.30	Why don't we have more openness in education	FCB(M)
N.31	Some 'love' by forcing (people) to be same	BJA(F)

| N.32 | Acts on negative images | AJA(F) |

ISSUES TO DO WITH PEACEMAKING

P.1	Mutual respect,	AJA(F)
P.2	Understanding	AJA(F)
P.3	Common ground	AJA(F)
P.4	Loving our neighbours together	ACA(F)
P.5	Understand difference	ACB(F)
P.6	Historical differences/Messiah/dividing land	ACB(F)
P.7	Difference expressed in attitudes	ACB(F)
P.8	Teach love God and neighbour	BJA(F)
P.9	Define neighbour	BJA(F)
P.10	Love not sufficient for peacemaking	BJA(F)
P.11	Tension loving neighbour/holding true to faith	BCB(M)
P.12	Loving neighbour to include everyone	BJA(F)
P.13	Parable Good Samaritan	BCB(M)
P.14	Recognizing good in people you disagree with	BCB(M)
P.15	Don't tolerate evil, unacceptable	BJA(F)
P.16	Recognize good and wrong	BCB(M)
P.17	Start with common ground	DMA(F)
P.18	Compassion	DMB(F)
P.19	Respect	DMB(F)

P.20	Love	DMB(F)
P.21	Tolerance	DMB(F)
P.22	Peace has to be bilateral	FJA(F)
P.23	The other side has to agree to peace	FJA(F)
P.24	Justice you shall pursue	FJA(F)
P.25	Put money spent on defense into dialogue	FCA(F)
P.26	People have to like forgiveness	FMB(M)
P.27	Go to negotiating table ready to negotiate	FMB(M)
P.28	Go into peace for the sake of peace	FMA(F)

REMEDIATION

R.1	Many ways to connect with God	AJA(F)
R.2	Christian/Muslim dialogue groups	ACA(F)
R.3	Share pain, wait for God's Guidance	ACA(F)
R.4	Images change and develop	ACA(F)
R.5	Enlightenment from interfaith Unity of Human Kind	ACB(F)
R.6	Remediation as tears	ACB(F)
R.7	Sat and talked with Muslims-searching for nearest synagogue	BCA(F)
R.8	Blessed with many interfaith friends, hopes for positive response from those who meet Jews	BJA(F)
R.9	Respect fundamental spiritual characteristic	BCB(M)

R.10	Work harder to open ourselves to the neighbour who is different	BJA and BCA
R.11	Act on good images	BJA(F)
R.12	Control negative responses	BCB(M)
R.13	Remediation with hospitality	DCA(M)
R.14	Interfaith dialogue began 1991 National Dialogue since 2002	DJB(M)
R.15	Interfaith organized prayers after 9/11/01	DJB(M)
R.16	Remediation dialogue thorough Christian Church	DCA(M)
R.17	Some people have knowledge of Abrahamic communities	DMA(F)
R.18	Act positively	DJB(M)
R.19	No trouble now overcoming xenophobic images	DCA(M)
R.20	Affirmation for People of the Book with human face	DMA(F)
R.21	Acts on positive images	DMB(F)
R.22	Hatred not accepted positive images affirmed	FJA(F)
R.23	Positive images for neighbour	FJA(F)
R.24	Accepting difference faith/or social	FCB(M)
R.25	Put yourself in other's shoes	FCB(M)
R.26	Education helps	FCB(M)
R.27	(interfaith helps) you understand Jesus better	FJA(F)
R.28	Two way relationships lessen fear	FCB(M)

Appendix 7: Codification of Themes 377

R.29	Movement from no preconception to One-on-one understanding	FMA(F)
R.30	Don't categorize	DMA(F)
R.31	Home visits help fear	FJA(F)
R.32	Remediation invite Lord Mayor to Matzah making	FJA(F)
R.33	Spoke to overcome negatives	FMB(M)
R.34	Learn/enriched by other faiths	AJA(F)
R.35	Connections from stories	ACA(F)
R.36	By their fruits you will find the People of God	ACB(F)
R.37	Interfaith strengthens faith/trust	all in Group B
R.38	Trust established	BCA(F)
R.39	Many paths to God	BCA(F)
R.40	Personal positive experiences with Christians	DJB(M)
R.41	Create experiences with other faiths/learn	DCA(M)
R.42	Understanding the other not too difficult	FCB(M)
R.43	Openness, understanding, other not too different	All agreed Group F
R.44	Accept and love, try not to judge	AJA(F)

SIMILARITIES IN FAITH TRADITIONS

| S.1 | Similarities in faith traditions | DMA(F) |

ISSUES TO DO WITH VALUES

V.1	Torah central to my life	AJA(F)
V.2	Family, making world a better placed	AJA(F)
V.3	Integrity,	ACA(F)
V.4	Wait for wisdom	ACA(F)
V.5	Humanness, honesty, love, justice, community	ACB(F)
V.6	Cross boundaries of difference	ACB(F)
V.7	Many paths, One God	BCB(M)
V.8	Mystical experience	BCB(M)
V.9	Humility	BJA(F)
V.10	Making world better place	DJB(M)
V.11	Involve others (making world a better place)	DJB(M)
V.12	Offer the hand of friendship	DJB(M)
V.13	Value people, do not stereotype	DCA(F)
V.14	Appreciate diversity	DMA(F)
V.15	Get to know, find common intersection	DMA(F)
V.16	My connection (with) God	DMB(M)
V.17	Honesty and straight forward	FJA(F)
V.18	Compassionate	FCA(F)
V.19	Respectful	FCB(M)
V.20	Speak from the heart	FMA(F)
V.21	Compassion	FMA(F)
V.22	Humble about their faith	FMB(M)

APPENDIX 8: FINAL ETHICS APPROVAL

Research Office
Research Hub, Building C5C East
MACQUARIE UNIVERSITY NSW 2109

Phone +61 (0)2 9850
Fax   +61 (0)2 9850
Email   edu.au

Ethics
Phone +61 (0)2 9850
Email   edu.au

28 April 2009

Mrs Hilarie Roseman
30 Metung Road
Metung
VIC 3904

Reference: HE27MAR2009-D06402

Dear Mrs Roseman

FINAL APPROVAL

Title of project: Intercultural Remediations: Truth, Reconciliation and Forgiveness in Multi-Ethnic Abrahamic Religious Organizations

Thank you for your recent correspondence. Your response has addressed the issues raised by the Ethics Review Committee (Human Research) and you may now commence your research. This approval also applies to the following amendment:

1. The recruitment poster will be placed in the Early Childhood Health Centre, Marsfield

Please note the following standard requirements of approval:

1. Approval will be for a period of twelve (12) months. At the end of this period, if the project has been completed, abandoned, discontinued or not commenced for any reason, you are required to submit a Final Report on the project. If you complete the work earlier than you had planned you must submit a Final Report as soon as the work is completed. The Final Report is available at: http://www.research.mq.edu.au/researchers/ethics/human_ethics/forms

2. However, at the end of the 12 month period if the project is still current you should instead submit an application for renewal of the approval if the project has run for less than five (5) years. This form is available at http://www.research.mq.edu.au/researchers/ethics/human_ethics/forms If the project has run for more than five (5) years you cannot renew approval for the project. You will need to complete and submit a Final Report (see Point 1 above) and submit a new application for the project. (The five year limit on renewal of approvals allows the Committee to fully re-review research in an environment where legislation, guidelines and requirements are continually changing, for example, new child protection and privacy laws)

3. Please remember the Committee must be notified of any alteration to the project.

4. You must notify the Committee immediately in the event of any adverse effects on participants or of any unforeseen events that might affect continued ethical acceptability of the project.

5. At all times you are responsible for the ethical conduct of your research in accordance with the guidelines established by the University http://www.research.mq.edu.au/researchers/ethics/human_ethics/policy

If you will be applying for or have applied for internal or external funding for the above project it is
responsibility to provide Macquarie University's Research Grants Officer with a copy of this letter as soo
possible. The Research Grants Officer will not inform external funding agencies that you have final approva
your project and funds will not be released until the Research Grants Officer has received a copy of this
approval letter.

Yours sincerely

PP Ms Karolyn White
Director of Research Ethics
Chair, Ethics Review Committee (Human Research)

Cc: Professor Naren Chitty, Faculty of Arts

ETHICS REVIEW COMMITTEE (HUMAN RESEARCH)
MACQUARIE UNIVERSITY

Bibliography

138 Muslim Scholars, 2007, *A common word between us and you* <http://www.acommonword.com/index.php?lang=en&page=option1>

Academic Dialogue on Applied Ethics, <http://caae.phil.cmu.edu/cavalier/Forum/meta/background/Rawls.html>

Abbott, WM SJ (gen. ed.) 1966a, 'Declaration on the relationship of the Church to non-Christian religions (Nostra Aetate)' in *The documents of Vatican Council II, translation editor, Very Rev. Msgr. Joseph Gallagher*, Guild Press, America Press, Association Press, New York

Abbott, WM SJ (gen. ed.) 1966b, 'Decree on ecumenism (Unitatis Redintegratio)' in *The documents of Vatican Council II, translation editor, Very Rev. Msgr. Joseph Gallagher*, Guild Press, America Press, Association Press, New York

ABC Online, 17/12/2005, *Cultural program to ease Sydney tensions.* <http//:www.abc.net.au/news/newsitems/200512/S1533272.htm>

Abu-Nimer, M 1999, *Dialogue, conflict resolution, and change: Arab-Jewish encounters in Israel*, State University of New York Press, Albany, NY. Adorno, TW, Frankel-Brunswik, E, Levinson, DJ & Sanford, RN, 1950 *The authoritarian personality*, Harper & Brothers, New York

Affinity Intercultural Foundation, <http://www.info@affinity.org.au>

Aldridge, M 1997, 'Evolution consciousness and the new technologies: crisis in communication for the twenty-first century', in *Communicatio, vol. 23 No. 1*, <http://www.unisa.ac.za/default.asp?Cmd=ViewContent&ContentID=247>

Ali, MA, 'Forgiveness, the importance of forgiveness in Islam' from *Institute of Islamic Information and Education*, <http://iiie.net/node/52>

Amnesty International Australia, 21st November, 2007, *Atefeh Rajabi Sahaaleh was hanged in public for 'crimes against chastity'. She was just 16 years old*, Locked Bag 23 Broadway NSW 2007 and at <http://www.action.amnesty.org.au/news/comments/1860/>

Anderson, JW, *Globalizing politics and religion in the Muslim world*, <http://www.press.umich.edu/jep/archive/Anderson.html>

Armstrong, K 2001, *The battle for God, fundamentalism in Judaism, Christianity and Islam*, Harper Collins Publishers, London.

Arquilla J & Ronfeldt, D 1999, *The emergence of noo politik: toward an American information strategy*, RAND Corporation, Santa Monica, CA.

Atkinson, D & Shakespeare, P 1993, 'Introduction' in *Reflecting on research practice: issues in health and social welfare*, Atkinson, D Shakespeare, P & French, S (edit.) Open University Press 1 – 10, Buckingham.

Augsburger, M, 1985, "Reconciliation as a lifestyle" *Program 2910, 30 minutes org.* < http://www.csec.org/csec/sermon/augsburger_2910.htm>

Augsburger, DW, 1989, *Conflict mediation across cultures: pathways and patterns*, Westminster/John, Knox Press, Louisville, Kentucky

Australian Bureau of Statistics 2011 Census, population born overseas <http://www.abs.gov.au/websitedbs/censushome.nsf/home/CO-59?opendocument&navpos=620>

Azar, EE 1973, *Probe for peace: small-state hostilities*, Burgess Publishing Company, Minneapolis, Minnesota.

Bachika, R (ed.) 2002, Bachika, R. 'Religion as a fundamental category of culture' in *Traditional religion & culture in a new era*, Transaction Publishers, New Brunswick (USA) and London (UK).

Back, KW 1989, 'Rhetoric as communication and performance', *Communication Research, vol. 16 no. 1*, p. 130–148.

Bailey, A & Smithka, P 2002, *Community, diversity and difference: implications for peace*. Rodopi, Amsterdam, New York, NY.

Bainbridge, WS 1997, *The sociology of religious movements*, Routledge, New York NY, London, p. 55

Balfour Report <http://fourdocs.gov.au/item-did-24.html>

Bar-Tal, D 2000, 'From intractable conflict through conflict resolution to reconciliation', *Political Psychology, vol. 21* no. 2, pp. 351–365.

Bartos, R 1986, 'Qualitative research: what is it and where it came from', *Journal of Advertising Research, vol. 26*, RC3–RC6.

Bash, CE 1987, 'Focus group interviews: an underutilized research technique for improving theory and practice in health education', *Health Education Quarterly, vol. 14*, p. 411–448.

Bellah, R, Madsen, R, Sullivan WM, Swidler, A & Tipton, SM 1985, 'Habits of the heart, individualism and commitment' in *American Life*, University of California Press, Berkeley, Loss Angeles, London.

Bellah, RN 1970, B*eyond belief, essays on religion in a post-traditional world*, Harper & Row, Publishers, New York, Evanston and London.

Berg, BL 2004, *Qualitative research methods for the social sciences*, 5th edition, Pearson, Boston, New York, San Francisco, Mexico City, Montreal, Toronto, London, Madrid, Munich, Parish, Hong Kong, Singapore, Tokyo, Cape Town, Sydney.

Berger. PL 1969, *The sacred canopy, elements of a sociological theory of religion*, Anchor Books, Doubleday & Company, Inc., Garden City, New York.

bin Laden, O 2001, *Version one, in Osama bin Laden's own words* – al-Jazeera TV October 7, 2001, <http://www.september11news.com/OsamaSpeeches.htm> page 2 of 7

bin Laden, O. Excerpts – *Al-Jazeera TV Broadcast, from Dubai on 27th December 2001*, pp. 4–5 <http://www.september11news.com/OsamaSpeeches.htm>

Blaiklock, EM 1983, *The confessions of Saint Augustine, a new translation with introductions*, Hodder and Stoughton, London, Sydney, Auckland

Boraine, A 2000, *A country unmasked. Inside South Africa's truth and reconciliation commission*, Oxford University Press, Oxford.

Borko, H, Peressini, D, Romagnano, L, Knuth, E, Yorker, C, Wooley, C, Hovermill, J, & Masarik, K 2000, 'Teacher education does matter: a situative perspective of learning to teach secondary mathematics' in *Educational Psychologist*, 35(3), 193-206

Brown, R *Teaching international communications*, a textbook survey, <ttp://www.bisa.ac.uk/bisanews/0109/teaching%20IC.htm>

Boulle, L 2005, *Mediation, principles process practice, 2nd edition*, LexisNexis Butterworths, Chatswood.

Bouma, G, Cahill, D, Dellah, H, Zwatz, A, 2011, Freedom of religion and belief in 21st century Australia, 2011 Human Rights Commission

Burns, RB 1996, *Introduction to research methods, 3rd edition*, Longman, South Melbourne, Australia.

Burton, J (ed) 1990, *Conflict: human needs theory, centre for conflict analysis and resolution*, George Mason University, Virginia, St. Martin's Press, New York.

Cahill, D 2003, *Paradise lost: Religion, cultural diversity and social cohesion in Australia and across the World* National Europe Centre Paper No.79, Paper presented to conference entitled "The challenges of immigration and integration in the European Union and Australia 18-20 February 2003, University of Sydney <https://digitalcollections.anu.edu.au/bitstream/1885/41762/3/cahill_paper.pdf>

Cahill, D. Bouma, G, Dellah H, and Leahy, M 2004, *Religion, cultural diversity and safeguarding Australia, a partnership under the Australian Government's Living in Harmony initiative*, Department for Immigration and Multicultural and Indigenous Affairs and Australian Multicultural Foundation, in association with the World Conference of Religions for Peace, RMIT University and Monash University

Camara, DH 1974, *The desert is fertile*, Orbis Books, Maryknoll, New York

Camilleri, JA 2006, 'Citizenship in a globalizing world' in M Tehranian, & BJ Lum, (eds) *Globalization & identity, cultural diversity, religion, and citizenship, peace and policy, Volume 10*, Transaction Publishers, New Brunswick (USA) and London (UK).

Campi E, & McLelland JC 2006, *Commentary on Aristotle's Nicomadean Ethics, volume LXXIII, sixteenth century essay & studies, The Peter Martyr Library volume 9, Peter Martyr Vermigli*. Kirksville, Missouri, Truman State University Press.

Caritas News 2007, *Crisis in Darfur, tribute for advocate of the Cambodian people*, No. 111, p. 13.

Carter, President J 1982, *Keeping faith. Memoirs of a President*, New York, Bantam Books.

Catholic Church 1994, *The catechism of the Catholic Church*, Australian edition, St. Pauls/Liberia Editrice Vaticana, Homebush, NSW.

Catholic Encyclopedia, *Anglicanism*, <http://www.newadvent.org/cathen/01498ahtm>

Centre for Advanced Research in Phenomenology, <http://www.phenomenologycentre.org/>

Chitty, N 2004, 'Configuring the future, framing international communication within world politics in the 21st century' in *The Journal of International Communication*, vol 10, no. 2, pp. 42–66.

Chitty, N 2005, 'International communication: into the 21st century as an academic 'Commons"' in *International Communication Gazette, no.* 67, pp. 555–559.

Chitty, N 2007, 'Introduction: rivers of time, the flow of systems' in *The Journal of International Communication*, vol. 13, no. 1, p. 6

Christie, DJ, Wagner, RV & Winter, DDuN 2001, *Peace, conflict and violence, peace psychology for the 21st Century*, Prentice Hall, Upper Saddle River NJ.

Clark, M 1990, 'Meaningful social bonding as a universal human need' in Burton, J (ed.) 1990, *Conflict: human needs theory, centre for conflict analysis and resolution, George Mason University, Virginia*, St. Martin's Press, New York.

Co-intelligence Institute <www.co-intelligence.org/P-dialogue.html>

Coleman, PW 1998, 'The Process of Forgiveness in Marriage and the Family.' In *Exploring Forgiveness*, ed. R. D. Enright and J. North. Madison, WI: The University of Wisconsin Press.

Collins, R 1974, *Conflict sociology*, Academic Press, New York, pp. 565–61.

Combatants for Peace, *Homepage*, <http://www.combatantsforpeace.org> Conflict theory, <http://www.sociology.org.uk/p2t3.htm>

Cook, JA and Fonow, MM 1986, 'Knowledge and women's interests. Issues of epistemology and methodology in feminist sociological research' in *Sociological Inquiry*, vol. 56, no. 1, pp. 2–29.

Cowie, AP (chief ed.) 1994, *Oxford advanced learner's dictionary of current English*, Oxford University Press: Oxford.

Crim, K 1981, *Abingdon dictionary of living religions: Keith Crim general editor Roger A. Bullard, Larry D. Shinn associate editors* Parthenon press, Nashville Tennessee.

Croft, A 2008, 'Calls for Anglican leader to resign' in *The Age*, 11th February, World page 7.

Crutchfield, RD and Wadsworth, T 2004, "Poverty and Violence", *Handbook of Research on Violence,* Westview Press, published in German 2002, published in English 2004.

De Chardin, T 1966, *Man's place in nature,* Collins, Fontana Books, London and Glasgow.

Deegan, MJ (ed.) 1999, *Play, school, and society, George Herbert Mead,* Peter Lang, New York, Washington, D.C./Baltimore, Boston, Bern, Frankfurt am Main, Berlin, Vienna, Paris.

De Grandis, R SJ 1986, *Healing through the Mass,* USA:Ellie Emmanuel, 60 Thomas Street, West End Brisbane, Q 4101 Australia,. now available at <http://www.Marianland.com/degrandis/degrandis001.html>

De la Rey, C 2001, 'Reconciliation in divided societies' in DJ Christie, RV Wagner & DA Winter (eds.) 2001, *Peace, conflict and violence, peace psychology for the 21st Century,* Prentice Hall, Upper Saddle River NJ.

Deng, FM., & Zartman, IW, (eds) 1991, *Conflict resolution in Africa ,*The Brookings Institution, Washington, D.C.

Derrida, J 2004, 'The global theatre of forgiveness', in *The Future of Values,* Jerome Binde (ed.) UNESCO Publishing: Berghahn Books and published in The Village Voice.

Derrida, J 2001, *On cosmopolitanism and forgiveness, thinking in action,* Routledge, London.

Deutsch, M 1973, *The resolution of conflict, constructive and destructive processes,* Yale University Press, New Haven.

Dewey, J 1933, *How we think,* D.C. Heath and Company, Boston, New York, Chicago, Atlanta, Dallas, San Francisco, London.

Dicklitch, S 2002, 'NGO and democratization in transitional societies – lessons from Uganda', in DN Nelsonard. & L Neak (eds) 2002, *Global society in transition, an international political reader*, Kluwer Law International, N.Y. The Hague, London.

Dinges, NG & Baldwin, KD 1996, 'Intercultural competence, a research perspective', in D Landis & RS Bhagat (eds.) 1996, *Handbook of intercultural training, 2nd edition*, SAGE Publications, Thousand Oaks, London, New Delhi, pp. 106–123.

Dolphin, L. "A short summary of Islamic Beliefs and Eschatology" <http://www.ldolphin.org/islam.shtml>

Dupuis, J SJ 2002, *Christianity and the religions. From confrontation to dialogue*, Maryknoll, NY, Orbis Books.

Eastman, Moira 1989, *Family, the vital factor, the key to society's survival*, Melbourne, Australia, Collins Dove.

Economist Intelligence Unit ViewsWire 2009, <http://www.economist.com/displayStory.cfm?story_id=11486461>

EIC (Ecumenical & Interfaith Commission, Melbourne), 1st February 2011, posting from David Schutz, "Glimmer of Hope" from *Document for renewal of religious discourse*, 23 Leading Egyptian Muslim Scholars, <http://cam.org.au/eic>

EIC (Ecumencial and Interfaith Commission) 2011, reporting "Egypt's Muslims attend Coptic Christmas mass, serving as 'human shields'", extract from article "Egypt's Muslims attend Coptic Christmas mass, serving as 'human shield'" by Yasmine El- Rashidi, Friday 7th January, 2011: <http://english.abram.org.eg/News/3365.aspx> in http://cam.org.au/eic

Eid al Fitr Prayer/Supplication, Islam, <http://www.qul.org.au/islamic-occasions/eid-ul-fitr/1117-eid-al-fitr-prayer--supplication>

Eisenstadt, S.N. 1976, 'The changing vision of modernization and development'. in *Communication and change the last ten years – and the next,* W Schramm & D Lerner (eds.), The University Press of Hawaii, Honolulu.

Elshinnawi, M 2007, 'Religious leaders launch new effort to resolve Israeli-Palestinian Conflict' in Voice of America, 8th November, 2007, <http://voanews.com/english/2007-11-08-voa8.cfm>

Encyclopaedia Britannica: Islam <http://www.britannica.com/EBchecked/topic/295507/Islam>

Encyclopaedia Britannica: Judaism <http://www.britannica.com/EBchecked/topic/307197/Judaism>

Enright, RD 2001, *Forgiveness is a choice, a step by step process for resolving anger and restoring hope,* American Psychological Association, Washington, DC.

Episcopal polity – Wikipedia < http:en.wikipedia.org/wiki/Episcopal_polity>

Fairchild, M, Presbyterian History, <http://christianity.about.com/od/presbyteriandenomination/a/prebyhistory.htm>

Feuerverger, G 1997, 'An educational program for peace: Jewish-Arab conflict resolution in Israel' in *Theory and practice, volume 36, number 1, Winter 1997.* Fincham, FD, Hall, J and Beach Steven RH 2006. *Forgiveness in marriage: current status, future directions* <http://fincham.info/papers/2006-fr.pdf>

Fisher, RJ 1972, 'Third party consultation: a method for the study and resolution of conflict' in *The Journal of Conflict Resolution, vol. 16, no.1,* pp. 67–94.

Fisher, RJ 1997, *Interactive conflict resolution,* Syracuse University Press, Syracuse, NY.

Fisher, RJ 1990, 'Needs theory, social identity and an eclectic model of conflict' in J Burton (ed.) 1990 *Conflict: human needs theory, centre for conflict analysis and resolution, George Mason University, Virginia,* St. Martin's Press, NY.

Fitzduff, M & O'Hagan, L 2000, 'The northern Ireland troubles: INCORE background paper' in CAIN Web Service, <http://cain.ulst.ac.uk/othelem/incorepaper.htm>

Fitzduff, M 2004, *Meta-conflict resolution, September 2004,* <http://www.brandeis.edu/coexistence/linked%20 documents/meta%20conflict%20readi ng.pdf>

Fitzduff, M 2002, *Beyond violence, conflict resolution process in northern Ireland,* United Nations University Press INCORE, Tokyo, New York, Paris.

Focus, The Magazine of Australia's Overseas Aid Program, May-Aug 2007, p. 19.

Forgiveness – forgiveness as an intervention, family/marital http://family.jrank.org/pages/643/Forgiveness-Forgiveness-an-Intervention-in-Family- Marital-Relationships.html)

Frederick, HH 1993, *Global Communication and International Relation,* Wadsworth Publishing Company, a Division of Wadsworth Inc., Belmont California.

Friedman, Y 1990, 'The role of knowledge in conflict resolution' in J Burton, (ed.) 1990 *Conflict: human needs theory, centre for conflict analysis and resolution, George Mason University, Virginia,* St. Martin's Press, New York.

Fry, DP. & Bjorkqvist, K 1997, 'Conclusions: alternatives to violence' in DP Fry. & K Bjorkqvist (eds.) 1997, *Cultural variation in conflict resolution; alternatives to violence,* Lawrence Erlbaum Publishers, Mahwah, N.J.

Fry, P & Fry, CB 1997, 'Culture and conflict-resolution models: exploring alternatives to violence' in DP Fry. & K Bjorkqvist (eds.) 1997, *Cultural variation in conflict resolution; alternatives to violence,* Lawrence Erlbaum Publishers, Mahwah, N.J.

Galtung, J 2007, 'Towards a model relating conflict, violence and peace' in C Webel & J Galtung (eds) 2007 *Peace and conflict studies: looking back – looking forward. The handbook of peace and conflict studies,* Routledge, Taylor & Francis Group, London, New York.

Gardiner, P 2007, *The clash of civilizations* from First Theme Session in JCMA 4th Annual Conference, July 2007 held at Pallotti College, Milgrove, Victoria.

Gay, P 1966, reissued 1995, *The Enlightenment, an interpretation, the rise of modern paganism,* W.W. Norton & Company, New York, London. Geneva Accord, October 2003, <http://www.fmep.org/documents/Geneva_Accord.html>

Glock, CY, & Stark R 1965, *Religion and society in tension,* Rand McNally & Company, Chicago.

Goleman, D 2006, *Social intelligence, the new science of human relationships,* Hutchinson, London.

Goulet, D 1973, *The cruel choice: a new concept in the theory of development,* Atheneum, New York.

Goulet, D 2002, *Development ethics at work: explorations: 1960–2002.* Routledge, UK.

Gouldner, AW 1970, *The coming crisis of western sociology,* Basic Books, New York.

Grayling, AC (ed.) 1995, *Philosophy, a guide through the subject,* Oxford University Press, Oxford, New York.

Grice, Paul 1989, *Studies in the way of wards,* Harvard University Press, Cambridge, Massachusetts, London, England

Groff, L 2006, 'The dialogue or clash of civilizations' in M Tehranian & BJ Lum (eds.) 2006, *Globalisation & identity, cultural diversity, religion, and citizenship, peace and policy, volume 10,* Transaction Publishers, New Brunswick(USA) and London (UK).

Guneratne, S 2005, *The Dao of the press: humanistic theory,* Hampton Press, Cresskill, N.J.

Guneratne, S 2007, 'World-system as a dissipative structure' in *The Journal of International Communication, vol. 13* no. 1.

Gurdin, B 1996, *Amite/friendship: an investigation into cross cultural styles in Canada and the United State,* Austin and Winfield, Benesada MD.

Haber, JG 1994, *Absolutism and its consequential critics,* Rowman & Littlefield Publishers, Lanham, Maryland.

Habermas, J 1984, *The Theory of communicative action, volume 1, Reason and the rationalization of society, Translated by Thomas McCarthy,* Beacon Press, Boston.

Habermas, J 1987, *The Theory of communicative action, volume 2, Lifeworld and system, a critique of functionalist reason, Translated by Thomas McCarthy,* Beacon Press, Boston.

Habermas, J 1990, *Moral consciousness and communicative action,* translated by C Lenhardt & SW Nicholson, introduction by T McCarthy, Polity Press, Cambridge.

Hahn, S 2003, *Lord, have mercy,* Darton Longman & Todd, London.

Halafof, Af and Wright-Neville, DP 2010, *Terrorism and Social Exclusion, Misplaced Risk, Common Security,* Cheltenham, Edward Elgar, in Monash series on Global Movements.

Hall, ET 1976, 1981, *Beyond culture*, Anchor Books, Division of Random House, New York.

Hamel, J 2001, 'The Focus group method and contemporary French sociology', in Journal of Sociology, vol. 37 no. 4, p. 341–254.

Hamelink, CJ 2000, *The Ethics of cyberspace*, SAGE Publications, London, Thousand Oaks, New Delhi.

Heaps, Bishop J 1998, *A Love that dares to question*, Aurora Books, David Lovell Publishing, Richmond, Victoria.

Heritage M & Bailey A 2006, *Educational assessment*, Lawrence Erlbaum, Mahwah N.J.

Hervieu-Leger, D 2000, *Religion as a chain of memory*. Polity Press, Cambridge.

Hieronymi, P 2001, 'Articulating an uncompromising forgiveness' in *Philosophy and Phenomenological Research, vol. 62 no. 3*, pp. 529–555.

Hill, B, Knitter, Paul F and Madges, W 2003, *Faith, religion and theology, a contemporary introduction*, Revised nd Expanded, Twenty-third publisher, a division of Bayard, Mystic CT 66355.

Hirsch, ED Jr. 1989, *Cultural literacy, introduction by Barry Jones*, Schwartz Publishing, Moorebank NSW.

Hofstede, G 1984, *Culture's consequences: international differences in work-related values*, SAGE, Beverley Hills, California.

Honderich, T (ed.) 1995, Prof. Shapiro S 'Spinoza, Baruch' in *The Oxford companion to philosophy*, Oxford University Press, Oxford, New York.

Honderich T (ed.) 1995, Murphy JG & Hampton, J 'Forgiveness and mercy' (Cambridge, 1988) in *The Oxford companion to philosophy*, Oxford University Press, Oxford, New York.

Hudock, AC 1999, *NGOs and civil society. democracy by proxy?*, Polity Press, Cambridge.

Humility – definition. Wikipedia <http://www.en.wikipedia.org/wiki/humility#Islam>

Huntington, S 1993, 'The clash of civilizations,' *Foreign Affairs*, vol. 72, pp. 22–49.

Interfaith Encounter Association (IEA) P.O. Box 3814, Jerusalem 91037. Israel website < http://www.interfaith-encounter.org>

Interfaith Encounter Association (IEA) Data Sheet 2011 <http://interfaithencounter.wordpress.com/groupseventsprojects/related- documents/>

International Jewish Committee for Interreligious Consultations, *Seek peace and pursue it: a Jewish call to Muslim-Jewish Dialogue.* <http://www.pr-inside.com/jewish-representative-body-welcomes-muslim-r468622.htm>

International Medical Corps: Newsroom: <http://www.imcworldwide.org/content/article/detail/1609>

Islam: Major Religions of the World Ranked by Number of Adherents. http://www.adherents.com/religions_by_adherents.htm

Jacobsen, C 2002, 'The process of secularisation: toward a theory-oriented methodology' in B Phillips, H Kincaid & TJ Scheff (eds.) *Toward a sociological imagination: bridging specialized fields,* University Press of America, Inc, Lanham, New York, Oxford.

Jamieson, AG. 2006, *Faith and the sword, a short history of Christian-Muslim conflict,* Reaktion Books, London.

Jandt, FE 2001, *Intercultural communication, an introduction,* 3rd edition, SAGE Publications, Thousand Oaks, London, New Delhi.

JCMA 2007, Fourth JCMA Conference at Pallotti College Milgrove. Conference Secretary Philip Newman, email: jcmavic@yahoo.com.au

JCMA, Jewish Christian Muslim Association <http:// www.jcma.org> Judaism: Answers < http://www.answers.com.topic/judaism>

Judaism: Effective Board Membership <http://www.tbi.org.au/home/tbi-board/board-of-governance-roles-responsibilites/>

Judaism 101: Torah <http://www.Jewfaq.org/torah.htm>

Jones Knowledge Group, <http://www.earthtimes.org/articles/show/news_press_release,221635.html>

Juergensmeyer, M 2003, *Terror in the mind of god, the global rise of religious violence,* University of California Press, Berkeley, Loss Angeles, London.

Jupp, J 2001, *The Australian People. An Encyclopedia of the nation, its peoples and their origins,* Cambridge University Press, Cambridge

Kant, I 1795, *Perpetual peace: a philosophical sketch,* <http://www.mtholyoke.edu/acad/intrel/Kant/Kant1.htm>

Kaplan, A 1961, *The new world of philosophy,* Random House, New York.

Kelman, HC 1979, 'An interactional approach to conflict resolution and its application to Israeli-Palestinian Relations', In *International Interactions; A Transnational Multidisciplinary Journal,* vol. 6. no. 2, pp. 99–122.

Kelman, HC 1987, 'The political psychology of the Israeli-Palestinian Conflict: How can we overcome the barriers to a negotiated solution?', in *Political Psychology,* vol. 18, no. 3, p. 347–363.

Kelman, HC 1990, 'Applying a human needs perspective to the practice of conflict resolution: the Israeli-Palestinian Case', in J Burton (ed.) 1990, *Conflict: human needs theory, centre for conflict analysis and resolution, George Mason University, Virginia*, St. Martin's Press, New York.

Kelman, HC 2006, 'Interests, relationships, identities: three central issues for individuals and groups in negotiating their social environment', in *Annual Review of Psychology*, vol. 57, p. 1–26.

Kelman, HC 2007, 'Anti-Semitism and Zionism in the debate on the Palestinian issue: personal reflections', in M Polner & S Merken (eds.) 2007, *Peace, justice, and Jews: reclaiming our tradition*, Bunim & Bannigan, Ltd., New York, NY, and Charlottetown, Canada.

Kelman, HC 2008, 'Reconciliation from a social-psychological perspective', in A Nadler, TE Malloy & JD Fisher JD (eds.) *The social psychology of intergroup reconciliation*, Oxford University Press, Oxford and New York.

Kington, T 2008, 'Muslims displace Catholics at the top' in *The Age*, Tuesday, 1st April 2008 (page World 10)

Kington, Tom "Number of Muslims ahead of Catholics says Vatican" in *The Guardian*, 31st March, 2008 page 10 http://www.theguardian.com/world/2008/mar/31/religion

Knox, Monsignor, 1966, *The Holy Bible, Knox version, a translation from the Latin Vulgate in the light of the Hebrew and Greek originals, authorized by the* Hierarchy of England and Wales and the Hierarchy of Scotland, School Edition, Burns & Oates Ltd. MacMillan & Co. Ltd., London.

Kolnai, A 1977, *Ethics, value and reality*, Athone Press, London.

Koran: Muhammad in *The Koran*, Sura LXX111, *The Enfolded*, First published 1909, last reprint, 1948, J.M. Dent & Sons Ltd., London, E.P. Dutton & Co. Inc., New York.

Kowalska, Saint Faustina, *Chaplet of Divine Mercy* <http://www.ewtn.com/devotionals/mercy/backgr.htm>

Kvale, S 1996, *InterViews, an introduction to qualitative research interviewing*, SAGE Publications, Thousand Oaks, London, New Delhi.

Landau, SF 1997, 'Conflict resolution in a highly stressful society: the case of Israel', in K Bjorkqvist & DP Fry (eds) 1997, *Cultural variation in conflict resolution, alternatives to violence*, Lawrence Erlbaum Publishers, Mahwah N.J.

Lengua, LJ, Roosa, MW, Schupak-Neuberg, E, Michaels, ML, Berg, CN, & Weschler, LF 1992, 'Using focus groups to guide the development of a parenting program for his difficult-to-research high-risk families', *Family Relations, vol. 41*, p. 163–168.

Lernoux, P 1989, *People of God, the struggle for world Catholicism*, Viking, New York.

Levantine Cultural Centre and the Raoul Wallenburg Institute for Ethics, Encounter Point, <http://levantinecentre.org/page/encounter.point.htm>

Lewes, GH 1875, in *Blitz 1992*, page 412, in 'Emergence' in *Wikipedia*, <http://www.en.wikipedia.org/wiki/Emergence>

Libresco, JD 1983, 'Focus groups: Madison Avenue meets public policy', in *Public Opinion*, August/September, 1983, pages 51–53, Montmorency, Vic., Index Press.

Lindner, EG 2006, *Making enemies*, Praeger Security International, Westport, Connecticut, London.

Lindner, EG 2004, *Theory of humiliation by Lindner, longer paper,* <http://www.humiliationstudies.org/whoweare/evelin13.php>

Lindner, EG August 2006, *Humiliation, Iran, and the Middle East Crisis,* <http://www.humiliationstudies.org/news/archives/001339.html>

Lindsay, H 1990, *The road to Holocaust,* Bantam books, New York, Toronto, London, Sydney, Auckland.

Liu, JH 2004, *A Cultural perspective on intergroup relations and social diversity,* <http://www.ac.wwu.edu/~culture/liu.htm>

Lodge, T 1991, 'Perspectives on conflict resolution in South Africa', in FM Deng & IW Zartman, (eds) 1991, *Conflict resolution in Africa,* Brookings Institute Press, Washington DC, p. 115.

Lowry, RJ (ed.) 1973, *Dominance, self-esteem, self-actualization: germinal papers of A. H. Maslow,* Brooks/Cole Publishing Company. A Division of Wadsworth Publishing Company Inc., Monterey, California.

Lynch, J & McGoldrick, A 2007, 'Peace journalism' in C Webel & J Galtung (eds.) 2007 *Peace and conflict studies: looking back – looking forward. The Handbook of Peace and Conflict Studies,* Routledge, Taylor & Francis Group, London, New York.

Madigan, D SJ 2001, *The Qur'an's Self Image. Writing and authority in Islam's scripture,* Princeton University Press: New Jersey, UK.

Mattelart, A 1994, *Mapping world communication – war, progress and culture,* translated by Emanuel S & Cohen, JA, University of Minnesota Press, Minneapolis, London.

Mead, GH, 1934, *Mind self and society,* University of Chicago, Chicago.

McLeod, Saul, 2009 updated 2012, "Jean Piaget" in *Simply Psychology,* <http://children.webmd.com/piaget-stages-of-development>.

McCullough, ME, Exline, JJ & Baumeister, RF 1998, 'An annotated bibliography on research on forgiveness and related topics' in EL Worthington (ed.) 1998 *Dimensions of Forgiveness, Psychological Research, Theological Perspectives,* Templeton Foundation Books, Pennsylvania.

McGarry, J & O'Leary, B 1995, *Explaining northern Ireland, broken images,* Blackwell, Oxford UK & Cambridge USA.

McGilchrist, Iain 2009, *The master and his emissary. The divided brain and the making of the western world,* Yale University Press, New Haven and London.

McLuhan, M & Powers, B 1989, *The global village, transformations in world life and media in the 21st Century,* Oxford University Press, New York, Oxford.

Merton, RK 1987, 'The focused interview and focus groups' in *Public Opinion Quarterly,* vol. 51, pp. 550–566.

Merton, RK, word origin: role model <http://www.answers.com/topic/moral-example>

Miceli, P 1985, reviewing White, RK 1984, 'Fearful warriors: a psychological profile of U.S.-Soviet relations, Don Mills: Collier Macmillan Inc. 1984', in *Peace magazine,* <http://archive.peacemagazine.org/v01n1p31.htm>

Michel T SJ and Omar IA 2010, *A Christian view of Islam. Essays on Dialogue,* Orbis Books, Maryknoll NY.

Mills CW 1959, *The Sociological Imagination, Fortieth Anniversary Edition,* Oxford University Press, Oxford.

Mitchell, C 1990, 'Necessitous man and conflict resolution: more basic questions about basic human needs theory', in J Burton (ed.) 1990 *Conflict: human needs theory, centre for conflict analysis and resolution, George Mason University, Virginia*, St. Martin's Press, New York.

Mitrovic, L 1999, "New social paradigm: Habermas's theory communicative action" in Philosophy and sociology, vol. 2, no. 6/2, pp. 217–223.

Montell, F 1999, 'Focus group interviews, a new feminist method' in NWSA Journal, vol. 11, pp. 44–71.

Moore, B (Ed) 1999, "Islam" in *The Australian Oxford Dictionary*, p. 695, Oxford University Press, Oxford.

Moore, B (Ed) 1999, "Muhammad" in *The Australian Oxford Dictionary*, p. 887, Oxford University Press, Oxford

Moran, WT 1986, 'The science of qualitative research', in *Journal of Advertising Research*, vol. 26, pp. RC16-RC19.

Morris, B 2002, 'Camp David and after: an exchange, 1. An interview with Ehud Barak', in *The New York Review of Books*, 13th June, 2002, pp. 42–45.

Mowlana, H 1986, *Global information and world communication, new frontiers in international relations,* Longman, New York, London.

Mowlana, H 1996, *Global communication in transition: the end of diversity?* SAGE Publications, Thousand Oaks, London, New Delhi.

Mowlana, H 1997, *Global information and world communication, second edition,*: SAGE Publications, London, Thousand Oaks, New Delhi.

Mowlana, H 2003, 'Communication philosophy and religion' in *The Journal of International Communication*, vol. 9 no. 1, p. 19.

Mowlana, H 2004, 'International communication, the journey of a caravan', in *The Journal of International Communication*, vol. 10 no. 2, p. 11.

Murphy, JS. 2003, *Getting even, forgiveness and its limits.* Oxford University Press, USA,

Muslim scholars from the Centre for the Study of Muslim-Jewish Relations, part of The Woolf Institute of Abrahamic Faiths, Cambridge. 25/2/08, *An Open Letter: A Call to Peace, Dialogue and Understanding between Muslims and Jews.* These Muslims scholars have facilitated this Letter , with the support of Muslims scholars throughout the world. <http://www.tariqramadan.com/article.php3?id_article=1370>

Muslim population in percentage: <http://en.wikipedia.org/wiki/List_of_countries_by_Muslim_population>

Nair-Venugopal, S 2003, 'Approximations of social reality as interpretations of culture: extending a framework of analysis in intercultural communication', in G Weaver (ed.) 2003, *Intercultural Relations, The Journal of International Communication*, vol. 9 no. 2, pp. 13–28.

Nathanson, DL 1992, *Shame and pride, affect, sex, and the birth of the self,* W.W. Norton & Company, New York, London.

Nayef HS 2002, 'Human rights regimes and the emergence of international political community', in DN Nelsonard & L Neak, (ed.) 2002, *Global society in transition, an international political reader,* Kluwer Law International, N.Y. The Hague, London.

Neal, Sister MA S.N.D., 1965, *Values and interests in social change,* Prentice-Hall, inc. Englewood Cliffs, New Jersey.

Nelsonard, DN & Neak, L (ed.) 2002, *Global society in transition, an international political reader,* Kluwer Law International, NY, The Hague, London.

Neuman, WL 1997, *Social research methods, qualitative and quantitative approaches,* Allyn and Bacon, Boston, London, Toronto, Sydney, Tokyo and Singapore.

Nicholson, H & Nicolle, D 2005, *God's warriors, Knights Templar, Saracens and the battle for Jerusalem,* Osprey Publishers, Oxford.

North, J 1998, 'The ideal of forgiveness, a philosopher's exploration' in *Exploring Forgiveness,* ed. R. D. Enright and J. North. Madison, WI: The University of Wisconsin Press.

Northern Ireland Hunger Strike < http://en.wikipedia.org/wiki/1981_Irish_hunger_strike>

Northern Ireland Peace Movement <http://womenshistory.about.com/od/peace/tp/nobel_peace_prize_women.htm>

Northern Ireland Women's Coalition <http://en.wikipedia.org/w/index.php?title=Northern_Ireland_Women%27s_Coalition&oldid=477764018>

Nucifora, A 'Alf's Articles, *Internet is revolutionizing use of Focus Groups*' <http://www.nucifora.com/art_146.html>

Nudler, O 1990, 'On conflicts and metaphors: toward an extended rationality', in J Burton (ed.) 1990 *Conflict: human needs theory, centre for conflict analysis and resolution, George Mason University, Virginia,* St. Martin's Press, New York.

Ohlson, T, Stedman, SJ with Davies, R 1994, *The new is not yet born, conflict resolution in southern Africa,* The Brookings Institution Press, Washington, D.C.

Ohlson, T 1991, 'Strategic confrontation versus economic survival in southern Africa', in FM Deng & IW Zartman (eds) 1991, *Conflict resolution in Africa* The Brookings Institution, Washington, D.C., p. 222.

O'Leary, B & McGarry, J 1996, *The politics of antagonism, understanding northern Ireland*, 2nd edition, The Athlone Press, London & Atlantic Highlands, NJ.

Onuf, Nicholas, 1989, *The world of our making*, Columbia: University of South Carolina Press.

Patten Report from Independent Commission on Policing in Northern Ireland, <http://cain.ulst.ac.uk/issues/police/patten/patten99.pdf>

Paige, R Michael and Martin, Judith N., *Ethics in intercultural training*, in D Landis & RS Bhagat (eds.) 1996, *Handbook of intercultural training, 2nd edition*, SAGE Publications, Thousand Oaks, London, New Delhi, pp. 35–60.

Jewish-Palestinian Living Room Dialogue of San Mateo County, USA, 2005, DVD *Dialogue at Washington High*. Peninsula Conflict Resolution Centre (PCRC) – Middle East Dialogue, c/- Dialogue, 1448 Cedarwood Dr., San Mateo, CA.

Pettigrew, TF and Tropp, LR 2011, *When groups meet, the dynamics of intergroup contact*, Psychology Press, Taylor & Francis Group, New York and Hove.

Pettit, G, *Dr. Pettit's forgiveness process*, <http://www.iloveulove.com/forgiveness/Pettitforgive.htm>

Pettman, R 2000, *Common-sense constructivism or making of world affairs*, Sharpe publisher, M.E.

Philips, B 2002 'Reconstructing the scientific method', in B Philips, H Kincaid & TJ Scheff (eds.) 2002, *Toward a sociological imagination, bridging specialized fields*, University Press of America, Lanham, New York, Oxford.

Phillips, B, & Christner, D 2011, *Saving society, breaking out of our bureaucratic way of life*, Paradigm Publishers, Boulder, London.

Pope Benedict XVI, *Papal address at University of Regensburg* <www.zenit.org/asrticle-6955?1=english>

Pope Paul VI Pastoral Constitution on the Church in the Modern World, 16. Guadium et Spes <http://www.vatican.va/archive/hist_councils/ii_vatican_council/documents/vat- ii_cons_19651207_gaudium-et-spes_en.html>

Porush, Israel 1977, *The House of Israel*, The Hawthorn Press, Melbourne.

Potter, NN (ed.) 2004, *Putting peace into practice, evaluating policy in practice, local and global levels.*, Rodopi Press, Amsterdam/New York NY.

Prophet Muhammad 'The Enfolded' in *The Koran, Sura LXXIII*

Psychologists for Social Responsibility 1989, *Dismantling the mast of enmity, an educational resource manual on the psychology of enemy images*, <http://www.psysr.org>

Ramsbotham, O, Woodhouse, T & Miall, H 2005, *Contemporary conflict resolution, the prevention, management and transformation of deadly conflicts*, 2nd edition, Polity Press, Cambridge.

Ratzinger, Joseph Cardinal (now Pope Benedict XVl) 1998, *Many religions – one covenant, Israel, the Church and the world*, foreword by Scott Hahn, Ignatius Press, San Francisco.

Rausch, DA 1990, *A legacy of hatred: why Christians must not forget the Holocaust*. Baker Books, Grand Rapids, p. 29

Rawls, J 2005, *Original edition, a theory of justice*, Cambridge, Massachusetts, The Belknap Press of Harvard University Press, London England.

Rebirth Africa Life on the Continent, <http://www.rebirth.co.za/apartheid_history1.htm>

Religion & Ethics, <http://www.abc.net.au/religion/stories/s817757.htm>

Roseman, H 2009, *The attraction of the common good in comprehensive awareness. National soft power building.* For Tsinghua International Centre for Communication Studies, First International Conference on Soft Power and Nation Branding. Beijing 8-9 September, 2009.

Ross, Marc, 2000, "Creating conditions for peacemaking theories of practice in conflict resolution in *Ethic and racial studies*, vol. 23 no. 6.

Rouhana, NN. & Bar-Tal, D 1998, 'Psychological dynamics of intractable ethnonational conflicts', in *American Psychologist*, vol. 53 no. 7, pp. 761–770.

Ruane, J & Todd, J 1996, *The dynamics of conflict in northern Ireland, power, conflict and emancipation,* Cambridge University Press, Cambridge.

Ruthven, M 2002, *A fury for God,* Granata, London, New York.

Saeed, A and Akbarzadeh, S 2001, *Muslim Communities in Australia,* UNSW Press, Sydney.

Saeed, A, 2003. *Islam in Australia,* Allen and Unwin, Crow's Nest, NSW.

Sambal, NH 2002, 'Human rights regimes and the emergence of international political community', in DN Nelsonard & L Neak (eds) 2002, *Global society in transition, an international political reader,* Kluwer Law International, N.Y. The Hague, London.

Sandole, DJD, van der Merwe, H, (Eds), 1993, *Conflict resolution theory and practice, integration and application, foreword by*

Professor Herbert C. Kelman, Manchester University Press, Manchester and New York.

Sands, Bobby, 1981, Hunger Strike, Northern Ireland, <(http://en.wikipedia.org/wiki/1981_Irish_hunger_strike)>

Sawin, MM 1979, *Family enrichment with Family Clusters,* Judson Press, Valley Forge.

Saunders, 1999, *A public peace process: sustained dialogue to transform racial and ethnic conflicts,* Palgrave, New York.

Schadewitz, N & Jachna, 2007, T *Comparing inductive and deductive methodologies for design patterns identification and articulation,* <http://www.sd.polyu.edu.hk/iasdr/proceeding/papers/Comparing%20Inductive%20and%20Deductive%20 Methodologies%20for%20Design%20Patterns%20 Identification.pdf>

Schaefer, H 2005, 'Network identity and religious harmony: theoretical and methodological reflections', paper prepared for the conference on Religious harmony: problems, practice, education, Yogyakarta and Semarang, Java, Indonesia. 27.9 to 3.10.2004 in *Marburg Journal of Religion, Volume 10, No.1 (August 2005)* <http://web.uni- marburg.de/religionswissenschaft/journal/mjr/art_schaefer_2005.htm>

Scheff, TJ 1997, *Emotions, the social bond, and human reality. Part/whole analysis,* Cambridge: Cambridge University Presse & Editions de la Maison des Sciences de l'Homme, Paris.

Scheff, T, 1994, <http://www.soc.ucsb.edu/faculty/scheff/16.html>
Scheff, T 1994, *Bloody revenge,* Westview, Boulder.

Scheff, TJ 2002, 'Working class emotions and relationships: secondary analysis of Sennett and Cobb, and Willis,' in B Philips, H Kincaid & TJ Scheff (eds), 2002, *Toward a sociological imagination, bridging specialized fields*, University Press of America, New York, Oxford.

Schubert, M, Murphy, K & Murdoch L 2007, 'National emergency: PM acts' in *The Age*, Friday, 22nd June, 2007, front page.

Schultz, D, posted 1/2/2011, 'A Glimmer of Hope for the future of Islam in Egypt?' in *Ecumenical and Interfaith Commission* newsletter, <http://www.melbourne.catholic.org.au/eic/>

Scimecca, JA 1990, "Self-reflexivity and freedom: toward a prescriptive theory of conflict resolution" in J Burton (ed.) 1990, *Conflict: human needs theory, centre for conflict Analysis and Resolution, George Mason University, Virginia*, St. Martin's Press, New York.

Sherif, M 1967, *Group conflict and co-operation: their social psychology*, Routledge K. Paul, London.

Showalter, DK December 19, 1997, *Eight forgiveness questions to ponder*, <http://www.vsg.cape.com/~dougshow/webdoc2.htm>

Shriver, Donald W. Jr. 1995, *An ethic for enemies, forgiveness in politics*, Oxford University Press, New York, Oxford.

Siraj Islam Mufti, "Major Principles of Islamic Governance" in *Muslim Access* <http://muslimaccess.com/articles/misc/islamic_governance.asp>

Simons, HW 1986, *Persuasion, understanding, practice, and analysis*, 2nd Edition, Random House, New York.

Simmons, Rabbi, *Forgiveness in Judaism,* from About. Com:Judaism, http://judaism.about.com/library/3_askrabbi_o/bl_simmons_forgiveness.htm>

Sites, P 1990, 'Needs as analogues of emotions' in J Burton (ed.) 1990, *Conflict: human needs theory, centre for conflict analysis and resolution, George Mason University, Virginia,* St. Martin's Press, New York.

Smith, C 2007, "Why Christianity works, an emotions-focused phenomenological account: in *Sociology of Religion, vol. 682,* p. 165.

Sorrells, K 1998, interview with Hall, ET. "Gifts of wisdom: an interview with Dr. Edward T. Hall, from *The Edge, the E-Journal of Intercultural Relations,* Summer 1998, Vol. 1(3) and published on "InterculturalU, Online Community of Interculturalists, <http://www.cms.interculturalu.com/node/144/print>

South African Truth and Reconciliation home page <http://www.doj.gov.za/trc/>

Stanford Encyclopedia of Philosophy, first published March 11th, 2003, substantive revision February 3rd, 2010, Memory 2010, <http://plato.stanford.edu/entries/memory>, pp. 4–5.

Stand for Israel, Balfour Declaration <http://www.ifcj.org/site/pagenavigator/sfi_about_war_balfour>

Staub, E 2001, 'Genocide and mass killing: their roots and prevention' in DJ Christie, RV Wagner & DDuN Winter (eds.) 2001, *Peace, conflict and violence, peace psychology for the 21st Century,* Prentice Hall, Upper Saddle River NJ.

Stolov, Y 2007, email to author on *The Interfaith Encounter Association, PO Box 3814, Jerusalem 91037, Israel.* <http://www.interaith-encounter.org> email yehuda@interfaith-encounter.org

Stolov, Y 2005, 'On overcoming anti-Semitism and Islamophobia – we must gain a true, deep and sincere knowledge of each other' in *Palestine-Israel Journal*, vol 12, no.2&3.

Story, J 1993, *An introduction to cultural theory and popular culture*, Prentice Hall, Harvester Wheatsheaf, London, New York, Toronto, Sydney, Tokyo, Singapore, Madrid, Mexico City, Munich, Paris.

Subkoviak, M, Enright, R Wu, C, Gassin, E, Freedman, S, Olson,L & Sarinopoulos, I 1992, Robert Enright and The Human Development Study Group 'Defining forgiveness: psychological & theological perspectives' in Forgiveness Bibliography in *The Forgiveness Web*, page 1, <http://www.forgivenessweb.com/RdgRm/Bibliography.html>

Tauran, Cardinal, President of the Pontifical Council for Interreligious Dialogue, 2007, 'Message for the end of Ramadan 'Id al-Fitr 1428 H./2007 a.d. Christians and Muslims: called to promote a culture of peace', http://www.vatican.va/roman_curia/pontifical_councils/interelg/documents/rc_pc_interelg_doc_20070928_ramadan2007_en .html

Taylor, C 1991, *The Ethics of Authenticity*, Harvard University Press, Cambridge, Massachusetts and London, England.

Teams of Our Lady, *Love and marriage, the covenant of conjugal love*, Study Topic for the First Year, Equipes Notre-Dame, General Secretariat, 49, Rue de la Glaciere, Paris XIIIe, France, <http://www.teamsgb.org.uk/documents/Teams%20The%20Study%20Topic.pdf>

Teams of Our Lady, 1963, *Charter of the Teams of Our Lady*, Imprimatur, Bourges, le 4 Decembre 1963, C. Baillargeau, v.g. also available online from Equipes Notre Dame International, <http://www.equipes-notre-dame.com/pages_en/Lex_Charte_en.html>

Teams of Our Lady, *The Rome pilgrimage, if only you knew what God is offering*, Britain-Ireland Region, September 1982

Tehranian, M & Lum, BJ (eds) *Globalization & identity, cultural diversity, religion, and citizenship, peace and policy, Volume 10,* Transaction Publishers, New Brunswick (USA) and London (UK).

The 99 attributes of Allah, <www.en.wikipedia.org/wiki/99_Names_of_God_in_the_Qur'an>

The Guardian, "Gaza, my child was killed and nothing has changed" <guardian.co.uk/world/Gaza>

Thompson, J 2005, 'On forgiveness and social healing', for *A panel discussion on the role of forgiveness in social healing, Harvard Divinity School, October 31, 2005* <http://www.humiliationstudies.org/documents/ThompsonForgiveness.pdf>

Tomlinson, J 1999, *Globalization and culture*, Polity, Cornwall.

Traubman, L and L, *Expanding identification* <http://www.traubman.igc.org/bw.htm>

Traubman, L, Jewish-Palestinian Living Room Dialogue Group <http://traubman.igc.org/mission.htm and http://traubman.igc.org/passover.htm>

Trompenaars, F & Hampden-Turner, C 1997, *Riding the waves of culture, understanding cultural diversity in business*, 2nd edition, Nicholas Brealey Publishing, London.

Tutu, Bishop D 2000, *No future without forgiveness*, Doubleday, New York New York. US Catholic Bishops, 1983, *The challenge of peace. God's promise and our response, Part 1* <http://www.osjspm.org/the_challenge_of_peace_1.aspx>

United Nations Interfaith Harmony <www.un.org/en/eventsinterfaithharmony week> United Nations resolution General Assembly World Interfaith Harmony Week <http://www.worldinterfaithharmonyweek.com/attachments/GhaziUNSpeech20.10.10,v.12%20as%20given.pdf>

United Nations. The speech of HRH Prince Ghazi, introduction to resolution A/65/L5, UN <http://www.worldinterfaithharmonyweek.com/attachments/Ghazi_UNspeech Advisory.pdf>

United Nations, video of HRH Prince Ghazi speaking to the UN resolution on interfaith harmony <http://worldinterfaithharmonyweek.com/120/photos- videos/video-of-prince-ghazis-speech-at-the-un/>

United Nations Resolution <http://www.worldinterfaithharmonyweek.com/attachments/UNGA%20Resolutio n%20WIHW%2020.10.10.pdf>

Van der Horst, B,a *Edward T. Hall a Great Grandfather of NLP* <http://www.cs.ucr.edu/`gnick/bvdh/print_edward_t_hall_great_.htm>

Van der Horst, B,b *What's important about values, criteria and belief,* <http://www.cs.ucr.edu/~gnick/bvdh/print_whats_important_about_values.htm>

Van der Merwe, HW 1989, *Pursuing justice and peace in south Africa,* Routledge, London.

Van der Merwe, H 1993, 'Relating theory to practice in south Africa' in *Conflict resolution theory and practice, integration and application,* (ed.) Sandole, JD., Van der Merwe H, Manchester University Press, Manchester and New York.

Walk, K, *How to write a comparative analysis,* copyright 1998 for Writing Centre at Harvard University, <http://www.fas.harvard.edu/~wricntr/documents/CompAnalysis.html>

Wallensteen, P 2002, *Understanding conflict resolution,* SAGE Publications, London, Thousand Oaks, New Delhi.

Weaver, G (ed.) 2003, 'Introduction' to *Intercultural relations, the Journal of International Communication, vol. 9 no. 2,* pp. 5–12.

Weber, M 1947, *The theory of social and economic organizations,* OUP, New York.

White, RK 1984, *Fearful warriors: a psychological profile of US-Soviet Relations,* Collier Macmillian. Inc., Done Mills.

Willett, G 1989, *Global communication: a modern myth,* <http://www.unisa.ac.za/default.asp?Cmd=ViewContent&ContentID=7149>

Wolfsfeld, G 1997, *Media and political conflict, news from the Middle East,* Cambridge University Press, Cambridge.

Worthington, E (ed.) 1998, *Dimensions of forgiveness, psychological research, theological perspectives,* Templeton Foundation Books, Pennsylvania.

Worthington, E, Jr. 2001, *Five steps to forgiveness – the art and science of forgiving,* Crown Publishers, New York.

Yale Law School, The Avalon Project, *Hamas Covenant, 1988,* http://avalon.law.yale.edu/20th_century/hamas.asp

Zionism, definition, Jewish Virtual Library <http://www.jewishvirtuallibrary.org/jsource/Zionism/zionism.html>

Zivatz, L 1991, *Doing good, the Australian NGO community,* Allen & Unwin Pty. Ltd., North Sydney.

Zwartz, B 2007, 'Interfaith chair at Catholic Uni a world first' in *The Age,* Wednesday, 7th November, 2007, page News 11.

Intercultural Understanding

Books from World Dignity University Press and Dignity Press
More information at: *www.dignitypress.org*

Michael H. Prosser, Mansoureh Sharifzadeh, Zhang Zhengyong
FINDING CROSS-CULTURAL COMMON GROUND

Cui Litang, Michael Prosser (eds.)
SOCIAL MEDIA IN ASIA

Li Mengyu, Michael H. Prosser
CHINESE COMMUNICATING INTERCULTURALLY

Victoria Fontan
DECOLONIZING PEACE

Ada Aharoni
RARE FLOWER

Francesco Cardoso Gomes de Matos
DIGNITY – A MULTIDIMENSIONAL VIEW

Evelin G. Lindner
A DIGNITY ECONOMY

Howard Richards, Joanna Swanger
GANDHI AND THE FUTURE OF ECONOMICS

Deepak Tripathi
A JOURNEY THROUGH TURBULENCE

www.ingramcontent.com/pod-product-compliance
Lightning Source LLC
Chambersburg PA
CBHW072322170426
43195CB00048B/2203